# Executing Freedom

# Executing Freedom

*The Cultural Life of Capital
Punishment in the United States*

DANIEL LaCHANCE

THE UNIVERSITY OF CHICAGO PRESS     CHICAGO AND LONDON

The University of Chicago Press, Chicago 60637
The University of Chicago Press, Ltd., London
© 2016 by The University of Chicago
All rights reserved. Published 2016.
Paperback edition 2018
Printed in the United States of America

27 26 25 24 23 22 21 20 19 18    2 3 4 5 6

ISBN-13: 978-0-226-06669-1 (cloth)
ISBN-13: 978-0-226-58318-1 (paper)
ISBN-13: 978-0-226-06672-1 (e-book)
DOI: https://doi.org/10.7208/chicago/9780226066721.001.0001

Publication of this book has been aided by a grant from the Bevington Fund.

Library of Congress Cataloging-in-Publication Data

Names: LaChance, Daniel, 1979– author.
Title: Executing freedom : the cultural life of capital punishment in the United States /
Daniel LaChance.
Description: Chicago ; London : The University of Chicago Press, 2016. | Includes
bibliographical references and index.
Identifiers: LCCN 2016001655 | ISBN 9780226066691 (cloth : alk. paper) | ISBN
9780226066721 (e-book)
Subjects: LCSH: Capital punishment—United States.
Classification: LCC HV8699.U5 L33 2016 | DDC 364.660973—dc23
LC record available at http://lccn.loc.gov/2016001655

FOR MY PARENTS, KAREN AND JOHN LaCHANCE

# Contents

Acknowledgments   ix

INTRODUCTION   When Bundy Buckles Up   1

PART I.   **From Rehabilitation to Retribution**

CHAPTER 1.   "Inside Your Daddy's House": Capital Punishment
and Creeping Nihilism in the Atomic Age   27

CHAPTER 2.   "The Respect Which Is Due Them as Men":
The Rise of Retribution in a Polarizing Nation   51

PART II.   **Executable Subjects**

CHAPTER 3.   Fixed Risks and Free Souls: Judging and Executing
Capital Defendants after *Gregg v. Georgia*   79

CHAPTER 4.   Shock Therapy: The Rehabilitation of
Capital Punishment   103

PART III.   **The Killing State**

CHAPTER 5.   "A Country Worthy of Heroes": The Old West and
the New American Death Penalty   129

CHAPTER 6.   Father Knows Best: Capital Punishment
as a Family Value   155

EPILOGUE   Disabling Freedom   183

Notes   195

Index   253

# Acknowledgments

This book has come to feel, in many ways, like a domestic pass-port. It has traveled with me literally—on flash drives, in files, and on laptops—these past five or six years as I have moved throughout the United States, from the Midwest to the Northeast and now to the South. From the University of Minnesota, where it was conceived in an American studies department, to Emory University, where it was completed in a history department, conversations with mentors, colleagues, and students in five academic institutions have added their own stamp to it.

At the University of Minnesota, scholars affiliated with the American studies program provided immense support for this project in its early stages. My mentors there, Elaine Tyler May, Barbara Welke, Lary May, Joachim Savelsberg, and Ellen Messer-Davidow, offered everything from methodological advice to friendly skepticism to line edits of chapters in progress. The members of Lary and Elaine May's monthly workshop for works in progress provided insightful feedback on the work in its early stages. Jason Stahl, Jeff Manuel, and Matthew Schneider-Mayerson responded in especially helpful ways to numerous chapters. The work was enriched, too, by interactions I was fortunate to have, in a number of contexts, with Elizabeth Ault, Susanna Blumenthal, Regina Kunzel, Miranda McGowan, Kevin Murphy, Michael Tonry, and Eugenia Smith, who deftly edited an early version of the manuscript.

As an assistant professor of legal studies in the Department of Political Science at the University of Massachusetts, Amherst, I was fortunate to be mentored by Barbara Cruikshank, whose generous feedback on my work, kindness, sound advice, and friendship I hope to pay forward someday to a future junior colleague. Jen Fronc provided invaluable feedback on chapters in progress. I am grateful for the interactions I had in the Pioneer Valley—intellectual, pedagogical, professional, or social—with Amel Ahmed, Ivan Ascher, Trish Bachand, Jim Ben-Aaron, Angelica Bernal, Steve Boucher, Diane Curtis, Alan Gaitenby, Shelly Goldman, Michelle Goncalves, Kevin Henderson, Allen Linken, Khary Polk, Britt Rusert, Robert Samet, Fred Schaffer, Jillian Schwedler, Libby Sharrow, Nina Siulc, Amanda Waugh, Leah Wing, Nick Xenos, and Diana Yoon. I'm especially grateful to Lauren McCarthy, who joined the legal studies faculty when I did and who provided constant friendship, support, and advice.

A year-long fellowship in the Law and Public Affairs Program (LAPA) at Princeton University's Woodrow Wilson School of Public Affairs gave me not only the time I needed to revise the manuscript, but also the opportunity to meet scholars who engaged with my work in new and exciting ways. Stéphanie Hennette-Vauchez, Dan Kelemen, David Lieberman, Georg Nolte, and Bertrall Ross filled the year with lively discussions and laughter that modeled an ideal combination of intellectual rigor and warmth. Conversations with Naomi Murakawa over the course of my year at Princeton transformed my thinking about criminal justice. Her own work strongly informs the arguments in this book. I feel fortunate, as well, for exchanges I had at Princeton with Jen Bolton, Peter Brooks, Margot Canaday, Leslie Gerwin, Dirk Hartog, Stan Katz, Kevin Kruse, Judi Rivkin, and Keith Wailoo. My experience there also introduced me to Jessica Zou, whose research assistance was so remarkable that I breathed a sigh of relief when she agreed on short notice, over a year later, to cite check and copyedit the final draft of the book in the summer of 2015. Throughout my stay in Princeton, Paul Frymer and Sarah Staszak offered a heaping helping of friendship and irreverent commentary on academia. They also modeled a love of cats that inspired me to adopt Max, my Maltese buddy who these past few months has dutifully watched me complete this book from a windowsill perch.

Finally, I feel so fortunate to have landed at Emory University, where colleagues in the History Department and Emory College have been welcoming and supportive of this work in its final stages. Thanks especially go to Patrick Allitt, Carol Anderson, Tonio Andrade, Elena Conis, Astrid Eckert, Michael Elliott, Nihad Farooq, Brett Gadsden, Leslie Harris, Becky Herring, Lynne Huffer, Jeff Lesser, Kay Levine, Judith Miller, Matt Payne, Michael Perry, Jonathan Prude, Mark Ravina, Jim Roark, Colin Reynolds, Alex Robins, Tom Rogers, Allison Rollins, Ellie Schainker, Sharon Strocchia, Allen Tullos, Brian Vick, Katie Wilson,

Yanna Yannakakis, and Kelly Yates. I owe a particular debt to Dawn Peterson, who offered extensive feedback on revised versions of chapters 1 and 2, and to Joseph Crespino, whose thorough reading of the penultimate version of the manuscript in the spring of 2014 improved the book immeasurably.

As this project has moved with me through various disciplinary and interdisciplinary homes, the law and society community has provided a crucial point of intellectual continuity. I have been grateful for opportunities to exchange ideas with, learn from, and get feedback on this work from Tom Blair, Birte Christ, Renee Cramer, Hank Fradella, Linda Meyer, Lisa Miller, and especially Keramet Reiter. Rob Owen patiently answered my questions about Texas's legal system, supplied important practical knowledge and advice, and welcomed me into his home for dinner while I was conducting research in Austin. Colleagues at the Hurst Summer Institute in Legal History at the University of Wisconsin, Madison, provided important perspectives as I began revision. I am extraordinarily grateful to Paul Kaplan and Benjamin Fleury-Steiner. Their work on capital punishment has substantially influenced my own. Both read and responded to complete drafts of this work, offering feedback that improved it significantly. I am in their debt.

In the acknowledgments to her own first book, historian Margot Canaday speaks of that rare friendship, forged at an academic institution, that eventually "transcends any institutional tie." I have been lucky to enjoy several of these relationships. Over the past decade of mentorship and friendship, Elaine Tyler May became a model in all things: writing with clarity and passion, thinking creatively and ambitiously about a project, generating intellectual community. Her confidence in my work often exceeded my own, and it is because of her ongoing support that this project evolved into the book it has become. Likewise, Barbara Welke has supported this project long since its departure from the University of Minnesota. In the years since I left Minneapolis, she has generously continued to read drafts and provide detailed feedback. Long telephone conversations with her have helped me work through innumerable intellectual and professional dilemmas. Her mentorship and friendship have been a gift.

Ryan Murphy and Caley Horan have always been this project's best and most influential interlocutors. Both read multiple versions of the manuscript, each time offering encouragement mixed with probing questions that caused me to return to the foundations of my thinking about punishment and political culture. I can't think of two better people with whom to have shared the highs and lows of writing a book.

Finally, this project owes its largest intellectual debt to Austin Sarat. In 2003, as a high school teacher, I landed in a three-week seminar for K–12 teachers he offered at Amherst College through the National Endowment for the Humanities. At each stage of the twelve years that followed, his support has been both generous and profoundly influential. Readers familiar with scholarship on the American death penalty will immediately recognize the influence of his work in the pages that follow; it is in many ways a response to his well-known cultural analysis in *When the State Kills*.

As a high school teacher turned professor, I have long noted that the acknowledgments sections of academic monographs seldom recognize those who influenced authors before their scholarly careers began. I am extraordinarily grateful to Gerard Herlihy, English teacher at Marian High School, for teaching me how to write and for encouraging me to make writing central to my life. I am also profoundly grateful to Barbara Allen, Deborah Appleman, Chiara Briganti, Nancy Cho, Greg Hewitt, Susan Jaret-McKinstry, Carol Rutz, and Ruth Weiner of Carleton College for the skills and knowledge they taught me when I was an undergraduate, both in the classroom and beyond.

In the world beyond my professional work, Dana Bontemps, Rachel Buchberger, Kevan Choset, Joe Christiani, Melanie Clarke, Sarah Davis, Drew Dupuy, Nick Eigen, Adam Ford, Andy Grover, Aundi Hammer, Jeff Hnilicka, Phil Lovegren, Amanda Mahnke, Annie Murray-Close, Marta Murray-Close, Greg Penta, Kevin Rasmussen, and Dan Weiner have supported me in innumerable ways. Thanks to them.

Generous fellowship support from various sources gave me the time and resources I needed to complete this work. Thanks to the donors who have underwritten the Stout Wallace Fellowship, the Erickson Legal History Fellowship, and the Mulford Q. Sibley Fellowship at the University of Minnesota; the Hurst Summer Institute in Legal History at the University of Wisconsin; and the Perkins Fellowship in the Law and Public Affairs Program at Princeton University. Professional development funding from the Department of American Studies at the University of Minnesota, the Faculty Development Fund at Riverdale Country School, the Political Science Department at the University of Massachusetts at Amherst, the Law and Public Affairs Program at Princeton University, and the History Department at Emory University has helped me travel to conferences and defrayed research expenses.

At the University of Chicago Press, I was fortunate to find in Doug Mitchell an editor whose enthusiasm for this project has been topped only by his ability to find consistently novel ways to express it. His confidence in the work has been sustaining. I'm also grateful to Alice Bennett, Timothy McGovern, and Kyle Wagner, who worked on the book in various capacities.

Parts of chapters 3, 4, and the epilogue have been published elsewhere in different forms. An earlier version of chapter 3 appeared in *Law and Social Inquiry* 32, no. 3 (2007): 701–24; the epilogue is the extended development of an op-ed that appeared in the *New York Times* on September 9, 2014; ideas in chapter 4 were presented in brief form in a news analysis that appeared online in *The Conversation* and was subsequently republished, online, by the *New Republic*.

Finally, I thank my parents, John and Karen LaChance, whose love and support have meant the world to me. From her leadership of everything from the town of Framingham Board of Library Trustees to the Greater Boston Real Estate Board, my mother modeled for me what it means to be an active citizen in a local community. And for nearly thirty years my dad, a now retired criminal defense attorney, defended the rights of the accused in Massachusetts, including many who had committed crimes that inspired widespread horror and disgust. His empathy and zealous advocacy for the most hated (and often least fortunate) among us are awe-inspiring. In very different ways, they each taught me what it means to be a citizen. This book is for them.

# When Bundy Buckles Up

In the late 1980s, some Florida residents vented their frustration at their state's new mandatory seatbelt law by affixing to their cars bumper stickers that read "I'll buckle up when Bundy buckles up."[1] The stickers linked the state's regulation of their behavior in cars with its own failure to strap condemned serial killer Theodore Bundy into its electric chair. When the objection appeared on bumpers, Bundy had been sitting on Florida's death row for years as his appeals wound their way through the state and federal courts. "Government has its priorities backward," Sunshine State drivers seemed to be complaining to anyone behind them on the road. It was infringing on the right of law-abiding folks to use their property in ways that harmed no one but themselves while bending over backward to respect the rights of a serial killer.

In just a few words, the Bundy bumper sticker articulated a larger sentiment underlying Americans' support for capital punishment in the late twentieth century. From the late 1950s through the end of the century, the amount of trust Americans placed in the federal government tracked their level of support for capital punishment.[2] The more confidence they had in big, centralized government like the one in Washington, DC, the less they supported the death penalty. In 1958, for the first time pollsters asked Americans, "How much of the time do you think you can trust the government in Washington to do what is right?" And 73 percent answered "Most of the time" or "Almost always."[3] That same year, in a separate poll, 42 percent of Americans said they supported the death penalty for a person convicted of murder, one of the lowest numbers ever registered by a polling firm since surveys on the topic began in the 1930s.[4]

Over the next forty years, Americans' answers to both of these questions would change dramatically. Faith in the federal government would plummet and demand for the death penalty would soar. In 1974, trust in Washington fell below 50 percent for the first time in the history of the poll, where it remained through the end of the century[5] (see fig. 1). Just two years later, the number of Americans who approved of the death penalty rose above 60 percent for the first time in over twenty years, and it has stayed above that mark ever since, rising steadily in the 1970s and 1980s. In 1994, when support for the death penalty peaked and 80 per-

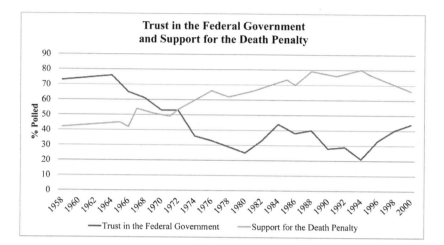

FIGURE 1. Trust in government and support for capital punishment, 1958–2004. National Election Studies, "Trust the Federal Government, 1958–2008," and Gallup, Inc., "Gallup Historical Trends: The Death Penalty."

NOTE: The source of the data about trust in the federal government is "Trust the Federal Government, 1958-2008," *American National Election Studies*, http://www.electionstudies .org/nesguide/toptable/tab5a_1.htm (accessed June 8, 2015). The survey was not conducted, and no data exists, for the years 1959–63, 1965, 1967, 1969, 1971, 1973, 1975, 1977, 1979, 1981, 1983, 1985, 1987, 1989, 1991, 1993, 1995, 1997, and 1999. With the exception of the data point for 1958, the source of the data about support for the death penalty is the Gallup Poll and is the percentage of respondents who said that they were "in favor of the death penalty for a person convicted of murder." Gallup, "Gallup Historical Trends: The Death Penalty," http://www.gallup.com/poll/1606/death-penalty.aspx (accessed June 8, 2015). The survey was not conducted, and no data exist, for the years 1958–64, 1968, 1970, 1973–1975, 1977, 1979–80, 1982–1984, 1987, 1989–90, 1992–93, and 1996–99. Gallup did not conduct its death penalty poll in 1958, the first year that the National Elections Survey began asking Americans about their trust in the federal government. For that year only, I have relied on a Roper Poll conducted that year. Cited in House Committee on the Judiciary, *Abolition of Capital Punishment*, Hearing before Subcommittee No. 2 of the Committee on the Judiciary. 86th Cong., 2nd sess., May 25, 1960, 87. The temporally closest available Gallup data is from 1957, when 47 percent of Americans indicated their support for the death penalty for a person convicted of murder.

cent of Americans polled expressed support for capital punishment, trust in the federal government hit an all-time low of 20 percent.[6] Such a finding raises the question, Why would Americans who have so little confidence in the government's ability to spend their tax dollars responsibly be so willing to let it take its own citizens' lives?

This book is a contribution to efforts by legal studies scholars to answer that question. Existing explanations center on long- and short-term accounts of American political institutions and the role they have played in controlling crime. Scholars taking the long view have noted that capital punishment in America has always been a predominantly local affair, with Washington playing little role in prosecuting the vast majority of death penalty cases. As a result, it has historically projected a distinctly populist character. Carried out mostly by local actors in state governments, executions have historically reflected the will of the people rather than the operations of an opaque, centralized government.[7] Other accounts have focused on the specific conditions of the death penalty's revival in the United States in the 1970s, arguing that rising violent crime rates and urban uprisings in the 1960s led conservative Americans to blame government bureaucracies they saw as too lenient with criminals.[8] Rising support for "law and order"-based approaches to punishment like the death penalty was a symptom of conservative Americans' disillusionment with liberalism.

These accounts, while compelling, are part of a much larger story about freedom in the United States since World War II. I argue that ideas about the freedom of middle-class white men underlay the death penalty's remarkable renaissance in the 1970s and its popularity over the last three decades of the twentieth century. Statistics showing a connection between support for the death penalty and attitudes toward government masked a racial divide: distrust in government promoted support for the death penalty among the white majority but weakened it among African Americans.[9] Middle-class white Americans' rising distrust during this period resulted from profound disillusion not simply with Washington but with the very particular type of government it embodied— one that was centralized, dispassionate, welfare-oriented, expert-driven, legalistic, paternalistic, and bureaucratic. In their minds it was not simply failing to keep the law-abiding safe from criminals, but was doing damage to a dominant culture that cherished the ideals of personal autonomy and self-governance. The revival of the death penalty in the

1970s and its growth in popularity over the ensuing decades was one of the most important symptoms of anxiety that modern government was undermining a spirit of individualism in the nation.

## Punishment and Freedom

Since the days of the early republic, punishment has lingered close to the heart of the meaning of political freedom in America. To Samuel Adams, punishment in a republic uniquely affirmed the sovereignty of the people. Urging death for farmers involved in Shays's Rebellion, an uprising against the state of Massachusetts in 1786, Adams reasoned that while such lawlessness could be pardoned in kingdoms, "the man who dares to rebel against the laws of a republic ought to suffer death."[10] Harsh punishment for crimes against the people reflected the importance of a free people compared with a single sovereign. Yet as a practice that suspended a person's freedom—sometimes permanently—punishment has also long stood as a source of debate about the proper nature and limits of the state's power over an individual citizen. The American penitentiary—an institution designed to uplift the wayward—had a dark side that Gustave de Beaumont and Alexis de Tocqueville identified after visiting several in the nineteenth century. They found that, despite its mission, it reduced men to slaves. "Whilst society in the United States gives the example of the most extended liberty, the prisons of the same country offer the spectacle of the most complete despotism," the men remarked in their report to the French government.[11] That contradiction did not go unnoticed by Americans. To some in the antebellum South, where the first penitentiaries would house white men, the penitentiary was a negation of republican ideals. Body-mutilating punishment respected freedom in a way that incarceration did not. "[For a] free-born American sovereign to be placed in this degrading institution," one critic of the penitentiary opined, "is far worse than death by any torture whatsoever."[12]

Nearly two hundred years later, these sorts of questions and observations about punishment's relation to freedom have remained as relevant as ever. Freedom, of course, is a term that is bandied about so carelessly that it is meaningless without a clear definition. I speak of it in political terms, a usage that always refers in some way to the relationship between a citizen and the state. And following a decades-old way of thinking about the concept first introduced by philosopher and historian Isaiah Berlin, I speak of the concept in "negative" and "positive" forms. In its negative form, freedom is the absence of unwanted government constraint, control, or influence over one's thoughts, speech, property, or action; one is free when one is not subject to coercive influences such as the will of others or the laws of a government. In its positive form, by contrast, freedom is a contingent capacity; one is free when one has sufficient material, social, and mental resources to maintain one's autonomy and achieve one's will.[13]

Historically, Americans have recognized both forms of freedom. We enshrined a negative vision of it in our founding documents. The Bill of Rights is largely a list of guarantees that the government will not take certain actions against its citizens. But attention to Americans' capacity to achieve their will and meaningfully participate as democratic citizens has also shaped their understandings of liberty and at times justified a robust role for government in helping them achieve autonomy. In everything from the development of free public education in the nineteenth century to the welfare bureaucracies of the twentieth, the student of American history finds examples of how positive freedom, too, has shaped governance in the United States. The way government has fulfilled the First Amendment's promise of protection of speech, for instance, might be understood in both negative and positive terms. The amendment itself protects negative freedom, forbidding the federal government to suppress political speech. But the expenditure of resources by local, state, and federal governments to teach reading, writing, and thinking skills to the nation's children represents, in some small part, an effort to cultivate positive freedom, to endow citizens with the capacity to meaningfully exercise their right to free speech.

Over time, as local, state, and federal governments grew, so did their ability to enact and carry out legislation designed to enable positive freedom. But whether government ought to exercise that power—and on behalf of whom—has been the subject of much disagreement. Because it requires the expenditure of resources, positive freedom comes at the expense of negative freedom: the government that requires parents to educate their children, for example, is the government that overrides their negative freedom from coercive state influence, in the name of protecting the positive freedom of future members of the polity. The tension is politically fraught. From the Progressive Era onward, the push and pull of these negative and positive understandings of freedom have shaped the history of the nation. The modern history of the American death penalty is no exception. Its changing fortunes are a product of the changing emphases on positive and negative freedom in the United States since World War II.

## The Decline of Negative Freedom and Capital Punishment in Postwar America

In part 1 of this book, I chart a shift in middle-class white Americans' relationship with freedom, from a tentative embrace of a positive understanding of liberty in the decades following World War II to disillusionment and an adoption of a negative vision in the late 1960s and early 1970s.

By the late 1940s, having lived through nearly two decades of depression and war, many white Americans had warmed to a positive understanding of freedom. Efforts to engineer an economic recovery in the 1930s had led to new and unprecedented state regulation of people and corporations. The Depression had reminded many in the middle classes that freedom was meaningless if it simply entailed the right to sink or swim on one's own. In a speech he gave during the Depression, President Franklin Roosevelt illustrated this broader principle by calling one of the four fundamental kinds of freedom Americans cherished a "freedom from want": understood in this way, freedom was deeply intertwined with material well-being and opportunities that individuals might not always be able to secure on their own.[14] Autonomy—individual freedom from dependency—had long been an American value, but many had come to believe it was not an innate human capacity but a learned one; it required the acquisition of knowledge and skills that society must provide if, say, the family could not. Many became convinced that freedom required a certain degree of protection from the harsh realities of a market-based society, with its cycles of boom and bust. What good was an individual's freedom of contract, for instance, in a glutted labor market offering the unskilled below-subsistence wages? The notion that government should intervene in big and small ways to guarantee certain minimum conditions of freedom underlay the rise of a "New Deal order" in which welfare programs and social service agencies made the government seem, more than ever before, to be a guarantor of its citizens' well-being.[15] War, too, had reinforced the conditions for a more positive understanding of freedom. Hope for a peace that would secure American freedom in the future had required the sacrifice of personal liberties during wartime. Americans grew victory gardens and rationed sugar as "victory overseas required an unprecedented invasion of home front duties into the private lives of its citizens."[16] And as fears of a new war with the Soviet Union quickly arose in the late 1940s, that sense of togetherness was renewed.

In this context, the New Deal order was incorporated into Cold War liberalism, an expansive approach to governance that attracted Republican and Democratic adherents alike.[17] Fueled by a widely shared antipathy toward a foreign, Communist enemy and by an unspoken assumption that the beneficiaries of the welfare state's domestic policies were middle-class white citizens, Cold War liberals placed a good deal of faith in government's ability to engineer the social good.[18] Indeed, at its core was a technocratic ethos. A technocracy is political rule by highly trained experts, insulated from political interests, who are dedicated to maximizing some vision of the good using their elite knowledge about how the world works. While the nation was not, of course, formally a technocracy, Progressive Era legal reforms, Roosevelt's New Deal social programs, and economic planning during World War II had given social scientists their first opportunity to participate in the operation of a state that had assumed responsibility for the welfare of its citizens.[19] The postwar period would continue that trend, as politicians continued to defer to expert judgment in making decisions about public policies and individual lives.[20]

Elite attitudes toward the problem of crime and the purpose of punishment reflected this larger willingness in American politics to see individuals as vulnerable and in need of societal assistance. Crime, to many influential elites, was the result not of a wicked disposition, but of a frustrated one: in their minds, a dearth of positive freedom underlay much of the criminal behavior that had traditionally been ascribed to innate depravity. Punishment, it followed, ought to rehabilitate inmates rather than further deprive them of the opportunity to develop as human beings. Retribution, inflicting on criminals a penalty equivalent in magnitude to the pain their crimes cause, could no longer be the chief penological objective of a state that had come to see itself as responsible for cultivating well-being rather than merely securing order.[21]

Such thinking had achieved recognition by the Supreme Court as early as 1949. In a majority opinion he wrote for a case that year, Supreme Court Justice Hugo Black confidently declared, "Retribution is no longer the dominant objective of the criminal law. Reformation and rehabilitation of offenders have become important goals of criminal jurisprudence."[22] Indeed, in Black's language and that of others, the very word punishment had fallen out of use. Its retributive connotations made it a distasteful term from an outmoded past.[23]

Unsurprisingly, the rise of more sympathetic understandings of criminal offenders underlay rising criticism of the death penalty. An emphasis on rehabilitation suffused the public statements of those who thought to end it. "Only if it is assumed that such criminals have complete free will to counteract their early conditioning and emotional stunting can a rational case be put forward for vindictive punishment and the death penalty," one vocal opponent of the death penalty asserted in 1962. "If this cannot be assumed, then the foundation crumbles under every argument in favor of capital punishment."[24] And by the late 1960s that foundation was indeed crumbling. Nationally, executions had steadily declined over the postwar period until they plummeted in the 1960s and dropped to zero in 1968. The decline was not solely attributable to elite maneuvering. Public support for the death penalty, as we have seen, reached new lows in the late 1950s that were sustained well into the 1960s. Death sentences declined as juries, particularly those in the North, also seemed increasingly unwilling to mete out the penalty.[25]

The Supreme Court's willingness to take up the constitutionality of the death penalty in the 1960s followed these decades of shifting thought about punishment. It took a new justice, however, to push the Court into a position where it could take up the matter. In a dissent to the Supreme Court's refusal to hear a challenge to capital punishment in 1963, newly appointed Justice Arthur Goldberg suggested that the death penalty might successfully be challenged on Eighth and Fourteenth Amendment grounds.[26] Goldberg's dissent gave hope to abolitionists, who interpreted it as a cue to begin ramping up legal efforts to have the death penalty declared unconstitutional. In the years that followed Goldberg's dissent, the Legal Defense Fund of the National Association for the Advancement of Colored People (NAACP) launched a broad attack on the death penalty in the courts, clogging appellate court dockets with challenges to its constitutionality. This approach brought executions to a halt. In 1972, after several years of decisions on the matter, the United States Supreme

Court declared in *Furman v. Georgia* that the death penalty was unconstitutional because juries meted it out arbitrarily.[27]

## Dissent Goes Mainstream: The Revival of Negative Freedom and Capital Punishment

Thus far I have been summarizing a relatively straightforward story of the death penalty's decline in the decades following World War II: in a modern world, capital punishment stopped making sense as Americans' understanding of freedom became more positive. The amount of blame one could ascribe to a criminal depended, more than ever before, on the environment that had shaped him. Even—and perhaps especially—the worst crimes were not exercises in free will, but indicators of a mind that had never been free, one chained by defects that a strong state could remedy.

But beneath the surface of a postwar consensus about the importance of positive freedom were anxieties about the fate of individualism. Increasingly sophisticated institutions and forces, including the government, seemed to be growing in their influence over human behavior. A positive understanding of freedom may have underlain shifts in American policy, in the aggregate, in more welfare-oriented and technocratic directions, but a declining sense of autonomy and individuality had inspired a good deal of hand-wringing by cultural critics. Concern about the precarious nature of individual freedom in a world reshaped by homogenizing social and political forces surfaced in the middle-class imagination as early as 1951 in J. D. Salinger's *Catcher in the Rye*, which called attention to the phoniness of Americans who incessantly measured themselves against false ideals.[28] Dissatisfaction with pressures to conform to those ideals and distrust of the entities seen as producing them—the state, the corporation, policymaking experts, mass culture—filled the popular culture the middle classes consumed. It also underlay best-selling books about dronish "organization men,"[29] works of modern art,[30] free market critics of the regulatory state,[31] and the academic research undertaken in the late 1950s and early 1960s by sociologists like Erving Goffman or psychologists like Stanley Milgram, who documented with alarm the malleability of human morality in institutional contexts.[32]

White men, who had long appeared in the popular imagination as the ideal carriers of a negative form of freedom, were the principal authors and objects of these analyses. From the frontiersman to the entrepreneur, white men historically presented themselves as uniquely able to transcend the limitations placed on them by forces beyond their control, to discipline their bodily appetites, to shape the world in their image. Modern life seemed to be imperiling that capacity. In everything from gay baiting in national political rhetoric to warnings from experts about the emasculating effects of too much mothering of young boys to the capacity of white-collar work environments to turn independent-minded individuals into "other-directed" people pleasers, historians have found evidence of a tacit crisis of masculinity in Cold War America.[33] One need only look at the heroes of the western movies popular in the 1950s—men who maintained a separateness from the frontier societies their ruggedness had made possible—to see how Americans were nostalgic for a vision of the individual unfettered by the constraints of civilization.

Anxiety about the fate of personal freedom in a modern America initially surfaced in contexts that were not overtly political: the content of popular culture or academic research. In the 1960s and 1970s, though, as the nation responded to new social and economic challenges, Americans from across the political spectrum became convinced that the state bore responsibility for creating the social problems it claimed to be solving. Technocracy, many thought, was undermining the value of individual life, weakening the bonds of family, and replacing moral intuition with elite expertise. The consequences for the nation's criminal justice policy were dramatic. As social conservatives, civil libertarians, and free market reformers criticized welfare-oriented government for undercutting personal and familial autonomy, they set the stage for a revival of retributive approaches to punishment and, in turn, the renaissance of the death penalty.

## Social Conservatives and the Making of the Silent Majority

Developments in the nation's racial history threw a wrench into middle-class white Americans' mid-twentieth-century flirtation with positive freedom. Many had been willing to fund federal welfare programs, like those created by the GI Bill, when they were able to see themselves and their families as the beneficiaries of federal spending. But as the Civil Rights movement took on more radical directions and Lyndon B. Johnson began his ambitious war on poverty in the 1960s, the recipients of federal tax dollars became, in the middle-class imagination, urban people of color. Having suburbanized and distanced themselves from urban life, many white Americans now felt conscripted into a welfare system that had nothing to do with them.[34] They no longer identified as the beneficiaries of liberalism but instead saw themselves as unwilling benefactors.[35]

In this context, a doubling of the homicide rate in the nation between 1964 and 1974 tested middle-class Americans' fidelity to Cold War liberalism.[36] The symbolic threat that urban crime and rioting posed to middle-class white Americans was enormous: by the end of the decade they were among the many Americans who, Jonathan Simon has noted, "had come to believe that a personal confrontation with armed violence . . . was a distinct possibility."[37] The criminal law, moreover, no longer seemed to be on their side. As the decisions of Earl Warren's Supreme Court expanded the rights of defendants in criminal cases, conservatives came to see the law as filled with loopholes that stymied law enforcement's efforts to bring dangerous criminals to justice.[38] By the late 1960s and early 1970s, when the death penalty's death seemed imminent, the conditions that had led many Americans to accept more structural responses to problems like crime were falling apart.

## Civil Libertarians and the Problem of Discretion

Given the rightward turn in American politics that followed the 1960s, it is easy to forget that some on the left, too, grew disenchanted with parts of the government built around a positive conception of freedom. Policies aimed at generating positive freedom required a degree of trust in those who would administer the government programs designed to maximize it that many on the civil libertarian left simply did not have. Sentencing was the most salient example of leftist distrust of paternalistic government. With rehabilitation as the point of punishment, state and federal governments often sentenced offenders to an indeterminate time in prison, giving parole boards and prison administrators discretion to determine when an inmate was ready to return to society. But rather than seeing this as a humane practice that curtailed the needless confinement of rehabilitated offenders, many were becoming convinced that a treatment-oriented prison system enabled abuses of power by prison personnel. It also pushed the government perilously close to thought policing. There was a fine line between rehabilitating people and reprogramming them, and for progressive critics influenced by an antipsychiatry movement that arose in the 1960s, the therapeutic orientation of modern criminal justice policy was crossing it.[39] Just as troubling, critics suggested that racism shaped parole boards' assessments of prisoners' readiness to return to society.[40]

Thus, in the years surrounding the Court's 1972 decision in *Furman v. Georgia* to suspend the death penalty, many on the right and on the left felt embattled by the criminal justice system; they had come to see government as the enemy of freedom rather than its guarantor. Converging resentment and distrust of the state set the stage for a major shift in American policy away from a mission of rehabilitation and the sentencing practices designed to support that mission. And it underlay the speed with which state legislatures recrafted their death penalty statutes in response to the Court's *Furman* decision, hoping that capital punishment could be reborn and reinvigorated.

With the blessing of social conservatives, who thought them too soft, and civil libertarians, who thought them too arbitrary, state legislatures across the country abolished or dramatically curtailed the use of indeterminate sentences and parole. They established fixed, standardized sentences for crimes, limiting judges' discretion in deciding a convicted defendant's punishment. The civil libertarian left was drawn to the way this approach set upper limits to the state's punitive power while the right lauded its taking decisions about punishment out of the hands of bleeding heart judges. The effects were dramatic. As the retributive revolution got under way, sentencing ceilings became sentencing floors; tough-on-crime legislatures ratcheted up criminal penalties and established draconian mandatory minimum sentences for all kinds of crimes. The defense of individual autonomy that had motivated leftist critiques of prisons inadvertently supported a reactionary understanding of criminal offenders as the sole cause of their crimes, who deserved their increasingly harsher punishments.

The death penalty's revival, after a period of suspension by the Supreme Court, was likewise driven by a judicial commitment to protecting individuals from the arbitrary exercise of discretionary power. In *Furman*, the Court temporarily suspended the death penalty not because it was an affront to human rights but because, in failing to regulate how jurors went about deciding which capital murderers should live and which should die, the law was running roughshod over the due process and equal protection guarantees of the Fourteenth Amendment. Once states revamped their capital sentencing statutes to give guidance to jurors about how to separate those deserving of execution from those deserving of prison sentences, the Court permitted executions to resume. Such an emphasis on fairness was symptomatic of a criminal justice system that, as political scientist Naomi Murakawa has powerfully put it, essentially "permitted limitless violence so long as it conformed to clearly defined laws, administrative protocol, and due process."[41]

At the core of an emphasis on procedural guarantees was a civil libertarian vision of defendants whose vulnerabilities lay not in their own deficits—cognitive, economic, environmental—but in a lack of clarity about how the state would exercise its monopoly on violence. It was not the punishment itself that the defendant needed protection from, it was the arbitrariness of the person or persons charged with determining or administering it. Such a priority on procedure implicitly imagined criminal defendants in an antipaternalistic way: they were figures endowed with a negative freedom that theoretically allowed them, when the law was clear and the exercise of its power to punish consistent, to act in ways that would yield predictable and foreseeable consequences. They did not, as a rule, need protection from themselves—from the effect their own diminished capacities may have on their ability to adequately anticipate the consequences of their behavior. They needed, instead, protection from a capricious state that made the consequences of their behavior unforeseeable. Their trenchant criticisms of rehabilitation, moreover, also added to a climate that was increasingly imagining criminal offenders as rational, responsible actors whose innate capacity to advocate for themselves required a state that abstained not from life-ending violence, but from psychological violence against the mind, where the capacity for self-advocacy lay.

Civil libertarians, then, played an important role in the revival of the American death penalty. While many of them opposed capital punishment, it ironically met their demands for a withdrawal of the state's punitive intrusions into the mind. And the laws governing it could be reformed, they would find out, in an effort to make its use more predictable. In the end, the distrust of government that underlay the reversal of twenty-five years of declining support for the death penalty was not simply the result of growing reactionary sentiment among Americans;

it was also the consequence of critiques of the state made by the civil libertarian left.

## Neoliberalism and the Rise of Supply-Side Economics

As the politics of race and criminal justice were diminishing the attachment to positive freedom of social conservatives and civil libertarians, economic crises of the 1970s—spiraling inflation combined with economic stagnation—were creating a demand for radically different ways of thinking about economic policy. The political, cultural, and economic effects of this thinking would further reinforce the broader national turn away from public policies rooted in a positive conception of freedom.

The New Deal had given rise to econo.nic policies rooted in the principles of Keynesianism. Named for its architect, John Maynard Keynes, Keynesianism held that governments could mitigate the damage caused by capitalist cycles of boom and bust by spending money they did not have in order to stimulate growth in times of economic downturn. Government welfare programs would put money into workers' pockets, giving them the purchasing power to stimulate economic growth.[42] A positive understanding of freedom underlay Keynesianism. Economic downturns, it tacitly held, imperiled individual freedom; government provision could protect it.

This regulatory approach to the economy formed the heart of the New Deal order, and it dominated mainstream economic thought for nearly four decades. But then the economy weakened dramatically in the 1970s. Inflation spiraled out of control and productivity declined. To many, Keynesianism seemed to be failing Americans. Growing doubt brought about a renaissance in more classic economic ways of thinking about the economy that policymakers had marginalized in the postwar period. Neoliberalism, as scholars would come to call this backlash against Keynesianism, revived a classic economic argument that the "free" or unregulated market most efficiently maximizes human happiness. By trying to solve social problems, neoliberalism held, the government-run welfare programs of President Johnson's Great Society had only exacerbated them. Private enterprise, free from government regulation, most effectively and efficiently delivered the vast majority of social goods without creating harmful dependency on welfare. Charities and families, not big government welfare programs, were best suited as a social safety net for individuals.[43] As opposition to the welfare state grew, so too did the appeal of negative understandings of freedom. Optimistic visions of an autonomous, rational, and entrepreneurial self, free from the burdens of regulation and taxation, suffused neoliberal thought.[44]

Neoliberalism came of age after the nation began its punitive turn, so we cannot argue that it played a role in generating the shift from a criminal justice system rooted in principles of rehabilitation to one rooted in retribution and incapacitation.[45] Still, neoliberalism certainly reinforced the material and ideological conditions that filled prisons to unprecedented levels in the 1980s and 1990s. Materially, neoliberalism's emphasis on a global free trade system created labor surpluses among unskilled workers in the United States that helped ratchet up incarceration.[46] Ideologically, neoliberalism trafficked in a commitment to personal responsibility that justified harsher punishment. The individuals who were to take entrepreneurial responsibility for their own economic fate were the same ones who would be held criminally responsible for transgressions.

By the early 1970s, then, social conservatives, civil libertarians, and neoliberals were making appeals to negative freedom. And while these constituencies pursued different agendas, each saw freedom as endangered by technocratic forms of governance. As a result, at various points they each adopted antigovernment rhetoric to advance their political agendas. And they imagined alternatives to business as usual that, more often than not, revolved around idealistic notions of individual freedom.

In this ideological context, I argue, the death penalty was not simply a blunt instrument for managing anxieties about crime, but also a symbol of a state that was changing in response to criticism. In an age when governments and corporations were expanding their capacity to manipulate people ever more effectively, executions offered an image of government that was doing the opposite, simply yet powerfully holding people accountable for what they had done and whom they had chosen to be. The execution of condemned murderers affirmed their status as individuals endowed with free will who were bearing responsibility for their actions. It honored the value of the individual lives their crimes had taken. And it revealed the prowess of governors and district attorneys, who portrayed themselves as populist heroes who had achieved justice for victims in spite of a system that was rigged against them.

While I focus on the role that these three ideologies—social conservatism, civil libertarianism, and neoliberalism—played in shoring up a majoritarian consensus in favor of the death penalty, many of the sources I use to tell my story are not directly associated with these movements.[47] The legal arguments, fictional movies, journalistic stories, and political speeches I explore were sometimes the result of conscious ideological maneuvering, but more often than not they reveal how those not setting out to support capital punishment could affirm the ideologies that were foundational to Americans' support for it. For instance, I illustrate the influence of moral traditionalist and neoliberal ideologies in films about the death penalty directed or produced by well-known leftists like Tim Robbins and Gloria Steinem, who would be unlikely to see themselves as appealing to racist sentiments or quelling free market anxieties. Yet as those ideologies pervaded the cultural air of the late twentieth century, Robbins and Steinem were, I aim to show, their carriers.

## Image and Implementation: A Delicate Balance

Part 2 of the book explores the cultural life of the death penalty in the contemporary era, the decades that followed the Supreme Court's 1976 decision in *Gregg v. Georgia*. Shortly after the death penalty returned, a new gap emerged between the ideological frustration with government that underlay the emotional demand for the death penalty and the reality that agents of the state would continue to carry out the punishment of death. In the popular imagination, the death penalty promised Americans to deliver what a legalistic and technocratic government could not: personalized justice, moral clarity, satisfying closure. But soon after executions resumed in 1977, capital punishment became mired in the impersonal logics and bureaucracies it was supposed to transcend. Legally, the expansion of federal courts' oversight of death penalty cases meant that many judges, in many forums, on many occasions, would review a capital defendant's appeals before a state would carry out a death sentence. As a result, the period between sentencing and execution grew longer than it had ever been before the *Furman* decision. And with the emergence of lethal injections, the act of execution came to look more like a medical procedure than a punishment, suggesting not retribution against a criminal carried out by a prison, but the prophylactic eradication of a "biological danger" by a public health agency.[48] In the popular imagination, the death penalty was the opposite of legalistic and technocratic government, but these elements grew dramatically after executions resumed in the United States in 1977.

How did the distrust of government that underlay the revival of the death penalty coexist with new ways of putting people to death that were more bureaucratic, technocratic, and anti-individualistic than they had ever been? Initially, quite well. The legalistic and managerial trappings of the reborn death penalty helped to distance contemporary state killing from the racism and classism that had historically plagued the practice. District attorneys in the past had most easily won death sentences for those who lacked the social or economic capital to avoid them: Native Americans, African Americans, Asian Americans, Latinos, and poor whites. No population, though, had borne as high a risk of death at the hands of the state as African Americans. As recently as the 1960s, capital punishment seemed like a thinly veiled alternative to the spectacle of lynching black men accused of rape in the South in the late nineteenth and early twentieth centuries.[49] After World War II, the South's annual execution numbers reflected the national pattern of decline, but they remained consistently higher than, and occasionally doubled, the number of executions posted in all other census regions *combined*. And a general racial lopsidedness of the use of the death penalty against African Americans in the South was particularly noticeable in executions for rape. From 1945 to 1967, 232 men were put to death in the South for crimes other than murder that involved rape. Of those, 197 were black and 27 were white.[50] In the context of the 1970s, to revive the death penalty was to revive a potent symbol of a violent, racist past. The administration of the death penalty in the post-*Gregg* era, then, was caught between the politics of freedom that pushed public policy in punitive directions and a politics of pluralism that required excising overt racism from public policy.

This posed a significant problem. Consciously and unconsciously, racism had underlain the white middle class's embrace of negative freedom and the way public policy built around it shifted the state's power away from empowering the disadvantaged and toward policing and punishing them. Institutional racism was effective, though, because on the surface institutions were color-blind. An explicit, avowed commitment to white male supremacy was no longer tolerated in mainstream political discourse. In contemporary America, the disparate impact of policies, rather than the content of Jim Crow-like laws, achieved racist outcomes. And while the death penalty was no different, its visibility as a dramatic sanction and the sensitivity surrounding its past use would make it the object of heightened scrutiny.

In that context, the legal trappings and professional standards that now surrounded the act of putting a person to death worked to weaken the connection between contemporary capital punishment and a racist past. The development of an elaborate federal jurisprudence designed to standardize the use of the death penalty amounted to a makeover project; surrounding death sentences with a color-blind jurisprudence designed to ensure due process was the Court's way of transforming executions into "antilynchings," to disassociate them from past spectacles of populist punitiveness.[51] Protracted appeals were signs that the government was not imposing death hastily or enthusiastically in the manner of the lynch mob. Likewise, the standardized execution protocols that states developed and their turn toward lethal injection further veiled the appearance of an execution as a violent, body-mutilating expression of communal rage. Legal and executive bureaucracies, the very institutions that had inspired a sense of "unfreedom" in those who supported reviving the death penalty, were necessary to keep its historical baggage in check.

Rather than undermining the death penalty, the contradictory coexistence of a fiery rhetoric of retribution with an icy reality of sober restraint initially proved vital to securing its legitimacy. Fiery rhetoric and icy reality distinguished contemporary executions from distinctively shameful histories, one at home and the other abroad, of capital punishment in the twentieth century. The rhetoric of retribution, which celebrated aggrieved local communities getting justice on behalf of one of their own, distanced the death penalty from the horror of mechanized forms of state killing embedded in memories of the Holocaust. Conversely, the reality of a sentencing and execution process that was technically sophisticated and legally complex distanced it from the horror of public lynchings, which peaked in the 1890s in the United States but continued well into the twentieth century. Visions of the state as simultaneously technocracy and vigilante posse, and of its condemned inmates as both out-of-control monsters and responsible subjects, constituted elements of a rich and contradictory cultural reservoir from which support for the death penalty drew strength.

## A Delicate Balance: Functional Negations of Negative Freedom

Retributive representations of state killing not only expressed the virtues of negative freedom, they also worked to manage the anxieties that arose for individuals living in a more libertarian world. When, in the name of securing negative freedom, the neoliberal state shrank its affirmative obligations to securing the health and well-being of its citizens, it created an environment of high risk and high reward. Such a climate was as anxiety inducing as it was liberating, and it threatened to subvert cultural commitments to negative freedom.

As we will see, sympathetic portrayals of the death penalty reconciled, brilliantly at times, a commitment to negative political freedom with a more positive understanding of freedom as a spiritual release from bearing the burdens of one's life alone. We find this kind of freedom, for instance, in discussions of the psychological benefits an execution provides to the families of murder victims. By providing "closure," death penalty advocates argued, executions released families from the chokehold of an unresolved, traumatic past. The state delivered them from the weight placed on them by the very existence of their loved ones' killers. Conversely, we also find this kind of freedom in fictional portrayals of the psychological benefits an execution provides to the condemned. Important fictional portrayals of the death penalty in the 1990s, like *Dead Man Walking* and *The Chamber*, showed isolated and disenfranchised inmates gaining a much-needed compassion, and a sense of grace, by taking responsibility for their crimes in the period preceding their execution. They too achieved closure. By portraying executions as relieving the anxieties created by a government that left people on their own while also expressing its virtues, defenders of the death penalty strengthened its symbolic value.

In a similar manner, supportive portrayals of capital punishment wrestled with dark expressions of negative freedom. A heroic vision of rogue, negative freedom underlay support for the death penalty, but a different kind of negative freedom was often a source of anxiety: the selfish, predatory behavior that thrives in a world where people understand liberty in egocentric terms. In the contemporary era those who embodied the dark extremes of this type of freedom—the monstrous serial killer, the cold-blooded, calculating hit man for hire—were the ones most deserving of death. Death sentences and executions became opportunities to purge these toxic abusers of negative freedom from the culture. By acknowledging and working through the anxiety that can be created by negative freedom—the unrealistic expectations it creates about human autonomy, the destructive egocentrism it may cultivate— discourse about capital punishment embedded it all the more effectively in the cultural landscape.

## Scope and Sources

My arguments focus on two central elements of death penalty discourse: representations of the government that puts people to death (what I will refer to, following legal studies scholar Austin Sarat, as "the killing state") and representations of those persons deemed deserving of death (what I will refer to, following legal studies scholars Kerry Dunn and Paul Kaplan, as "executable subjects").[52] To make my claims I rely on nonfictional and fictional sources. Popular culture, which I define as widely disseminated fictional texts designed to appeal to broad audiences, plays a crucial role in the story I am telling about the American death penalty. First, by resolving the contradictions inherent in death penalty discourse into a larger vision of the good, popular culture reveals the fantasies underlying support for capital punishment that are often scattered across the cacophony of judicial opinions, political debates, trial transcripts, and execution manuals. In that sense I see popular culture as a tool that has worked to maintain majoritarian support for the death penalty.[53] But to shore up this support, these texts often had to depict and resolve the anxieties about racial and class inequalities and punitive violence that capital punishment generated. Thus I also examine popular culture texts as sources that uniquely reveal the insecurities and self-doubts inspired by the fantasies underlying support for the death penalty.[54] A significant number of Hollywood films in the 1990s showcased condemned white inmates triumphing existentially, purging their racist beliefs, and suffering from reverse racism. In distorting the reality of capital punishment, these films attempted to quash very real anxieties that the institution was dehumanizing and racist. When they functioned this way, films and other popular texts about the death penalty, like the player queen in *Hamlet*, protested too much, revealing a culture that, on an unconscious level, was deeply bothered by a reality it claimed to have left in the past.

Popular culture also provides a crucial link between nationally circulating ideas about the death penalty and the practices of local communities. As a work of discourse analysis, this book illustrates how nationally circulating ideas about state violence and freedom have been
expressed in locales that use the death penalty most, such as particular
counties in Texas and Oklahoma. Recent death penalty scholarship has
suggested that we must focus on counties, rather than states or regions,
to understand why the death penalty is used. Regional variations in customs, statutes, and political structures all impose significant limitations
in trying to tell a national story about the death penalty.[55] But by demonstrating how nationally circulating ideas about state violence and freedom have been present in those counties and states that execute the most
condemned inmates, I hope to show how implicated national political
culture has been in the localized use of the death penalty.

## Condemned to Be Free

After its judicial resurrection in the 1970s, the death penalty became
the most draconian extreme of what some have called the "punitive
turn," the ratcheting up of harsh punishment that began in the 1970s and
turned the United States into the most punitive nation in the world. By
2008, an unprecedented one in every one hundred American adults were
locked up on any given day.[56] Scholars of the punitive turn have shown
how harsh punishment expressed strong desires to demean, degrade,
and dehumanize criminals. From victim impact statements in which angry family members of victims tell offenders they will burn in hell to
"humilitainment" reality television programs in which vigilantes confront would-be sex offenders in on-camera sting operations, the delivery
of punitive pain once again became an occasion for the public denuncia-
tion of loathed folk devils.[57] One has only to look at the comments sections of online newspaper articles to get a sense of the way that punishment is imagined as an act that degrades. "Why waste tax payers' money
on feeding the fat pig just before she dies," one commentator on ABC
News's website wrote in response to a story it published about the last
meal request of Georgia death row inmate Kelly Renee Gissendaner.[58]

Harsh, punitive sentiment is not limited to the United States, of
course. But in the Western world its translation into public policy and
mainstream culture has been unique. No other Western democracy still

permits the death penalty. Nor do our peer nations permit, as we do, practices that publicly shame those convicted of crime. From the publication of sex offender registries to the use of chain gangs to "creative" sentences by judges like Ted Poe of Texas, who has required low-level offenders to wear placards in public announcing their crimes, Americans continue to mark criminals with scarlet letters.

To explain Americans' predilection for harsh, degrading punishment, historian James Q. Whitman has contrasted the history of class stratification in the United States and Europe. When egalitarianism swept the Western world in the late eighteenth and early nineteenth centuries, Continental Europeans gradually subjected all convicts to the less degrading and painful punishments that were once reserved for the elite, a practice Whitman calls "leveling up."[59] That ethos, he writes, underlies its comparatively moderate approach to punishment in the contemporary period: "For Europeans, it is an imperative consequence of the abolition of the ancien régime that dignity must be extended to all." Continental Europeans, he argues, identified with their "low-status ancestors. We were all, most of them can say, once at the bottom."[60] Most Americans, on the other hand, have felt no connection to those African slaves who existed at the bottom of the early American caste system. The result has been a greater willingness to degrade, to "level down," to equalize punishment by reducing anyone who was punished to the status of the slave.

In this book, however, I argue that in Americans' cultural imagination, capital punishment has not always been represented as an act of degradation. In both our distant and recent past, the penalty of death has been imagined as a punishment that recognizes and respects the humanity and legal personhood of the criminal. Americans have often tacitly adopted a normative understanding of the death penalty that resembles that of Enlightenment philosopher Immanuel Kant. Kant famously argued that a refusal to punish murder with death was itself a form of intolerable degradation to the murderer. The state that showed mercy was paternalistically reducing those offenders to subjects whose actions, like those of a child, could not be read as issuing from a fully developed, responsible will. *Not* to punish was to degrade.[61] Historically, the execution scene could offer a moment of self-presentation and community recognition that affirmed the criminal's status as a unique member of the polity. Indeed, literary scholar Jeannine Marie DeLombard reveals the political import of published accounts of the confessions and gallows speeches of slaves in the antebellum period. The act of speaking to a public audience about one's life and one's crime represented, albeit perversely, an "augmentation" of the slave's political status. "The slave's offenses activated his personhood," she writes. "Passage through the criminal justice system punitively affirmed the black individual's political membership, making it possible to envision him in alternative public, civic roles."[62] In our cultural history, executions, to use Whitman's formulation, have occasioned the "leveling up" of marginal subjects. A conception of the execution as an event that recognized the offender as a rights-bearing member of the polity underwent a renaissance in the late twentieth century and could, at times, challenge understandings of executions as degradation ceremonies.

Christianity has long shaped the meaning of the death penalty in American society. Writing in 2002, Supreme Court Justice Antonin Scalia, a Catholic defender of the death penalty, argued that it was telling that death penalty abolitionism had taken its firmest hold in "post-Christian Europe" instead of the United States. "For the believing Christian," he argued, "death is no big deal"; it was not an end to all existence, but merely to a bodily one.[63] Scalia's words tapped into a historical Christian connection between the endurance of harsh punishment and the experience of sublime transcendence. In both Europe and the United States, executions before the Enlightenment were religious affairs, dramas of sin and redemption in which the condemned occupied an almost privileged position. The imminence of execution provided an incentive for humbling oneself before God, asking for mercy, and, like Dismas, the penitent robber crucified next to Christ, feeling comforted by a sense that grace had been given. For the sinner the pious acceptance of the penalty was long a sign of the way punishment could redeem the soul.

While Christianity is now mobilized against the death penalty as often as it is mobilized for it, a conservative Christian tradition has operated in the post-*Gregg* era to soften the perception of state killing as a violation of a person's humanity. A celebration of the soul, that ineffable self that could be redeemed in life and become transcendent in death, suffused important death penalty films of the 1990s. Hundreds of years after authorities in colonial New England villages stopped bringing condemned persons to church services to pray with the community in the period leading up to their executions, Hollywood revived an image of a death sentence as a trigger for a process of rehabilitation in condemned inmates that culminated in the achievement of spiritual enlightenment. While Americans despise their criminals and are quick to denounce them as predators or psychopaths, they also continue to take seriously a belief in a transcendent soul, and that belief, in turn, has preserved punishment in our collective imagination as a drama of moral reckoning. In our discourses about punishment, degradation has been balanced by stories of how the pain of punishment can cultivate virtues in both criminal offenders and the citizenry that punishes them. Punishment revolves, as Philip Smith reminds us, around symbols of order and disorder, the sacred and the profane, purity and pollution. It is "a field of human activity vulnerable to eruptions of the primal, mysterious, and awe-inspiring."[64] Attention to the sacred is at the heart of this book: the death penalty has insidiously appealed to a desire to be noble as well as cruel.

French existentialist philosopher Jean-Paul Sartre famously proclaimed that humans are "condemned to be free." His words quite literally describe the plot lines of many important cultural works that feature the death penalty in the twentieth century, from James Cagney's *Angels with Dirty Faces* in 1938 to Tim Robbins's *Dead Man Walking* in 1995, from Richard Wright's *Native Son* in 1940 to Ernest Gaines's *A Lesson Before Dying* in 1993. Americans have long romanticized their death penalty, conceiving of it as a crucible in which a kind of existential freedom may finally be achieved. These execution scenes offer comfort in a world where large, structural injustices exist and regularly transform dispossessed figures into scapegoats or criminals. They show us the condemned transcending the structural forces that have disenfranchised them through an epiphany that can occur only when death looms.

These narrative moments are what initially brought me to this study of the cultural life of capital punishment in the United States. And as I will show, they became particularly emblematic of a world that lost faith in the collective, democratic problem solving that only government can undertake. In the name of guaranteeing our freedom, the state came to say no rather than yes. It shifted its focus toward maintaining order rather than expanding opportunity. The death penalty, and Americans' attachment to it, became perhaps the greatest symbol of that ethos. In the United States, we have condemned—and executed—to feel free.

PART I

# From Rehabilitation to Retribution

## CHAPTER ONE

# "Inside Your Daddy's House"

## *Capital Punishment and Creeping Nihilism in the Atomic Age*

Increasingly, I have come to believe that the death penalty is fundamentally a symptom of bewilderment and confusion in society. A culture that resorts to the death penalty as a method of coping with its troubled is evidencing the same desperation, panic and outrage as the emotionally twisted individual who, in his instability, kills a fellow human being.[1] — Byron E. Eshelman, *Death Row Chaplain* (1962)

"*Buried treasure.* Wake up, little boy. There ain't no caskets of gold. No sunken ship. And even if there was—hell, you can't even *swim*."[2] — Truman Capote, *In Cold Blood* (1965)

In 1966, hundreds of thousands of Americans flocked to bookstores to buy *In Cold Blood*, Truman Capote's true crime account of the murder of a midwestern family and "its aftermath."[3] The story had mixed all the salacious details of a thriller with the gravitas of a tragedy. Acting on false information, two inept ex-cons, Perry Smith and Dick Hickock, had traveled across the state of Kansas to rob a wealthy farming family, the Clutters, of the mountains of cash they thought they would find in a safe. When they arrived, though, they discovered that no safe existed. In frustration, the pair tied up members of the family in separate rooms and killed them—leaving with nothing more than a few dollars.

Capote followed the case from the hatching of the ill-fated plot to the hanging of Smith and Hickock on a rainy night some five years later. Reconstructing what had happened from extensive interviews he conducted with the killers and members of the community their crime upended, Capote told a complex story. He wrote not of a morally innocent world sundered by crime and repaired through punishment, but of a morally troubled world in which superficial innocence masked collective self-doubt. In his hands, the crimes of the deviant revealed a widespread sense of emptiness lingering beneath the surface of wholesome American values.

Nowhere was this moral ambiguity more evident than in Capote's description of the punishment of Smith and Hickock. The long-awaited punishment of the men seemed as devoid of purpose as the crime had been. The book's title had a double meaning, Capote told an interviewer at the time: "in cold blood" referred not only to the way the press had covered the murder of the Clutters, but to the chillingly antiseptic process of putting the two killers to death.[4] The writing subtly invited readers to compare the pointless violence of the executions with the pointless violence of the crimes. By the time they climbed the twelve steps of the Kansas gallows, life in the town their crime had disrupted had returned to normal. No members of the Clutters' extended family came to see the hangings. What there was to see, Capote reported, was violence as unnecessary and aimless in character as what it was punishing.

Although few knew it at the time, Vintage had released the book at a pivotal moment in the history of the American death penalty. In that same year, a team of lawyers from the Legal Defense Fund (LDF), a legal advocacy organization for African Americans with ties to the NAACP, launched a full-out attack on the constitutionality of the sanction. They would ultimately argue, among other things, that the death penalty was a cruel and unusual form of punishment banned by the Eighth Amendment to the Constitution. The Supreme Court had, in earlier decisions, pegged the definition of cruel and unusual to Americans' "evolving standards of decency." The LDF faced a number of indicators—like the failure of state legislatures to abolish capital punishment—that suggested that such standards had not yet evolved to encompass abolition of the death penalty. To overcome that hurdle, its lawyers planned to argue that it was only because the death penalty's use was so infrequent and biased that it was tolerable to a majority of Americans, who would never tolerate the widespread, frequent executions that a fair system would produce. Armed with this larger strategy, the LDF took on the case of any capital defendant who lacked counsel and flooded the courts with appeals. Executions stopped by the middle of 1967 as lower courts began delaying them to see how the Supreme Court would respond.[5]

By some measures the time seemed ripe for an all-out effort to end the death penalty. Both its use and its popularity had been in a slow decline since the end of World War II. Liberal elites had long challenged the wisdom of retributive, eye for an eye justifications for punishment. It was barbaric, they claimed, not only because it was an affront to human dignity, but also because, in light of the rehabilitative techniques the state had at its disposal, it was unnecessary. By the middle of the 1960s, their perspective seemed to be trickling down to many ordinary Americans. A 1966 poll had found that 42 percent of Americans were in favor of capital punishment,[6] one of the lowest numbers in decades.

But if optimism about the state's ability to rehabilitate criminals had grown, so too had concern about the nation's soul. In the 1950s and 1960s, acts of mass murder committed by white men periodically rocked the nation. To some these crimes seemed symptomatic of a nation whose culture had been infected by pernicious forces: a crass materialism that valued things more than people, a dangerous moral relativism that held all value judgments to be equally valid, and a profane secularism that prioritized momentary pleasure over long-term spiritual fulfillment. The result, many American critics warned, was a kind of nihilism—a belief that life was meaningless—that violent crime reflected. Some on the right associated the nation's reluctance to punish with the impoverishment of its soul. And they presented the death penalty as a way to regain what had been lost. Thus, while the death penalty was languishing in one corner of American culture, it was being reborn in another.

## Popularizing the Rehabilitative Ideal

Nurtured by the role experts had played in overseeing New Deal programs in the 1930s and the unprecedented part scientists played in winning World War II, a technocratic approach to government continued to flourish during the early years of the Cold War.[7] Government, Democratic and Republican liberals of the era agreed, had affirmative obligations to the well-being of the people, and experts ought to play a prominent role in helping it meet those obligations.

Such a philosophy extended to the state's power to punish. Across the country, prominent psychiatrists regularly spoke about the nation's criminal justice policy in public forums and advised progressive administrators in state and federal justice systems. Underlying the advice they tendered was the principle that the state had the means and the expertise to make rehabilitation, not retribution, the purpose of punishment.[8] For its most progressive proponents, rehabilitative psychotherapy would be a process of self-discovery that would guide inmates to law-abiding lives when they left prison. Caryl Chessman, an inmate on California's death row in the 1950s, became an international cause célèbre by writing best-selling books like *Cell 2455, Death Row* (1954) and *Trial by Ordeal* (1955). In them he presented himself as an amateur criminologist and advanced this vision of an empowering therapeutic state.[9] Turning the psychoanalytic lens on himself, Chessman told readers that his first contact with the criminal justice system had hardened rather than helped him:

> Emphasis, as it too often is, was placed on neutralizing my drives instead of finding legitimate and challenging outlets for them. I never felt or was led to feel that "straightening out" would mean other than a disastrous defeat. Indeed, defeat seemed to be the goal of those dealing with me. The youngster in trouble, if he is to be helped, must believe that society is a genuinely interested big brother, not a grim patriarch who demands submissive conformity or else.[10]

The assumption, for Chessman and the liberal criminologists his best seller channeled, was that repression led to antisocial behavior. If the criminal found prisons staffed by liberal psychiatrists instead of authoritarian guards, Chessman claimed, he would be more apt to abandon his antisocial stance toward society.

Chessman was not the only popularizer of liberal criminology. In a series of mass-market films about capital punishment in the 1950s and 1960s, Hollywood filmmakers consciously sought to win audiences over to the cause of abolishing the death penalty by showing them that the condemned were not rebels, but rather victims of a world that had beaten them down and left them powerless mentally as well as physically. In Walter Wanger's *I Want to Live!* (1958) and Irvin Kershner's *The Hoodlum Priest* (1961), the condemned were not savvy heroes but pitiful souls, victims of social forces or the winds of fate who needed that "genuinely interested big brother," as Chessman put it.[11]

*I Want To Live!* shrewdly dramatized the rare case of a woman on death row.[12] In an Academy Award–winning performance, Susan Hayward played Barbara Graham, a California woman who is wrongly executed for the murder of a wealthy socialite during a burglary gone bad.[13]

Tough on the surface after a life of bad breaks, Barbara is soft underneath. Wanger had urged the film's director, Robert Wise, to create "the feeling that this girl is isolated, in a cage, from the rest of the world,"[14] and Wise had delivered with a film that exploited viewers' understanding of women as vulnerable, maternal figures incapable of real criminal agency. Barbara's baby boy visits her on death row, reminding audiences that her impending execution could never be a triumph of individual courage: it was a merciless severing of the sacred bond between a mother and her child. The execution scene, too, capitalized on Victorian gender roles to portray going to the gas chamber as a degrading, pornographic spectacle. To avoid facing the condemning or voyeuristic looks of witnesses, Barbara receives permission to wear a sleep mask to her execution. Mask on, she stumbles helplessly toward the gas chamber, at one point falling backward in fear (see fig. 2). Instead of offering closure, Barbara's last words are a rhetorical question. When a guard advises her to breathe the cyanide fumes deeply so as to avoid pain, she hisses back, "How would you know?" This—a condemned woman terrified by the unknown and literally unable to face her fate—was Wanger's denouement-

FIGURE 2. In contrast to films that had shown condemned men bearing their fate with courage, *I Want to Live!* (1958) presented execution as degrading and disorienting.

cized vision of death at the hands of the state: isolating, disorienting, humiliating, terrifying.

*The Hoodlum Priest*, released several years later, adopted a similar tack.[15] In it, a liberal priest takes Billy Lee Jackson, a sympathetic white hoodlum, under his wing. Billy goes straight, taking a job at a produce market, but he cannot shake his reputation as an outlaw. When his employer unjustly fires him for stealing from the company, he gives up on a legitimate life and burglarizes the market in retaliation. Caught red-handed, he kills his former employer in a panic and is sentenced to death for the crime.

Like *I Want to Live!* the film depicted the condemned as a victim of social forces, his good-faith efforts to become a law-abiding citizen stymied by a world that does not give second chances. It too sought to unsettle audiences with its execution scene. Whereas older Hollywood renderings of capital punishment kept viewers aware of how much time the condemned had left—usually by shots of a clock ticking inexorably toward the appointed time—*The Hoodlum Priest* kept audiences unsure of how much time Billy has left once his execution day arrives. He is moved from his regular cell to a holding cell to the gas chamber in one dizzying, continuous sequence. Without the ritual buildup, the punishment is both disorienting and mechanical. *Time* magazine's movie critic pointedly adopted impersonal language to describe an execution scene he found profoundly moving: "The condemned object is swiftly, efficiently prepared for the gas chamber. In the boy's eyes, wide with horror, the spectator reads the incredulous realization: in a few short minutes his life, the only life he has or will ever have, is with absolute certainty going to end."[16] The execution was not a sublime moment of moral closure, but an unceremonious death by assembly line.

But perhaps the most explicitly liberal film of the bunch was Richard Brooks's 1967 film version of Capote's *In Cold Blood*. Before filming began, Brooks, who both wrote and directed the film, traveled to the Menninger Clinic in Topeka, Kansas. Headed by Karl Menninger, a prominent liberal psychiatrist, the clinic was a nationally renowned therapeutic training and treatment center at the forefront of making the case that psychiatry could and would revolutionize the criminal justice system.[17]

Over the course of two days of meetings, Brooks got a crash course in the tenets of liberal criminology. Criminals, he learned, were not like normal people. Their criminal behavior stemmed from an internalized sense of inferiority that had itself been caused by a variety of environmental conditions. Poverty, a dysfunctional family, or humiliating childhood experiences had stunted their moral and emotional development, leaving them bereft of self-esteem and unable to respond to provocations in the way normal people would. Crime was not something they chose. It was more like something that happened when they stumbled blindly into situational traps and saw violence as their only means of escape. One of the Menninger clinicians compared committing murder to losing a chess game: "You make one move and you are caught by that. You have to make another move, then you have to make another move, you know? Many times we say, 'How did I ever get caught in something like that?' We got caught . . . without even being aware. We made one small move after the other."[18] In such circumstances, who could justify the death penalty? It was not punishment, but one final act of cruelty from a world that had often been tormenting a person for decades. It was especially cruel because it was unnecessary. Modern psychiatric research conducted at places like the Menninger Clinic promised a near future in which psychologists could defuse these ticking human time bombs. As he sat in meetings with their researchers and clinicians, Brooks confirmed his suspicions: psychiatry had changed the criminological landscape, yet Americans still stubbornly clung to a retributive way of thinking about punishment.

Energized by his two days at the clinic, Brooks decided to make the Menninger perspective central to the film. The opening titles prominently acknowledged his debt to the experts at the clinic. Menninger research, audiences learned, showed that every "senseless" murderer had issued a cry for help before he killed. And Perry Smith, Brooks pointedly showed them, had done just that, only to be ignored by a prison staff that lacked the training to recognize it. "Maybe if they'd had a head doctor here during my first stretch, he'd have known I had a bomb ticking inside of me. He'd have known I wasn't ready for parole," Perry tells the prison chaplain shortly before his execution, driving home the film's heavy-handed faith in psychiatric expertise.[19]

Liberal criminologists and enlightened jurists applauded these films. Donald E. J. MacNamara, dean of criminology at the New York Institute of Criminology and chairman of the Annual Meetings Program for the American Society of Criminology, screened *I Want to Live!* for criminologists at the society's annual conference. Afterward, he wired Wanger that those who had watched it saw it as a documentary—its criminology was right on the money, and its educational value, he thought, would be a real boon to criminal justice reform efforts.[20] The progressive Supreme Court justice William O. Douglas, who had granted a stay of execution to the real-life Barbara Graham and would vote to suspend the death penalty a decade and a half later, screened the film for his fellow justices in Washington, DC—one of the first such screenings at the US Supreme Court—and sent Wanger a note of appreciation.[21]

If the movies had any effect on the nation's mood, these liberal elites hoped, opposition to capital punishment might finally be trickling down to ordinary Americans. Richard Brooks thought that might be the case. Speaking to an interviewer two years after the release of *In Cold Blood*, Brooks was proud. "You obviously can't give the movie anything like full credit for this," Brooks told the *Los Angeles Times*, "but the fact is that there hasn't been a single public execution in this country in the period since the movie was released. And that's what 'In Cold Blood' was about as I saw it."[22] A modern faith in the state and revulsion at the gratuitous cruelty of executions, he hoped, had changed Americans for good.

## Rumblings beneath the Surface

In 1966, as the Legal Defense Fund's efforts to get a Supreme Court ruling declaring the death penalty unconstitutional got under way, support for the death penalty was as low as it had ever been, with just 42 percent of Americans supporting it. The next year, however, support had jumped twelve points to 54 percent. By 1976, 66 percent of Americans would support the death penalty. In the mid-1980s, approval would surge to over 70 percent, where it would remain through the end of the century.[23] What accounted for such a dramatic about-face?

Some accounts of the punitive sentiments that swept the nation in the 1970s have rightly focused on the role that antiblack racism played in the demand by a white "silent majority" that politicians get tough on crime (or, conversely, on how politicians, for political gain, stoked racially charged fear of crime).[24] Support for the death penalty was no exception. White southerners' disproportionate use of it against African Americans for the crime of rape in the decades following World War II testifies to the sanction's function as a thinly veiled expression of white supremacy in an era when lynching had declined.[25] The death penalty's historical connection to racism and resurgent white anxiety about black criminality in the late 1960s undoubtedly generated support for capital punishment when its abolition seemed imminent.

As we shall see, however, the part that horrifying crimes of young white men played in generating support for the death penalty serves as an important counterpart to our conventional understanding of the role race played in its renewed popularity. Responses to white men who would come to be known as psychopaths formed a distinctive, though related, current of thought in the conservative demand that the nation abandon rehabilitation and bring back the death penalty.[26] In contrast to black criminality, white psychopathy evoked a sense that mainstream culture, generated by whites, was to blame for a world infected by a nihilism that whites themselves had actively wrought or passively permitted. In this climate, a spate of young white men who killed for no apparent reason were a source of profound angst. They haunted the middle-class imagination, embodying an existential threat to the dominant culture that came from within it.

Capote's book, unlike Brooks's film version of it, had made this clear. In Capote's hands, the American culture that Perry Smith and Dick Hickock had attacked was as tortured as they were. While Brooks had fastened on Capote's sympathetic presentation of Smith as a candidate for rehabilitation, he ignored Capote's very different take on Hickock. Unlike Smith—a racial and class outsider—Hickock had grown up in the kind of traditional nuclear family that had been exalted in the aftermath of World War II. And he had, by his own account, had a wholesome high school experience, earning nine varsity letters and winning two unused college athletic scholarships. Digging into his psyche, however, psychiatrists found a psychopathic personality. Capote quoted liberally from one of Dick's psychiatric reports: "His self-esteem is very low, and he secretly feels inferior to others and sexually inadequate. . . . He is uncomfortable in his relationships to other people, and has a pathological inability to form and hold enduring personal attachments. Although he professes usual moral standards he seems obviously uninfluenced by them in his actions."[27] Hickock, Capote had shown, had a particularly horrifying desire for sex with prepubescent girls.

None of this psychopathy had a discernible point of origin in Dick's upbringing. Hickock's psychopathic qualities—his inability to feel remorse, his shallow, manipulative relationships with others—could not be ascribed to the social-structural problems that liberals in the 1960s saw as the root cause of crime. He was not the victim of poverty or racism or abusive parents. He was instead part of a broader kind of crime that Capote and others called attention to at the time: the alarming rate at which white men, without any apparent warning or motive, embarked on killing jags. In the book, Capote quoted extensively from a Menninger Foundation article on the topic, "Murder without Apparent Motive." In it, four psychiatrists had chronicled patterns in a small sample of men who murdered persons they had no rational reason to kill. Their irrationality stemmed from "disturbances in affect organization":

> [T]he men displayed a tendency not to experience anger or rage in association with violent aggressive action. None reported feelings of rage in connection with the murders, nor did they experience anger in any strong or pronounced way, although each of them was capable of enormous and brutal aggression. . . . Their relationships with others were of a shallow, cold nature, lending a quality of loneliness and isolation to these men. People were scarcely real to them, in the sense of being warmly or positively (or even angrily) felt about. . . . The three men under sentence of death had shallow emotions regarding their own fate and that of their victims.[28]

Capote found this psychopathic profile compelling enough that he took a significant detour to highlight other men on Kansas's death row who fit it. One evening in 1958, Lowell Lee Andrews, a twenty-two-year-old University of Kansas student whom one neighbor had called "the nicest boy in Kansas" calmly shot to death all the members of his immediate family, without warning or provocation. In a similarly unpredictable manner, George York and James Latham, two AWOL white soldiers in their late teens, went on a cross-country killing jag in 1961, killing seven people for the pleasure of it. Capote devoted pages of his book to describing the remarkably similar qualities of the senseless crimes that those on Kansas's death row had committed.

Other cases that surrounded the release of *In Cold Blood* fit a similar pattern. Readers of the book would likely have recalled Charles Starkweather, a nineteen-year-old who, with his fourteen-year-old girlfriend Caril Ann Fugate, gained national attention when they went on a multiday killing spree in Nebraska and Wyoming in 1958, the year before the Clutter murders. In 1965, just as *In Cold Blood* was released, twenty-three-year-old Charles Schmid killed three girls in Tucson over the course of a year, burying their bodies in the desert on the outskirts of town. The next summer, twenty-four-year-old Richard Speck would break into a Chicago townhouse functioning as a dormitory for student nurses and systematically lead eight of them, one by one, to their slaughter. Several weeks later, twenty-five-year-old Charles Whitman would climb to the top of a tower in the middle of the University of Texas-Austin campus, load a gun, and kill eleven people on the grounds below and three inside the building. These men represented a violent, psychotic, extreme iteration of the white juvenile delinquent, a figure who had become a source of anxiety for middle-class whites in the 1950s. While liberals had presented technocratic, therapeutic expertise as the solution to the problem of juvenile delinquency, these young men represented the limits of Americans' tolerance for therapeutic solutions. With the exception of Whitman, who was killed at the scene of his crime, each of them was sentenced to death at a moment when executions were in sharp decline.[29]

These cases occurred just on the cusp of a significant rise in the incidence of mass murder that began in the mid-1960s.[30] The local and national publicity they generated presented Americans with a much more discomforting face of crime than Hollywood had been feeding them. Investigators found Andrews, who had massacred his family, sitting on a sun porch yards away from the corpses of his family, petting the family dog. "He was the most unconcerned murderer I ever met," Ralph Athey of the local sheriff's department told the Associated Press.[31] Andrews himself agreed with that assessment: "I don't feel anything—period," he had told the police. "I'm not sorry and I'm not glad I did it."[32] Officials who interviewed York and Latham likewise emphasized their nonchalance. "It didn't seem to bother them one way or the other," Colorado Sheriff W. H. Terrill told the press. "I mean, no more than what you'd think about going out and shooting a rabbit." Another official told reporters, "They talked as if they might have robbed a peanut machine. . . . There wasn't any remorse. They even laughed at some of their victims."[33] These were not the sympathetic souls of the recent spate of liberal anti–death penalty films. Articles about the crime noted the boys' atheism, their desire for the death penalty, and Latham's "I hate the world" tattoo.[34]

The nihilism of these young men stoked long-standing neurotic suspicions that modern life had created an imperceptible emptiness within ordinary persons. Since the nineteenth century, Western thinkers had been wringing their hands about what technology, classic liberalism, urbanism, and capitalism were doing to human beings. Émile Durkheim's

"anomie," Karl Marx's "alienation," Max Weber's "iron cage" all described a kind of hollowness, malleability, and subsequent hunger for
purpose that the conditions of modern life created.[35] Modern social science had created the figure of the delinquent whose crimes were the result of exclusion from the bounty of a virtuous middle-class American
culture, but the modern world had created a very different sort of criminal: young men like Dick Hickock, Charles Starkweather, Lowell Lee
Andrews, and Charles Schmid. Defying liberal criminological explanation, they had grown up near the center of a culture that they had one
day turned on. They were grotesque expressions or exploiters of a spiritually unsatisfying middle-class American culture rather than the tragic
casualties of a failure to access that culture.

Concern about the emptiness these men embodied or manipulated
had been simmering in the middle-class white imagination since World
War II. The war had demonstrated how easily humans could use reason
and technology to end life on a massive scale. It had shown how regular
people could become the instruments of vile cultural and political forces.
In its aftermath, Americans had begun critically examining their own
culture. In 1951, at the height of the first deep freeze of the Cold War,
psychologist Solomon Asch began a number of now-famous psychological experiments revealing that persons will lie about what they see in
front of them if they become convinced that those near them have seen
something different. In an "Emperor Has No Clothes" moment, subjects
lied about the relative length of a line presented to them to avoid being
the lone truth teller.[36] The experiment raised questions about the integrity of average persons: their willingness—or perhaps ability—to sacrifice social approval in order to speak the truth.

In the early 1960s, Stanley Milgram of Yale University, who had been
Asch's student, conducted experiments demonstrating just how obedient
average Americans could be when an expert ordered them to administer
shocks to a fellow human being. Led to believe they were assisting him
in conducting memory experiments, most of Milgram's subjects (65 percent) administered to an unseen "learner" what they believed to be a
massive, 450-volt shock, despite the learner's pleas that they stop. When
subjects asked him about proceeding, the "expert" ordered them to continue in language devoid of agency: "It is absolutely essential that you
continue," or "The experiment requires that you continue," he would
say. Their obedience was a clear indicator of the power of institutional
authority that had no discernible human will driving it.[37] Milgram's work

called into question Americans' ability to abide by their understanding of right and wrong when push came to shove. At best, it showed how a modern world had loosened the influence that traditional forms of authority had over people, allowing them to be more easily guided by morally rudderless totalitarian or bureaucratic or scientific logics. At worst, the malleability of Milgram's subjects called into question whether free will and moral agency really existed. A capacity for negative freedom— to resist outside pressure and think independently—was at the heart of ennobling visions of human beings. Those visions now seemed built on false pretenses.

Murderous boy-men like Hickock, York, Latham, and Andrews embodied the feelings of emptiness that lay beneath the surface of middle-class, postwar prosperity. While social critics imagined that emptiness as creating a hunger for meaning that authoritarian regimes could exploit, these young men stood as another consequence of it: people who responded to an internalized sense of emptiness not by running toward authority, but by denying its existence altogether. In stark contrast to the criminal imagined by liberals, whose crimes reflected a stymied desire to lead a good life, journalists and social critics presented the young white serial or spree killer as the product of a world that had lost its moral foundation. He was perilously unmoored and reveled in a kind of narcissistic, nihilistic freedom.

Alarmist journalists wondered whether this kind of nihilistic freedom was infectious. Charles Schmid, for instance, was nicknamed the "Pied Piper of Tucson" by *Life* magazine because some in the Tucson adolescent community had worshiped him; some local teenagers likely knew of his murderous behavior and kept quiet about it.[38] That thought haunted coverage of the case. "According to the verdict, Schmid will die in the gas chamber," the *Los Angeles Times* reported shortly after his sentencing. "It is debatable to most observers here, however, whether his unsavory and unwanted legacy to the local teenage world will die with him."[39] In 1959, teenagers in Nebraska had inspired similar angst by "blaring rock 'n' roll" outside the prison on the night of Charles Starkweather's execution.[40]

Several notable fictional works portrayed these young white men, or figures like them, as extreme expressions of a nihilism that permeated contemporary American culture. In Flannery O'Connor's hands, the murderous white man was a self-fashioned truth teller, exposing the meaninglessness of modern life. In "A Good Man Is Hard to Find," the title work of a prizewinning collection of short stories published in 1955, O'Connor portrayed a vacuous middle-class white family traveling across Georgia on a vacation road trip. From the story's opening paragraphs, a mood of existential isolation and loneliness surround an otherwise traditional family. Mom and Dad and their preteen son and daughter are remarkably contemptuous of one another; each embodies the self-absorption of a modern, consumer-driven culture. Even the baby has a "faraway smile."[41] The children's grandmother, reluctantly brought along for the ride, comes off no better. She voices righteous indignation about the modern generation's values, but the values she is nostalgic for, we quickly see, are the product of a racist and paternalist view of the world. Neither the younger nor the older generation seems capable of empathy.

A car crash cuts short the unhappy vacation. A man named the Misfit, recently escaped from the state penitentiary and wanted for murder, comes across them. He informs the dazed family that he has been punished for a crime he did not commit, and he asserts that his experience is common: the world is filled with cases in which "one [person] is punished a heap and another ain't punished at all."[42] Nobody, he notes, seems to care. His random killing of strangers, it appears, is a way to make literal the psychological deadness to the world that those who are alive demonstrate in their everyday failure to recognize the pain and injustice that surrounds them. In two waves, the Misfit has his associate march the members of the family into the nearby woods, where they are shot dead: first the boy and the father, then the mother, the girl, and the baby.[43]

As the Misfit prepares to shoot the grandmother, she begins to understand that she is being executed for the crime of complicity in an unjust world. Overcome with a radical, Christlike love, she reaches for him and calls him her son. Thrown off by her capacity for love, the Misfit recoils and abruptly shoots her. Early in his appearance, he asserts that there's "no pleasure but meanness," both exposing and reveling in a world that has lost its spiritual foundation.[44] The grandmother's demonstrated capacity for empathy in her final moments seems to alter that appraisal. She "would have been a good woman if it had been somebody there to shoot her every minute of her life," he realizes in the story's final moments.[45]

O'Connor sympathized with her Misfit without adopting his fatalism. "If you live today you breathe in nihilism," she had opined to a friend in the same year she introduced the Misfit to America. But the end of

her story shows that such nihilism is not an intractable reality but a surmountable mentality. The white spree killer was a window into all of
us.[46] He unveiled a capacity for goodness and love that had been buried,
but not lost, in the postwar world.

Joyce Carol Oates's fictional treatment of Tucson killer Charles
Schmid in a 1966 short story also captured the fear that the seeds of murderous violence lay within mainstream life. In "Where Are You Going,
Where Have You Been?" she created a devilish countercultural antago-
nist named Arnold Friend—Oates's stand-in for Schmid—who shows up
at a suburban home to lure away Connie, a curious fifteen-year-old girl.
Connie has refused to join her family on a picnic, choosing to stay home,
listen to rock 'n' roll, and indulge in "trashy daydreams." One daydream
in particular—about a tryst with a local teenage boy in an alleyway the
night before—seems to summon the fiendish Friend, who parks in the
driveway, walks up to the house, chats with her through a screen door,
and psychologically rapes her in short order. He leads her off, in the end,
into the desert.[47]

The story was no cautionary tale. Oates did not present Connie's abduction as a kind of punishment for her rebellion against family values.
The text instead revealed both suburban domesticity and the countercultural rebellion that promised an escape from it as symptoms of the
same existential emptiness. Arnold Friend initially embodies an excite-
ment that lay beyond the security of home. But as he stands talking to
her through a flimsy screen door, she realizes that his countercultural
coolness is a ruse, the product of pancake makeup and elevator shoes.
Beneath it is a disorienting nihilism that preys on adolescent desire for
rebellion. And yet the story does not, Wizard of Oz–style, affirm the virtues of domestic tranquility against cosmopolitan temptations. Arnold
forces Connie to recognize, correctly, that her desire for escape was
more than a symptom of immaturity; it was a tacit recognition that the
security against which she sought to rebel was never there in the first
place. Her father ignores her and her mother badgers her in fights that
"kept up a pretense of exasperation, a sense that they were tugging and
struggling over something of little value to either of them." The home,
an "asbestos ranch house," was supposed to be the source of moral security but as those in an age of home-grown psychopaths were discovering,
its moral insulation, like its literal insulation—the cancer-causing asbestos—was a dangerous fiction.[48]

Arnold is, in the end, not a source of moral corruption but a mirror who reveals to Connie just how devoid of moral foundation her existence has always been. Before he leads her away, he tells her, hauntingly, "The place where you came from ain't there anymore, and where you had in mind to go is cancelled out. This place you are now—inside your daddy's house—is nothing but a cardboard box I can knock down any time. You know that and always did know it."[49] In a final image, as Connie leaves the house, consenting to her own abduction, she moves with Arnold toward the "vast sunlit reaches of land" she had never noticed before, a desertlike emptiness that had surrounded her all along.[50]

In its own contemplation of the white multiple murderer, Capote's *In Cold Blood* called into question the broader state of the culture that surrounded both the criminals and their victims. The Clutters may have been the town's darlings, but the family had its demons. Doubts about the value of life gnawed at Bonnie Clutter, the mother of the family, whose debilitating depression confined her to bed most of the time.[51] The teetotaling Herb Clutter's fastidiousness, Capote showed, came with an unhealthy obsession with control.[52] Their daughter Nancy's journal, moreover, contained paranoid entries in which she claimed someone had purposely killed her cat. Their reputation as the town's darlings masked a more complex psychological reality, Capote frequently showed.

The area's postwar prosperity, moreover, seemed built on distrust that the murders exposed. Rather than assuming that a drifter had murdered the family, the residents of Holcomb eyed one another suspiciously. The disillusion and despair that Smith's and Hickock's crimes elicited was latent in Holcomb before the crime had even been committed. Myrtle Clare, the town's postmistress, embodied the nihilistic malaise that Capote found lingering underneath the community. She taunts her elderly, religious mother with a cavalier attitude about the death of the Clutters:

> "When your time comes, it comes. And tears won't save you." She had observed that her mother had begun to shed a few. "When Homer died, I used up all the fear I had in me, and all the grief, too. If there's somebody loose around here that wants to cut my throat, I wish him luck. What difference does it make? It's all the same in eternity. Just remember: if one bird carried every grain of sand, grain by grain, across the ocean, by the time he got them all on the other side, that would be only the beginning of eternity. So blow your nose."[53]

Moments like this in the text may have driven *Harper's* critic Rebecca West's response to *In Cold Blood*. West placed the murders that Capote described in the context of modern literature. "What air do these peo ple breathe not permeated with the culture we have made?" she asked of Perry Smith and Dick Hickock. "Where else could they have caught this infection but from us? There is a hateful continuity between the world of literature and the world of Mr. Capote's criminals." Modern literature had explored the idea that life was unbearable, she explained. The idea "passes into general currency, in films, on television, in chatter, and so it happens that one day a naïve person . . . comes to believe that sophisticated people believe life to be unbearable, and therefore it is not terrible to carry the belief to its logical conclusion and to deprive his fellowmen of their lives." Nihilism, West suggested, was a literary trope gone awry; authors needed to assert the value of life.[54] Fellow literary critic Malcolm Muggeridge also found nihilistic continuity between the world of Holcomb and the world of "Mr. Capote's criminals." *In Cold Blood*, he said, had called attention to "a violence, a criminality, a death wish at the very heart of our kind of society."[55]

In an era when elite faith in rehabilitation was peaking, inexplicable acts of multiple murder by young white men exposed a nihilism that was at stark odds with the technocratic confidence of the age. Artistic explorations of these crimes and their context by O'Connor, Oates, and Capote captured a broader doubt about the modern world that contested the liberal assumptions that filmmakers like Richard Brooks and public intellectuals like Karl Menninger took for granted. They and others who argued for the virtues of rehabilitation had assumed that those who broke the law had been denied the benefits of integration into society. They had assumed that the society the criminal would return to was healthy. The rising presence of the unfeeling white male who committed motiveless murder called each of these assumptions into question. More and more Americans were beginning to think that the criminal was not a pitiful other but a homegrown reflection of a moral rot lurking beneath an edifice of modernity and prosperity. Screenwriter Abby Mann, who went to Tucson in 1966 to investigate the Schmid case for a screenplay he was writing, voiced this perspective. His work in the world of criminal justice, he told the *New York Times*, had left him "with the feeling that under given circumstances, anyone could be a murderer."[56]

## Regeneration through Punishment

A growing crisis of confidence in the nation's moral integrity, stoked by a rising awareness of white psychopathy and a sense that it was a symptom of cultural decadence, contributed to what followed: tumbling support for a prevention- and rehabilitation–based approach to criminal justice and a dramatic uptick of public support for capital punishment.[57] Writing in support of the death penalty in the late 1970s, after public opinion had swung decisively back in favor of capital punishment, Cornell University professor Walter Berns defended the practice as an antidote to nihilism. The death penalty was the symbol of a virtuous society, Berns charged, one whose members held humanity in high regard. The execution of criminals was not a warning to would-be offenders but a declaration that the condemned were aberrant exceptions. They had proved themselves unfit to belong to a moral community of persons who, "even in the absence of a policeman, will not assault our bodies or steal our possessions, and might even come to our assistance when we need it, and who stand ready, when the occasion demands it, to risk their lives in defense of their country."[58] Those good people vastly outnumbered the Charles Mansons of the world, and an execution was an affirmation that they, not the psychopath, embodied what it meant to be human. A nation that executes, he promised, "will remind its citizens that it is a country worthy of heroes."[59]

Berns's work also revealed how, in the culturally conservative imagination, the death penalty was becoming consonant with an understanding of freedom that was suspicious of the state. In their objectification of human life, white mass murderers seemed to embody the white abandonment of a way of life—prebureaucratic, prerelativistic, prelegalistic—that had historically endowed each individual with a sense of honor and self-restraint. Men like Charles Manson and Charles Schmid were symptoms of a world in which tight social relations and moral instruction no longer prepared citizens for a life in which they exercised their freedom with an unselfish civic-mindedness. Indeed, the sense of nihilism their crimes reflected and stoked was a form of negative freedom run awry—irresponsible, megalomaniacal, untethered.

As we will see, throughout the seventies, conservatives increasingly blamed big, bureaucratic centralized government for this perceived change in American culture. The rise of a paternalist government run by experts and jurists who were out of touch with the moral essence of local communities had undermined relationships of mutual obligation within those communities. In hubristically purporting to have the knowledge and capacity to socially engineer the good life, moreover, welfare-oriented government fostered dangerous dependency on the state and, in doing so, created a culture in which individuals did not feel the importance of developing individual self-control.

As an antipaternalist state action, the death penalty represented a rebuke against this vision of the state. The death penalty was, instead, the symbol of a state that recognized the primacy of family and local community in the development of Americans who were capable of altruism and self-control. It was a tacit assertion that shared values, rather than regulatory frameworks, held communities together. As a quasi-religious, sacrificial act, execution offered proof that the criminal law was not just an instrument humans used to ensure their collective survival but was subordinate to a sacred moral order that existed before the state. As Berns put it,

> The criminal law must possess a dignity far beyond that possessed by mere statutory enactment or utilitarian and self-interested calculations; the most powerful means we have to give it that dignity is to authorize it to impose the ultimate penalty. The law must be made awful, by which I mean awe-inspiring, or commanding "profound respect or reverential fear." It must remind us of the moral order by which alone we can live as human beings, and in our day the only punishment that can do that is capital punishment.[60]

As a kind of sublime violence, capital punishment abolished the nihilism that infected the world and reconciled men's desires to be both heroic individuals and selfless members of a moral enterprise much larger than themselves. Capital punishment upheld an understanding of community as "people who do not value their possessions more than their citizenship, who do not think exclusively or even primarily of their own rights, people whom we can depend on even as they exercise their rights, and whom we can trust."[61] Nihilism, cynicism, relativism—the sins of the modern world—had challenged this understanding. It followed that it would take an antimodern practice to reassert it. In elegant, erudite prose, Berns articulated what it meant when juries rejected the pleas of psychiatrists and sentenced young men like Charles Starkweather, Charles Schmid, James York, George Latham, Richard Speck, and Charles Manson to death.

## Rage against the Machine: The *Longue Durée* of "Law and Order"

Continually contrasting despicable criminals to "heroes," Berns revealed an important current in the reactionary thought of his age. Support for the death penalty was about more than repressing threats to society; it was about reviving a way for communities to demonstrate, through the punishment of bad men, the existence of heroes, exceptional human beings who embodied the persistence of responsible, yet vigorous freedom in a world generally afflicted by a corrosive moral paralysis.

After a decade of dramatically rising rates of violent crime, by the early 1970s a bureaucratic and legalistic criminal justice system had come to seem the embodiment of that modern moral paralysis. Journalists and filmmakers began suggesting to Americans that the fear they felt for their safety had been magnified by a prison system built around rehabilitation. The failure of rehabilitation had "become paramount," *Baltimore Sun* editorial writer Richard O'Mara told readers in 1976. "It is forcing students of the criminal justice system to a radical conception of that system's purpose. They are moving back to the conviction that the best response to crime is punishment—punishment for the sake of retribution and deterrence, only secondarily for rehabilitation."[62] Like many reporters of the day, O'Mara quoted a study of studies published by criminologists Douglas Lipton, Robert Martinson, and Judith Wilks, which Martinson had famously distilled for a wider audience in a 1974 article in *Public Interest*.[63] The researchers had surveyed 231 rehabilitation programs and found no discernible influence, positive or negative, on recidivism. Journalists summed up the study, later called "the most politically influential criminological study of the last half century," with the phrase "Nothing Works."[64] Appearing on the CBS newsmagazine *60 Minutes*, then one of the top-rated programs on television, Martinson came across as a "heroic iconoclast" willing to speak the dirty truth that rehabilitation was a failure.[65] The segment ended with reporter Mike Wallace telling the audience that criminals needed not rehabilitation but "[a] swift, sure painful kick in the backside."[66] In many minds, moreover, the problem was not limited to the management of prisons; the law too was to blame. New criminal jurisprudence produced over the 1960s by Earl Warren's Supreme Court had bestowed on criminal defendants new rights that, they thought, made it easier than ever for criminals to evade justice. A right to counsel, to be told of one's right to be silent, and above all, to have illegally obtained evidence excluded from one's trial, had neutered law enforcement, endangering not only Americans' physical security, but also their capacity to recognize and fight evil.

The death penalty represented an antimodern alternative to these institutions. Those who championed it in legislatures, governors' mansions, and courtrooms presented themselves as populist heroes dismantling a modern system that had left ordinary Americans feeling morally and physically insecure. In this context, demand for the death penalty was not simply a punitive, retributive response to criminals or a reversion to harshness when other tools of social control seemed to be failing. It expressed, rather, a desire for heroes in a technocratic world that, in seeking to manage problems rather than vanquish evil, had no use for heroism. As Garry Wills noted at the time, Richard Nixon's law and order platform was not only a coded appeal to racism, but to many it was "the last clause left from our old moral creed . . . the ideal of self-government, of the self-disciplined, self-made man."[67]

Indeed, well before the backlash created by urban rioting in the 1960s, popular culture revealed an existing connection, in the popular imagination, between law and order and a pleasurable sense of liberation from the alienating forces of modern life. In the 1950s, the western movie and the hard-boiled detective story revealed the psychic tension that many in the white middle classes experienced in a world transformed by bureaucracies and mass consumption. The sometimes lawless yet always righteous, violent energy that frontier heroes displayed on the big screen or that private detectives like Mike Hammer channeled in pulp fiction satisfied yearnings for a world where individuals could heroically bring order to chaos.[68] Filmmaker John Ford's last western, *The Man Who Shot Liberty Valance* (1962), openly mourned the loss of lawless yet noble energy in the modern world.[69] Ford presented the tragic hero of the film, Tom Doniphon, as a rugged frontiersman who heroically kills Liberty Valance, a predatory cattleman who had terrorized the frontier town of Shinbone. Shooting Valance from the shadows, Doniphon intentionally creates the illusion that Ransom Stoddard, an eastern lawyer, fired the lethal shot in a fair-and-square duel. Hailed as a hero, Stoddard goes on to lead the territory into civilized statehood and becomes its first senator, while the self-sacrificing frontiersman Doniphon is forgotten. For Ford, that amnesia was troubling. The mournful final notes of *Liberty Valance* suggested the psychological cost that came from a modern culture's failure to honor its origin in the lawless violence of rough yet morally good men.[70]

In the early 1970s, a spate of new movies transposed the frontier ethos to the inner city and celebrated rogue, antitechnocratic, antilegalistic white men who meted out death vigilante-style to menacing threats to the social order. The most notable of these films were Don Siegel's *Dirty Harry* (1971) and Michael Winner's *Death Wish* (1974).[71] In *Dirty Harry*, Clint Eastwood was Harry Callahan, a San Francisco cop who goes rogue and pursues a psychopathic killer who evades justice. In *Death Wish*, Charles Bronson starred as Paul Kersey, a New York City architect who patrols the streets at night and kills would-be muggers after his wife is killed during a home invasion and the police do nothing but offer sympathy. These heroes demonstrated the lawless, civilizing violence whose loss Ford had grieved in *The Man Who Shot Liberty Valance*. If Ford mourned the construction of a democratic, disembodied political order at the beginning of the 1960s, Siegel and Winner celebrated its deconstruction, its reembodiment at the beginning of the 1970s in violent white male vigilantes.

The first *Dirty Harry* film, which was the fifth-highest-grossing film of 1971 and spawned numerous sequels, condemned just the sort of legalism that conservatives had come to see as paralyzing communities' efforts to defend themselves against criminal predators. Harry brings smoking-gun evidence of the killer's guilt to the district attorney, but the DA refuses to press charges because the evidence, seized without a warrant, would be inadmissible in court. Harry's commonsense recognition that the law had drained common sense out of law enforcement pushes him to disregard the rules and hunt down the psychotic killer on his own time. Harry was a kind of fantastical embodiment of a death penalty that was no longer used.

The considerable box office success of *Dirty Harry* and *Death Wish* prompted countless sequels and knock-offs that reinforced anxieties about crime and cultivated skepticism about the bureaucratic state's ability to stop it. Vigilante heroes were fearless in a world of fear, confident in a world of nervous backward glances, and free in a world of self-imposed imprisonment behind locked doors. But while these films voiced frustration with a flawed system of justice, they also inspired ex-hilaration. They could generate that sense of the sublime that Corey Robin suggests conservatives have long experienced "when violence is performed for the sake of creating, defending, or recovering a regime of domination and rule."[72] In his review of a *Dirty Harry* knockoff, *Walking Tall* (1973), Gene Siskel could barely contain his enthusiasm for the newly established genre of films that depicted a man in blue "throwing away his badge and substituting a quick revolver for the slow criminal courts." Watching a rogue cop in *Walking Tall* exact speedy justice, Siskel confessed, "One feels like joining in the mayhem and yelling in one's best vigilante voice, 'Forget the trial; let's string 'em up!'"[73]

By the time Walter Berns wrote his political philosophical defense of the death penalty in 1979, popular culture had already expressed many of its themes through vigilante films. Like Harry, capital punishment's effectiveness was certain in a time of profound doubt. It was individual-izing in an age of structural analysis. It expressed a vision of the world in which bold moral commitments, not bureaucratic tinkering, shaped his-tory. It saw righteous violence as sublime rather than scandalous. The retributive punishment of death expressed a clarity, a forcefulness, and a narrative tidiness that rehabilitation could never match. With the cli-mactic death of the offender came the tangible proof that the pain of his crime had been returned to him. The same could not be said for reha-bilitation, which was not guaranteed to work and left no physical mark on the offender when it did. Retribution offered the opportunity for cul-tural regeneration through violence that rehabilitation never could.

Indeed, as we will see in the chapters to come, the popularity of what *Dirty Harry* represented was evident not only in the film's box office re-ceipts, but also in the extent to which pro–death penalty voices chan-neled Harry in the decades to come. Proponents of "tough on crime" policies like the death penalty would cast themselves as vigilantes who would cut through the red tape and replace it with something much sim-pler: righteous violence. When James David Raulerson was put to death in Florida for the murder of an on-duty police officer in 1985, some of the fifty law enforcement officials who gathered outside the state prison in Starke on his execution day wore *Dirty Harry*–themed T-shirts that said "Raulerson Make My Day," an allusion to the famous line from the franchise's latest film, *Sudden Impact* (1983).[74] By the late 1980s, presi-dential candidates would get in on the act. Alluding to Michael Duka-kis's opposition to the death penalty and support for weekend prison furloughs for well-behaved prisoners, George H. W. Bush presented his own support for capital punishment as part of a larger rogue response to the criminal justice system. "Clint Eastwood's answer to crime is 'Go ahead: Make my day,'" Bush explained to audiences on the 1988 campaign trail. "My opponent's answer is slightly different. His answer is 'Go ahead: Have a nice weekend.'"[75]

## Conclusion

Commenting on Walter Berns's defense of the death penalty, columnist Colman McCarthy noted how odd it seemed for the death penalty to operate as a symbol of American society's moral vigor. "Previously, executionists had the temperateness to defend capital punishment with the standard clichés: deterrence, meting out eye-for-an-eye justice, or the 'public demands it.' Those arguments were shameless and hollow, but at least those advancing them came on with no pretensions to a moral vision," McCarthy wrote. But that had all changed. "America—if Walter Berns is to be believed—may be in for a moral revival of stirring magnitude. National leaders keep saying that America has lost its moral vision. Now we know where to find it—on death row."[76]

Capital punishment, however, had a long history of use by communities seeking to affirm, through the sacrificial ritual of punishment, the presence and holiness of a collective moral conscience.[77] This unofficial function of capital punishment was not novel; Americans' willingness to acknowledge and embrace it openly was. The commentary generated at the conclusion of Charles Schmid's case was illustrative. *Time* characterized the Tucson where Schmid had lived and killed as a boomtown filled with newcomers following an "aimless itch," who "did not care what their children were up to or else hesitated to check on their activities for fear of inhibiting them." On the eve of a ten-year pause in executions, the magazine suggested that a death sentence for Schmid was an indicator that community members were awakening from a moral slumber. "The community finally did something about Smitty," it said. "Last week a jury convicted him of murdering the Fritz girls and sent him to die in the Arizona gas chamber."[78] As the death penalty was dying in the nation's courts and execution chambers, it was being reborn in its people's collective imagination.

## CHAPTER TWO

# "The Respect Which Is Due Them as Men"

## *The Rise of Retribution in a Polarizing Nation*

"What some governments do to their people, you know . . . like lobotomies[?] . . . You don't interfere with somebody's life. You let people meet their own fate."[1] — Gary Gilmore, *The Executioner's Song* (1979)

In a utopian future, B. F. Skinner conceded to his readers in 1971, heroism would not exist. Since well-designed environments would condition good behavior, "little or nothing remains for autonomous man to do and receive credit for doing. He does not engage in moral struggle and therefore has no chance to be a moral hero or credited with inner virtues." These lines were one of many moments of candor in *Beyond Freedom and Dignity*, his book-length consideration of the role psychology should play in engineering a better world.[2] Skinner, a psychologist, had pioneered behaviorism, an approach to understanding human behavior that held that the environment, not some inner will, shapes every organism's behavior. "Freedom," he came to believe, was a prescientific, magical way of explaining human behavior that reflected just how little humans had historically known about the influence of environment on their behavior. Incentives and disincentives to act in particular ways saturated our daily lives, and they had profound consequences for how we behaved. In the world Skinner imagined behaviorism creating, environments would become carefully engineered landscapes of incentives and disincentives as humans collectively reshaped them to generate desired behavior.

Surveying the contemporary landscape, Skinner was frustrated with how attachment to the concepts of freedom and dignity got in the way of building a better society. The nation's criminal justice system was a prime example. Its punitive approach was scientifically unsound. Punishment, Skinner pointed out, was much less effective at deterring bad behavior than the alternatives behaviorism offered. A world designed to motivate good behavior would be "a world in which behavior likely to be punished seldom or never occurs."[3] But rather than change their world, he noted in exasperation, Americans preferred to attribute the cause of crime to a mythical "will" that lay within the offender. Indeed, that "will" was precisely at the heart of conservative intellectual Walter Berns's defense of the death penalty: to refuse to punish was to deny its presence and, in so doing, to degrade what it meant to be human.[4] But for Skinner the facts did not change because they were unpleasant to contemplate.[5] Clinging to outdated notions of freedom blinded us to behavior-shaping stimuli and left us powerless to do anything about them. "We Can't Afford Freedom," read the headline of *Time*'s 1971 cover story on Skinner's work, neatly summing up this point.[6]

Skinner's utopianism should have appealed to those on the left who had been seeking for years to replace retribution with social welfare programs that would prevent crime by proactively improving the lives of potential criminals and offering rehabilitative programs to those who slipped through the cracks and landed in prison. And it undoubtedly did appeal to Cold War liberals who remained committed to the New Deal order. Over the course of the 1960s, however, many on the left had grown increasingly wary of social engineering. If the right had come to associate the state's exercise of paternalistic power with a damaging form of cultural decadence, many on the left had grown worried about its repressive effects on vulnerable minorities. Indeed, by the 1970s, a civil libertarian consensus had formed among some on the left that negative freedom—and in particular the negative freedom to be oneself and think one's own thoughts—was under attack. The culprits, as they saw it, were scientists like Skinner working in conjunction with liberals who placed too much faith in the state to engineer the good. In some cases, these critics felt, technocracy was serving reactionary ends more than progressive ones. In the name of helping, social engineering was endangering the integrity of the individual's mind and undermining people's right to self-determination. It was, in other words, endangering freedom.

There was perhaps no greater expression of these feelings in popular culture than *One Flew over the Cuckoo's Nest*. In the middle of the 1970s, sandwiched between the second and third *Dirty Harry* sequels, the runaway hit film expressed antiauthoritarian discontent with repressive institutions. If *Dirty Harry* had captured reactionary frustration with the state's lack of competence and resolve in the exercise of its police powers, *One Flew over the Cuckoo's Nest* expressed anxiety about the state's exercise of its *parens patriae* power, its paternalistic, caretaking authority over those deemed unable to care for themselves. An adaptation of a 1962 novel by Ken Kesey, the film swept the Academy Awards and was the third-highest-grossing movie of the year.[7] Set in an Oregon mental hospital, it depicted a world in which persons declared mentally incompetent by the state became children, stripped of their right to determine what was in their own best interests. Using the *parens patriae* power vested in them by the state, hospital staff turned patients into docile automatons with treatments that seemed designed to increase their dependence on the institution. In the film, a free-spirited, rebellious white male patient, memorably played by Jack Nicholson, finds himself in exactly that situation: lobotomized when he goes too far in resisting the forces of institutionalization (embodied, tellingly, by an emasculating female nurse).

*One Flew over the Cuckoo's Nest* had located the horrors of paternalistic technocracy in a mental institution, but in the civil libertarian imagination, the prison had become a place where a similar "psychoauthoritarianism," as one critic called it, had taken hold.[8] Prisons, of course, were supposed to take away physical freedom, and civil libertarians did not question the propriety of imprisonment as a punishment for a person lawfully convicted of a crime. They did vehemently object, though, when prison authorities invoked their rehabilitative mission to justify expanding their control over prisoners' minds as well as their bodies.

Across the country in the late 1960s, the rise of behaviorism within psychiatry had been leading to new experimental programs aimed at altering the internal life of prison inmates. At the same time, existing parole practices faced criticism generated by participants in the new left's social movements. Critics accused prison administrators of abusing their discretionary power in a system of indeterminate sentencing. Based on recommendations from prison staff, parole boards could simply decide that a man serving a sentence of, say, one year to life for a relatively minor crime was not ready to return to society and keep him locked up for decades. That discretion, civil libertarians became convinced, had created an unfair system in which an inmate's race or political ideology or servility determined how quickly parole boards deemed him rehabilitated and returned him to society. Those who committed similar crimes served shockingly different lengths of time in prison.[9]

Civil libertarians' discontent with a paternalistic state attracted them to a retributive philosophy of punishment. With its emphasis on moral blameworthiness and its rejection of rehabilitation, retribution appealed strongly, as we saw in the last chapter, to social conservatives hostile to the welfare state and frustrated with its lack of moral clarity. In an age where large segments of the left had also come to distrust the state, however, retribution proved politically promiscuous. It attracted *Dirty Harry*–admiring and Bible-quoting conservatives, but it also came to appeal to journalists, law professors, and political activists on the civil libertarian left who had grown increasingly critical of the discretion the criminal justice system vested in judges, parole boards, and psychiatrists.[10] A retributive approach to the punishment of criminals, they came to believe, would curb the tyrannical effects of too much discretion. Retribution required that punishment be proportionate to the crime; it thus appealed to those who saw "rehabilitation" being used as a justification for detaining prisoners who had committed minor crimes for long prison terms. If the conservative right had been drawn to the way retribution could justify harsh punishment for the worst crime, the libertarian left was drawn to the way it placed limits on the amount of punishment that could be authorized for minor crimes and the kind of punishment that could be authorized for any crime.

In fictional works, political commentary, and legal analysis, civil libertarian critics associated the therapeutic state with an impermissible usurpation of the individual's right to psychological self-determination. To use punishment as an occasion for social engineering—as might be done when the state used "rehabilitation" to change prisoners against their will or detain them indefinitely—was to deny offenders' right, as citizens endowed with negative freedom, to get what they deserved for their actions and then resume their membership in society.[11] The solution, they thought, was to ban involuntary psychiatric treatment of prisoners without strict judicial oversight and to install transparent procedures that officials would be required to follow in determining the punishment for a crime or making any significant changes to the nature of that punishment while it was ongoing.

All this ideological fervor surrounded and informed the meaning of the death penalty at a key moment in its history. Perhaps because the actual use of capital punishment was declining, many civil libertarians of the age did not hesitate to invoke the death penalty as a standard against which technocratic intrusions into the souls of inmates compared unfavorably. Supposedly humane, therapeutic techniques of modern punishment, they sometimes suggested, were justifying a form of tyranny that was worse than medieval dungeons or chopping blocks. In its most extreme form, this rhetoric held that it was better to be dead than to become an object through which the state carried out a social agenda. As part of repudiations of the rehabilitative ideal, the death penalty became a symbol of a harsh punishment that nonetheless respected the mental integrity of those who suffered it.

In a legal context, commitment to the civil libertarian value of due process would underlie both the suspension of the death penalty in 1972 and the lifting of that suspension in 1976. When the Court imposed an official moratorium on executions, citing arbitrary sentencing outcomes, a civil libertarian concern with protecting the individual from the capricious exercise of state power was at the heart of its reasoning. Because the decision was not a flat-out declaration that the death penalty was inherently cruel, though, the Court left open the possibility that the problem could be remedied. State legislatures immediately set to work creating new procedural safeguards to guard against unfairness, and after the Court approved the changes in a 1976 decision, executions resumed.

In the opinions that demanded and then approved of the reforms legislatures made to the capital sentencing process, we can see how a commitment to honoring an individual's negative freedom—the central value of civil libertarianism—created a conundrum for the justices. On the one hand, their commitment to procedural fairness revealed a desire to protect a defendant's right to be free from the capricious exercise of the state's power to punish. Without clear formulas to determine the worst of the worst, juries would not produce fair outcomes and defendants would not be free from irrational, idiosyncratic decisions about their fate. On the other hand, strict adherence to formulas designed to make punishment fair and predictable could produce its own kind of injustices. No set of sentencing guidelines could anticipate the intangible qualities of individual defendants and their cases that could very well be relevant to the broader goal of ensuring that only the worst of the worst were executed. Without some discretion, how would defendants be protected from the unjust exercise of the state's power that rigid formulas might sometimes command?

Freedom from caprice and freedom from injustice, the Court discovered, could sometimes come at the expense of one another. The system they ultimately approved did nothing to resolve the conundrum. Indeed, its insolvability, and the Court's refusal to acknowledge it, would profoundly shape the exercise of capital punishment in its revived form. A civil libertarian commitment to negative freedom underlay, in the end, a modern death penalty ridden with internal tensions.

### "Lost Automatons": Civil Libertarian Anxiety about the Disciplinary State

Civil libertarians' anxiety about governments' use of psychiatric knowledge to manipulate people had its origins on the anticommunist right.[12] In the aftermath of World War II and then the Korean War, Americans anxiously studied how totalitarian regimes manipulated their subjects' thoughts. Published in the United States in 1949, George Orwell's *1984* imagined a future world in which a totalitarian government superintended the thoughts of its citizens through a rigorous program of surveillance, discipline, and torture.[13] Several years later, false confessions made by American captives during the Korean War stoked fears of communist states' abilities to use brainwashing, or "coercive persuasion" as experts called it.[14]

Fears over coercive persuasion spread to the left end of the political spectrum and into popular culture. Critics noted that McCarthyism used the very "thought reform" techniques of America's foreign enemies and that "democratic America was not immune to totalitarian impulses."[15] As we have seen, psychologists like Solomon Asch and Stanley Milgram had set out to see just how susceptible Americans were to the authority of the crowd or the expert, and they had come back with alarming results. In the late 1950s, sociologist Erving Goffman presented the institutions of modern government as potentially oppressive. In 1958 he published *Asylums: Essays on the Social Situation of Men-*

tal *Patients and Other Inmates,* in which he documented how "total institutions"—places like prisons, mental hospitals, and army barracks—transformed the psyches of those who lived and worked in them.[16] A process of "mortification" began, he argued, when an inductee to one of these institutions moved from private person to patient, prisoner, or soldier. He gradually grew more docile and dependent on the institution. Using chilling language, Goffman explained that new inductees were "shaped and coded into an object that can be fed into the administrative machinery of the establishment, to be worked on smoothly by routine operations."[17]

If Goffman's scholarship reflected anxieties about Americans' susceptibility to authoritarianism, it also tacitly celebrated the rebel as the bulwark against all the mortifying forces that threatened to undermine independent-mindedness in America. The last part of Goffman's book documented the creative ways patients sometimes resisted efforts to transform them into docile automatons. Resistance was possible.

Antiauthoritarianism had flourished in American popular culture as well. Amid the frosty political climate created by McCarthyism in the early 1950s, novelists, playwrights, and filmmakers revived a long-standing American romance with the dissident outsider. J. D. Salinger's *Catcher in the Rye* (1951) railed against a middle-class culture in which people exploited one another in both vulgar and socially approved ways. His disillusioned adolescent hero Holden Caulfield found phoniness at every turn in Cold War domestic culture.[18] At the height of the anticommunist purges, Arthur Miller's play *The Crucible* (1953) took aim at Joseph McCarthy and the US House of Representatives' Un-American Activities Committee, celebrating a man who martyrs himself for the truth rather than lie on behalf of a theocracy overrun by paranoia. Both of these texts marked the rise of sympathetic images of rebels in Cold War America and their coming ubiquity in popular culture.

While optimistic liberal visions of rehabilitation suffused death penalty films of the late 1950s and 1960s, the prison provided a place for some of the most notable antiauthoritarian stories circulating in popular culture. A number of films presented prisoners as the ultimate rebels. In films like *Brute Force* (1947), *The Last Mile* (1955), *Birdman of Alcatraz* (1962), and *Cool Hand Luke* (1967), they courageously confronted tyrannical wardens and guards.[19]

A 1962 movie set in a federal prison, *Birdman of Alcatraz,* gave cinematic voice to antiauthoritarian wariness of the rehabilitative ideal.[20]

After earning a last-minute commutation of his death sentence by Woodrow Wilson, Robert Stroud becomes, from his prison cell, a bird keeper and one of the foremost experts on bird diseases, demonstrating the rehabilitative potential of a man initially thought unredeemable. While the film extolled the value of rehabilitation, it was skeptical of institutions' ability to keep that value at the heart of their operations. Prison bureaucrats, it showed, were risk averse and irresistibly drawn toward policies that would maintain order, even at the expense of the positive personal growth of inmates. Citing the need for order, the warden takes Stroud's birds away. In the climactic showdown that follows, Stroud articulates the film's defiant individualism. The reforms the warden has made—abolishing the corporal punishment of prisoners, upgrading the conditions of cells—are only superficial, he argues. The philosophy of rehabilitation is as authoritarian as ever. In a heated argument with the warden, Stroud gives his keeper an etymology lesson, informing him that the word *rehabilitation*

> comes from the Latin root, *habilitas*, the definition is to invest again with dignity. You don't consider that part of your job, Harvey, to give a man back the dignity he once had. Your only interest is in how he behaves. You told me that once a long time ago, and I'll never forget it: "You'll conform to our ideas of how you should behave." And you haven't retreated from that stand one inch in 35 years. You want your prisoners to dance out the gates like puppets on a string, with rubber stamped values impressed by you with your sense of conformity, your sense of behavior—even your sense of morality. That's why you're a failure, Harvey, you and the whole science of penology, because you rob prisoners of the most important thing in their lives: their individuality. On the outside they're lost automatons, just going through the motions of living.[21]

Thus, while some in Hollywood were touting "enlightened penology" as a humane response to criminal behavior, *Birdman of Alcatraz* was foreshadowing a skepticism by some on the left that would grow stronger over the course of the 1960s. What good was dismantling the gallows, the film seemed to ask, if the life that was saved was ground into submission by mortifying (in Goffman's sense of that word) regulations or petty tyrants?

Released in 1962, the film presaged the growth, in the decade that followed, of a civil libertarian left's distrust of parole boards and prison psychiatrists. With rehabilitation as the rationale for removing persons convicted of crime from society, by World War II legislatures had authorized indeterminate prison sentences—sometimes with a maximum of lifelong incarceration—under the progressive presumption that offenders would be released when prison officials deemed them rehabilitated. But rather than preventing the unnecessary detention of persons who posed no threat to society, those on the left, from reform-minded civil libertarians to revolutionary antiprison activists, saw indeterminate sentencing as oppressive. Prisoners who failed to convince parole boards that they were rehabilitated, they argued, often ended up serving inordinately long sentences for the types of crimes they had committed.

Some critics of indeterminate sentencing laws saw the problem through the lens of race. Racial discrimination, they thought, was an "epidemic" in the criminal justice system, and it operated most egregiously through the unchecked discretion vested in correctional officials making parole decisions.[22] With ties to the Black Panther party, radical prison movements of the late 1960s and early 1970s called attention to the indeterminate sentence as a racist tool of repression.[23] In 1971, the manifesto of those who rioted at New York's Attica Correctional Facility following the death of Black Panther leader George Jackson at the hands of a California prison guard made indeterminate sentences a central part of their list of grievances. Four of their twenty-seven demands revolved around the premise that parole was, in one gloss of it, "unconstitutional, secretive, anti-rehabilitative, and rigged against black and brown people."[24]

The civil libertarianism that dominated much of the cultural and legal criticism of indeterminate sentencing in the 1970s, however, was often focused on protecting prisoners conceived of as citizens endowed with a right to negative psychological freedom rather than as victims of racial and economic inequality. The specter of technocratic tyranny tapped into a classical wariness, in an antimonarchical American political tradition, about power vested in those who were not directly accountable to the people. The objects of much of that anxiety were elite judges, prison officials, and psychiatrists, whose unchecked power was most horrifyingly presented in stories of thought policing.

Jessica Mitford's aptly titled muckraking account of American prisons, *Kind and Unusual Punishment* (1973), called attention to the way indeterminate prison sentences had become a tool for securing mental domination over prisoners. Quoting Thomas Szasz, the best-known critic of psychiatry at the time, Mitford likened the techniques of the parole board to those of clerics during the Spanish Inquisition. The deviant prisoner, she said, "is first discredited as a self-responsible human being, and then subjected to humiliating punishment defined and disguised as treatment."[25]

One of the first widely circulated critiques of rehabilitation in popular culture had come from overseas in the form of a novel. Released in the United States in 1962 and made into an American film ten years later, British writer Anthony Burgess's *A Clockwork Orange* imagined the dystopian consequences of the use of Pavlovian-style aversion therapy on juvenile offenders.[26] Alex, a Beethoven-loving juvenile delinquent, undergoes aversion therapy by the state to extinguish his appetite for violence. Strapped to a seat in a movie theater, his eyes held open by medical equipment, he watches images of violence flash across the screen as classical music plays in the background. The doctors then inject him with nauseating drugs. Alex soon associates violence with the feeling of being deathly ill and is, we see, unable to contemplate, much less commit, the kinds of crimes he reveled in as a delinquent. The therapy is too successful, though, and Alex becomes neutered, unable to defend himself against others in the world. Just as important, he becomes as nauseated by Beethoven as he is by thoughts of violence. The surgical removal of his primal instincts has had unintended negative effects on his ability to enjoy the best that civilization has to offer.

Burgess later explained that he had deliberately sought to challenge the technocratic assumption that people ought to be seen by science as programmable beings. Humans, he wrote, "stubbornly do not want to be anything but what we are—creatures aware of our faults and determined, more or less, to do something about those faults in our own way." And while Alex was indeed programmed, Burgess challenged the idea that humans were, like their animal counterparts, so easily manipulated by rewards and punishments. A human willingness to endure pain in order to uphold principle suggested otherwise: "That a man may be willing to suffer torture and death for the sake of principle is a kind of mad perversity that makes little sense in the behaviorist's laboratory."[27]

## From Dystopian Imaginings to Pressing Reality

A series of clumsy and cruel behavior modification programs in prisons in the late 1960s confirmed a burgeoning association between technocracy and tyranny. At Atascadero State Hospital in California, an institution housing sex offenders and the criminally insane, doctors punished ninety inmates for rule violations by injecting them with anectine, a drug that temporarily paralyzes muscles and causes feelings of asphyxiation. ("How severe is the anectine experience from the point of view of the patient?" asked a report for the California Department of Corrections. "Sixteen likened it to dying. Three of these compared it to actual experiences in the past in which they had almost drowned. The majority described it as a terrible, scary, experience.") By the department's own admission, doctors subjected five patients to the treatment without their consent.[28]

At about the time prison psychiatrists were administering anectine to inmates in California, officials in a federal maximum security correctional facility in Marion, Illinois, were launching Special Treatment and Rehabilitation Training (START), a behavior modification program. The most difficult inmates there were placed in sensory deprivation cells at the beginning of a behavioral program in which they would gradually earn back, in exchange for good behavior, what had been summarily taken away from them.[29] The program came under scrutiny after the American Civil Liberties Union sued the prison on behalf of several prisoners.[30]

Journalists invoked *Clockwork Orange* in stories about these studies and other behavior modification programs that had begun popping up in prisons across the country.[31] In 1955 the Maryland legislature had established the Patuxent Institution in Jessup to treat "defective delinquents" who might benefit from intensive psychiatric care. Founded with the advice of liberal psychologists like Karl Menninger and Robert Lindner, Patuxent's reputation as a modern, progressive institution was undermined by inmate lawsuits that told of behavior modification therapies that used sensory deprivation and electroshock therapy to control the inmates. An article on Patuxent published in the *New York Times*, titled "A Model, Clockwork-Orange Prison," noted that the indeterminate sentencing law meant 38 percent of inmates who had been admitted to the hospital as patients served a much longer sentence than they would have served for their crimes in a regular prison.[32] Classified as patients rather than prisoners, they had few constitutional grounds to challenge the authority of the Patuxent administrators. In a 1972 case, the Supreme Court found that one Patuxent inmate who had refused to cooperate in the diagnostic intake procedures had preserved his status as a rights-bearing prisoner. Because the staff could not diagnose him without his cooperation, he had never become a patient and had not forfeited his right to be treated as a prisoner serving a finite punishment. When it determined that he had been detained for as long as his original sentence mandated, the Court ordered him released.[33] Those who had been admitted, however, were stuck until doctors deemed them rehabilitated.

The staff at Patuxent vigorously defended the control their expertise gave them over the inmates' freedom. "No one likes to admit he's not normal," one doctor explained to the *Times*. "Everybody who's in here, their primary drive is toward getting back in society. This is part of their problem—the inability to delay gratification. From a treatment point of view, the indeterminate sentence is very helpful."[34] Such rhetoric, which would have inspired nodding in the 1950s, was becoming catastrophically impolitic in the early 1970s. Hostility toward technocracy was rising as an increasing number of social critics, from journalists to filmmakers to law professors, sought to codify convicted criminals' status as persons who had forfeited their liberty, but not their personality, to the state.

In response to the negative publicity generated by these programs, alarm bells began ringing in the nation's legislative and judicial chambers. In 1971 a Senate Judiciary Subcommittee on Constitutional Rights began investigating behavior modification programs in American prisons in the aftermath of experiments conducted at Marion. The furor that followed succeeded in shutting down the program before the hearings even began.[35] In 1973, the US Court of Appeals for the Eighth Circuit ruled that the involuntary injection of amorphine, a drug that induced vomiting, into prisoners at the Iowa Security and Medical Facility in order to condition them against infractions like swearing and lying was a violation of their Eighth Amendment rights.[36] In 1974, backlash against therapies that combined physical manipulation of the body with attempts to rewire thought processes led California legislators to amend the penal code. "All persons, including all persons involuntarily confined, have a fundamental right against enforced interference with their thought processes, states of mind, and patterns of mentation through the use of organic therapies," the code now stated.[37] In 1976 Congress passed federal human subjects regulations, which classified prisoners as "vulnerable subjects" and, in so doing, imposed new limits on the kinds of experiments that could be conducted using them as participants.[38]

Controversy over "psychiatric violence" also surrounded plans by the Federal Bureau of Prisons to make one of its new facilities in Butner, North Carolina, a behavior modification research center in which psychiatrists would test new rehabilitative therapies on federal inmates. Activists railed against the implications. Alluding to *1984* and, once again, *A Clockwork Orange*, columnist William Claiborne in the *Washington Post* spread the rumor that inmates at Marion who had been notified that they would be sent to Butner had committed suicide. "They chose death rather than to suffer the horror that was being perpetuated against them," he quoted an inmate as writing.[39] In the *Chicago Defender*, George E. Blue, a federal prisoner in Atlanta, encouraged his fellow inmates to engage in a one-day hunger strike against behavior modification techniques, which he described as "new measures our keepers have dreamed up to tighten the bonds of slavery."[40] In protest of the facility, five to ten thousand people gathered in Raleigh on Independence Day in 1974, where John Conyers, Ralph Abernathy, Jesse Jackson, Stevie Wonder, and Angela Davis spoke to crowds. Richard Nixon's "Southern Strategy" was threatening North Carolina's reputation of "New South progressivism," Angela Davis plainly warned the crowd, calling the federal facility "a laboratory for new forms of repression."[41] The campaign against the center led to a philosophical overhaul. Its initial director, a behaviorist, resigned, and the facility opened in 1976 under a much more civil libertarian philosophy of punishment that had eliminated compulsory rehabilitation.[42]

The outcomes in California, Iowa, and North Carolina showed that backlash against behavior modification programs did result in some substantive limits on what states could do to prisoners. But they were limited by a focus on protecting the integrity of the psyche rather than ameliorating the broader conditions of confinement. Because civil libertarian critics were so focused on protecting a sacred inner will that Skinner saw as so problematic, their rhetoric inflated the importance of certain negative, due process rights—like the right to object to the conditions of one's confinement—while doing little to articulate inmates' positive rights—the duties owed them by the state.[43] Courts, Edward M. Opton wrote in the *Mississippi Law Journal*, had come to grant leeway to the exercise of power over prisoners when officials called it "treatment" rather than punishment. It came as no surprise, he explained, that "prison administrators have from time to time labeled as 'treatment' acts which, if called 'punishment,' would be instantly recognized as of dubious morality or legality." The reform he suggested, indicative of the larger thinking about how to curb administrative tyranny, was to create procedural safeguards rather than to articulate a set of substantive values about the treatment of prisoners. The acts of prison psychiatrists, he argued, should be reclassified as acts of punishment, thus opening them to judicial scrutiny: "Prison psychiatrists are, in general, first and foremost functionaries in the disciplinary power structure of the prison bureaucracy. Their interests are as adverse to the welfare of the prisoners as are those of the prison keepers. Therefore, punitive psychiatric therapies in prisons should be subject to at least the same judicial scrutiny and standards as are administrative punishments."[44]

Opton's emphasis on subjecting treatments to "scrutiny and standards" of the courts was well intentioned, but it avoided the larger question of whether inmates had a substantive, positive right to certain minimum standards of living while incarcerated that proscribed certain treatments altogether. Historically, the Court had interpreted the Eighth Amendment ban on cruel and unusual punishment conservatively; there was no guarantee that the "standards of review" it would apply to practices of prison psychiatrists would be found to be of "dubious legality." The call for procedural review was thus rather toothless without an interpretation of the Eighth Amendment that was more sympathetic to the plight of prisoners.[45] Opton's proposed reform honored the right of the prisoner to object and be heard by courts while remaining mute about the substance of what the prisoner was opposing. It reflected a reform-minded approach to a system that was at bottom defined by a dominant reading of the Eighth Amendment that permitted harsh treatment.

This approach to the problem of unchecked punishment was neither unique nor confined to law reviews. It lay at the heart of the federal legislation that authorized a Sentencing Commission to overhaul the federal criminal code by replacing indeterminate sentences and parole with one-size-fits-all determinate sentences spelled out in sentencing guidelines.[46] Objective factors, like the severity of the crime and the criminal history of the offender, would trigger preordained, fixed sentences. The movement had begun with a single state—Minnesota had created the first state sentencing guidelines in 1978—but over the next three decades twenty states and the District of Columbia eventually adopted them in various forms, all with the goal of making sentences for a given crime similar for offenders with similar criminal histories.[47]

Eliminating judges' and parole boards' discretion would theoretically guarantee greater consistency in the sentences imposed on different persons for the same crime. Civil libertarian critics of the prison system may have initially hoped, moreover, that creating a formulaic set of sentencing guidelines would soften punishment across the board, that the modal time inmates would serve for a crime would be what the most privileged had served under the old system. But no such values were made part of the statutes. They tellingly said nothing about how harsh sentences should be—only that they should be uniform and "proportionate" to the crime. What was proportionate, though, was a matter of legislative judgment, and legislators faced constituents who were increasingly frightened by crime and demanding harsher punishment.[48]

In the end, then, an emphasis on fairness left offenders vulnerable to harsh treatment. By focusing on the procedures that courts and prisons followed in determining sentences, the authors of determinate sentencing laws guaranteed inmates fairness but not protection from excessively long sentences served in degrading conditions. As a war on drugs took off and lawmakers responded to anxiety about crime, determinate sentencing offered a way to expand the use of incarceration. In the 1990s, Congress increased the federal sentencing ranges for certain offenses. State and federal legislatures voted into law mandatory minimum sentences for crimes that increased the penalty for everyone. "Three strikes" laws brought a new level of harsh consistency to the sentences offenders served for their third felonies.

Thus, once it was built into the system via determinate sentencing laws, the defense of individual autonomy that had motivated civil libertarian critiques of the criminal justice system quickly came to serve a reactionary understanding of offenders as morally blameworthy men and women who deserved the harsher punishments legislators began enacting. A focus on equal protection and due process had won criminal defendants the guarantee that parole boards would not use rehabilitation to inflate the cost of their crimes, but it also ironically "won" them long stays in prison by legislatures determined to be tough on crime.

Antiauthoritarian concern with prisoners' rights had worsened not only the quantity of punishment defendants received, but also its nature. The treatment of prisoners worsened in the aftermath of behavior modification scandals. Rather than discontinue the use of solitary confinement after its scandalous use in the START program, officials

at Marion recast it as a technique necessary for maintaining prison order.[49] As a practice now justified by the unimpeachable imperative of
maintaining security, solitary confinement avoided the civil libertarian
objections that it was part of a behavior modification program aiming
to reshape the minds of inmates. The move was semantic, of course: as
scholars have grimly documented, solitary confinement has psychologically devastating effects on those who endure it regardless of the purpose given for its use.[50] In a climate transformed by a newfound sensitivity to negative mental freedom, however, semantics mattered. Suffering
that resulted from the necessity of maintaining prison security was not
the same as suffering that resulted from involuntary participation in a
behavior modification program. In the aftermath of the public outrage,
the former was acceptable, but the latter was not. Inmates had tragically
won a negative right to mental integrity that permitted their confinement
in a small box.[51]

The rebellion against indeterminate sentences and involuntary psychiatric treatment set the stage, in ways few civil libertarians anticipated,
for the punitive turn that followed. Americans were left with a government that cared about honoring, through procedural protections, prisoners' rights to be free from the discretion administrators had over the
length and psychiatric aims of their incarceration. When all the i's were
dotted and t's crossed, however, little was in place to curb the violence
the law could visit upon them.[52] The result was a state whose right to inflict punishment was focused on disabling the body.[53] Nowhere was that
principle better illustrated than in the state's right to kill.

## Rationalizing Death

In the late 1960s and early 1970s, as the death penalty's demise seemed
increasingly likely, capital punishment became a rhetorical foil in arguments about the limits of the government's control over prisoners'
thoughts. In attacks on behavior modification, critics used capital punishment as a point of comparison for mind-centered punishments in order to impress on audiences just how terrible certain techniques of rehabilitation were. Take, for instance, a 1972 opinion piece by Roy Spece
Jr. and J. Anthony Kouba, coeditors of *Southern California Law Review*. That year the California Supreme Court ruled in *People v. Ander-*

*son* that the death penalty violated the state constitution's prohibition of cruel and unusual punishment.[54] Writing in the *Los Angeles Times*, Spece and Kouba cited a passage in *Anderson* in which the court had clarified that "cruel and unusual" punishments did not include those "innovative types of punishment whose purpose is the rehabilitation or reformation of criminal offenders"—precisely the techniques that had been the source of recent aversion therapy scandals.[55] This was alarming, they told readers. The word rehabilitation had a "talismanic" quality, they argued. It "connotes that society is benevolent and helps people" but was, in reality, a form of state power designed to "neutralize their threat to society." There was, moreover, no way to ensure that the state would not one day use the techniques designed to rewire prisoners' minds on all citizens. "Americans must prepare quickly to choose whether they will surrender their free will to the state. If they delay, their apparatus of choice may be confiscated and the freedom of selection forever lost," the authors ominously intoned. Spece and Kouba predicted that state officials, "who no longer can eliminate prisoners by executing their bodies, will feel led to eliminate prisoners [by] executing their minds."[56]

Spece and Kouba were writing an op-ed, a genre of writing that by its very nature is reductive and inflammatory. Nevertheless, their concerns were shared by other legal scholars, who wrote law review articles that also used capital punishment as a metaphor for the grave threat behaviorism posed to mental freedom. Michael H. Shapiro, who participated in crafting the California statute limiting involuntary psychiatric treatment of California prisoners, acknowledged that the issue created certain dilemmas. What would happen, say, if a technocratic legislature were willing to forgo the death penalty if psychiatric treatment could transform the criminal into a new person? If forced on him, was an inmate's transformation the moral equivalent of an execution? Shapiro argued that it was: "If indeed there has been a change of identity, then there has been an execution, and instead of putting the prisoner's remains in a box, or burning his corpse, the state has recycled his body."[57]

That sentiment was evident in philosopher Herbert Morris's criticism of therapeutic approaches to punishment. In response to the creeping tendency of elites to ascribe bad behavior to mental illness, Morris argued in 1968 for a retributive, neo-Kantian vision of punishment as a sanction that offenders freely bring upon themselves and that offsets the unearned advantage they have taken by breaking the law. The undue power over persons that a rehabilitative rationale authorized disturbed him. In assuming that they are sick and need to have their values altered, Morris argued, "we display a lack of respect for the moral status of individuals, that is, a lack of respect for the reasoning and choices of individuals. They are but animals who must be conditioned." An inalienable right to be treated as a person implied a "right to punishment," an entitlement to endure the consequences for one's behavior without being treated as a mental patient. Morris even went so far as to invoke death as an outcome that could be preferable to forced rehabilitation: "I think we can understand and, indeed, sympathize with a man's preferring death to being forcibly turned into what he is not."[58]

This romantic notion that individuals preferred the literal death of suicide or capital punishment to the psychological death of behavior modification programming had plenty of precedent. From Socrates to Christ to Joan of Arc to John Brown, martyrdom for one's personal convictions had long been the stuff of antiauthoritarian myth. It was, such myth held, better to die as a dissident than to live as a slave. Many of the artists, activists, and intellectuals who attacked behavior modification and indeterminate sentences did not, of course, support the death penalty. As the nation's mood was becoming more punitive, however, their exaltation of the individual who prefers death to psychological coercion inadvertently softened the punishment of death. Advocating for prisoners' right to unencumbered "mentation," their rhetoric marginalized the importance of ensuring the humaneness of nonpsychiatric forms of punishment, like mandating high standards for conditions of confinement, establishing upper limits on the length of incarceration, or declaring the death penalty an inherently cruel, and thus unconstitutional, punishment. Indeed, in their arguments, the death penalty came to symbolize, perversely, a sanction that respected an offender's right to mentation.

By sanctifying the prisoner's negative psychological freedom, moreover, their rhetoric tacitly supported a vision of offenders as morally blameworthy and thus deserving of harsh punishment for their crimes. Some conservatives who defended the merits of capital punishment on retributive grounds adopted Morris's antitherapeutic vision of the individual as a moral agent. Arguing in favor of the death penalty in 1979, Walter Berns used language strikingly similar to Morris's. The anger underlying the demand for the death penalty, he explained, communicated respect for offenders' moral agency. It sprang from "an expression of that element of the soul that is connected with the view that there is responsibility in the world; and in holding particular men responsible, it pays them the respect which is due them as men. Anger recognizes that only men have the capacity to be moral beings and, in so doing, acknowledges the dignity of human beings."[59] While for Morris retribution was a philosophy that limited state power in an age of indeterminate sentences, for Berns it was a rationale for harsh punishment, grounds for authorizing the state to exercise its sovereign power over life and death. Assertions of moral autonomy meant to protect individuals easily morphed into assertions of moral blameworthiness used to justify their harsh treatment.

Beyond contributing to the broader national mood of distrust that bolstered support for retribution and the death penalty, civil libertarianism shaped the judicial logic that led to the temporary suspension of the death penalty in 1972 and its revival in a new form four years later.

On June 29, 1972, the Supreme Court of the United States issued its longest ruling ever: a one page per curiam decision followed by more than two hundred pages of concurring and dissenting opinions. The decision in *Furman v. Georgia* held that unacceptable arbitrariness in administering capital punishment had made the penalty unconstitutional.[60]

The decision was the result of a campaign against the death penalty that ultimately prevailed by arguing that states used capital punishment so arbitrarily as to violate defendants' Eighth and Fourteenth Amendment rights. In *Furman* the Legal Defense Fund, using a strategy devised by Anthony Amsterdam, called the Court's attention to the way defendants in the same jurisdiction whose crimes were similar often met dramatically different fates. Such arbitrary outcomes resulted from the discretion legislatures had given to juries. Over the course of the twentieth century, state legislatures had gradually abandoned mandatory death sentences for capital crimes. They instead allowed juries to return their verdicts with a punishment of death or imprisonment attached. The option of lesser sentences, legislatures had reasoned, would end juries' tendency to acquit defendants they wanted to spare from execution.[61] But the resulting system, one of unfettered discretion, produced dramatically inconsistent outcomes. Reviewing capital sentencing statutes in *Furman*, a majority of the Court was dismayed. Unchecked discretion, Justice William O. Douglas wrote, allowed juries to apply the death penalty "selectively to minorities whose numbers are few, who are outcasts of society, and who are unpopular, but whom society is willing to see suffer though it would not countenance general application of the same penalty across the board."[62] Where Douglas saw bias, other justices saw caprice: inconsistent outcomes were the inevitable product of random combinations of jurors with diverse dispositions. "It smacks of little more than a lottery system," complained Justice William J. Brennan Jr.[63] Justice Potter Stewart remarked that there was as much rhyme or reason in receiving a death sentence as in suffering from a lightning strike.[64] Given these irregularities, the Court ruled the death penalty unconstitutional, but only two of the justices declared the penalty itself cruel or unusual. If states could find ways to make the sentencing process fair, the decision implied, the death penalty might pass constitutional muster.

The Court's desire to eliminate arbitrariness and bias in death sentences amounted to a directive to state legislatures to impose rationality on the exercise of sovereign power, to demystify or tame the will that underlay juries' life-and-death decisions. The most logical way to protect the rights of unpopular minorities or unlucky defendants who drew a hostile jury, it seemed, was to regulate juries' subjective assessments of offenders' blameworthiness and crimes' heinousness. Juries needed guidance from statutes laying out the objective criteria that would mark capital defendants as members of one of two groups of offenders, the executable or the nonexecutable.

In its desire for objectively knowable criteria for distinguishing the very bad from the worst capital defendants, the Court's decision in *Furman* reflected the larger retributive turn away from entrusting the fate of criminals to the subjective judgment of anyone—psychiatrists, judges, or representatives from the community. Like the sentencing guidelines that would transform the country's penal codes, the Court's decision in *Furman* implicitly valued the offender's negative psychological freedom. Knowledge that courts will apply the law of criminal punishment uniformly, like knowledge that gravity affects everyone, is a condition of liberty because it reduces uncertainty about what one must do to achieve happiness and avoid pain. The arbitrary outcomes of a legal system steeped in discretion, by contrast, make the consequences of one's actions more uncertain. "People live or die, dependent on the whim of one man or of 12," Douglas wrote with dismay in his *Furman* opinion.[65] Thus, when the Supreme Court pushed states to develop rules that would make a death sentence more predictable, it was responding to the civil libertarian premise that a government ought to respect a person's individual freedom by announcing the law, enforcing it consistently, and treating an offender exactly as it treats others who have committed similar crimes.[66]

Responding to *Furman*, state legislatures almost immediately set to work drafting new legislation that might produce fair outcomes. Four years later, though, as the Court reviewed the various capital sentencing statutes the states had created to solve the problem of arbitrariness, the justices faced a new dilemma. As they considered the approaches of some states, the perils of too much rationalization—of too much predictability—became evident. Ten states, including North Carolina, seemed to give the Court exactly what it commanded: they eliminated jurors' and judges' discretion and created mandatory death sentences for those convicted of capital crimes. Indeed, when a Nixon-created Commission on Criminal Justice Standards and Goals sat down to evaluate the state of the death penalty after the Court's ruling in *Furman*, it came to the conclusion that the "only option open to a legislature appears to be to require capital punishment for all persons convicted of the crime to which it attaches, without any exercise of discretion."[67] In a truly fair system, the commission of a capital murder would be the sole criterion for separating the executable from the nonexecutable.[68] This approach to capital sentencing, though, was abhorrent to the Court for reasons it articulated in *Woodson et al. v. North Carolina* (1976). Practically, the Court feared that juries, knowing their verdicts would impose death sentences on defendants, would return to acquitting guilty murderers they did not see as deserving death. The Court's decision, however, was also rooted in a philosophical commitment. It was wary of authorizing a sentencing system so fair that it would outlaw mercy, which, the Court recognized, sovereigns historically granted on "factors too intangible to write into a statute."[69] Mercy, the refusal to punish when one is entitled to, had to remain a possible response to the "diverse frailties of humankind."[70] Mandatory death penalty rules did not take those frailties into account. They treated "all persons convicted of a designated offense not as uniquely individual human beings, but as members of a faceless, undifferentiated mass to be subjected to the blind infliction of the penalty of death," Justice White wrote.[71] As the Court's use of passive voice indicates, the specter of an impersonal, soulless state hovered over its decision. A respect for the individual required the Court to soften its insistence on sentencing consistency.

The Court gave its approval, instead, to statutes created by states like

Georgia that preserved juries' capacity to be merciful but sought to give more guidance to their decision making. In *Gregg v. Georgia* (1976), it approved formulas designed to "guide" juries in deciding whether a defendant they had convicted of capital murder ought to die. The nature of these algorithms would differ from state to state and would reflect different penal priorities. Juries would decide the punishment after a second trial, known as the penalty phase, that would follow conviction. Prosecutors and defense attorneys would present jurors with contextual evidence about the commission of the crime and the defendant's past. Jurors would then weigh the heinous, aggravating elements of the crime, defined by the state's sentencing statute, against any evidence they deemed mitigating. If the aggravating factors outweighed the mitigating ones, the Court ruled, they could issue a death sentence. The goal was to give juries "guided discretion," preserving a death sentence as a subjective act of judgment visited upon an offender by members of the community, but also ensuring its consistency with other death sentences.[72]

We will see that the Court's desire to have its cake and eat it too, to treat defendants equally yet consider them as unique individuals, failed. It is tempting to read that failure as evidence of the dysfunctional nature of capital punishment. This is just what Justice Harry Blackmun did when he proclaimed in 1994 that, after nearly twenty years of trying to fix broken sentencing schemes, he would "no longer . . . tinker with the machinery of death" and would vote against the government in future death penalty cases.[73] If the metric against which the jurisprudence is measured is ideological balance rather than fairness, however, the Court's tangled opinions actually boosted the legitimacy of the death penalty. By preserving discretion and unpredictability in sentencing, *Gregg* allowed capital punishment to appear both retributive and fair, something it could not do if the death penalty was mandatory or was left entirely to jurors' discretion. "Guided discretion," the legacy of *Gregg*, struck a balance between a sanction that appeared rational and one that expressed particularized, populist anger.

As sociologist David Garland has noted, in requiring clearer standards for death in *Furman*, the Court was working to distance capital punishment from its historical association with antiblack lynching; the creation of sentencing guidelines expressed the value of due process and color-blind fairness.[74] Writing in the aftermath of a world war that had revealed the devastating consequences of bureaucratized state killing, however, the Court also seemed haunted by the opposite kind of bogeyman: the modern hyperrationalized, eugenic state.[75] In voting to strike down the death penalty, Justice Thurgood Marshall wrote critically of eugenics as a justification for capital punishment: "This Nation has never formally professed eugenic goals, and the history of the world does not look kindly upon them. If eugenics is one of our purposes, then the legislatures should say so forthrightly and design procedures to serve this goal. Until such time, I can only conclude, as has virtually everyone else who has looked at the problem, that capital punishment cannot be defended on the basis of any eugenic purposes."[76] A mandatory death sentence on conviction for a capital crime is not necessarily a eugenic policy, of course, but it does treat the executable as a class of persons rather than as unique individuals. Automatic death sentences would make the state appear insensitive to the distinctiveness of each individual offender. It would appear too detached from those governed by it, more interested in managing populations than in achieving individualized justice.

Indeed, while the Court had sought to preserve a space for mercy, the pocket of discretion that *Gregg* retained called public attention to the retributive purpose of capital punishment in ways that objective sentencing schemes would not have. Had the Court allowed or required automatic death sentences for those convicted of capital murder, the act of conviction would have masked the act of condemnation; defendants would die because they committed the crime, not because they in particular deserved death. Individual blameworthiness would be implicit. Guided discretion schemes, on the other hand, made the death sentence elective, essentially requiring a jury to say to the defendant, in front of an observing public, "We know what *you* did. We know who *you* are. And *you* deserve to die." By requiring guided discretion, the Court had unintentionally struck a balance between caprice and determinism. Under schemes like Georgia's, death sentences would not appear biased or irrational. But by maintaining the unpredictable outcomes discretion entailed, neither would they appear too mechanized, too rational.

The creation of a penalty phase would make the act of condemnation more meaningful to those who saw the death penalty, as some reactionaries did, as a moral imperative. Intended to put the brakes on arbitrary punitiveness, civil libertarian reforms of capital sentencing resulted in a system that was more appealing to the punitive heart. By recognizing the unique blameworthiness of the offender and connecting the pain of punishment to the pain the crime had created, capital sentencing protocols now made death sentences *more* retributive when they were handed down. The defendant who has been automatically or summarily sentenced to death upon conviction of a capital crime has been assigned a punishment; the one who has been sentenced to death by a jury that has listened to days of testimony about his life and deliberated for hours solely about his fate has been *condemned*.

The Court's decisions in *Furman* and *Gregg* also foreshadowed the development of a second, separate tension that would also exert a profound influence over the practice of capital punishment in the modern, post-*Gregg* era. This was the nascent tension between capital punishment's symbolic meaning and its institutional practice. Social conservatives imagined the death penalty as a sublime antidote to a federal judiciary that, they felt, had become biased toward defendants. But the revived death penalty would remain under the supervision of the federal judiciary. Indeed, the legalism that had incensed Harry Callahan in *Dirty Harry* grew as a result of the Supreme Court's reauthorization of the death penalty in *Gregg v. Georgia*. *Gregg* represented the first application of an ambiguous new interpretation of the Eighth Amendment that the Court had set out in *Furman*. It raised countless new issues about state killing that the federal courts, until the 1970s, had never had to face. Opinion upon opinion would follow to resolve these issues, but as the composition of the Court changed and legal ideals bumped up against the messy realities of cases, the federal judiciary's attempt to create a logically consistent jurisprudence of death would ultimately prove a Sisyphean task.

Moreover, the bureaucracy that was so unresponsive to Paul Kersey in *Death Wish* would not be displaced by the revival of the death penalty; it would take over the death penalty. Indeed, as punitive sentiments pushed more and more funding to police departments and prisons, the institutions of the punitive state would grow increasingly standardized in their operations, reducing the capacity of individuals or local communities to do things their own way.[77] In this new age of retribution, expertise did not disappear, it only changed its character and orientation. The experts shaping policy in prisons were no longer psychiatrists aimed at transforming souls; they were risk managers charged with neutralizing as efficiently as possible the risks criminal offenders posed to public safety. The death penalty would be no exception to this trend, as prison personnel developed protocols that turned executions into what legal studies scholar Mona Lynch has described as acts of "waste management": soulless procedures that aim to dispose of inmates as efficiently as possible.[78]

In the 1970s, however, as it was getting back off the ground, the death penalty did not yet seem encumbered by a technicality-ridden jurisprudence and bureaucratic detachment. Indeed, it felt quite the opposite to some, who saw the death penalty as satisfying a reactionary imperative to punish while preserving an inmate's right to mentation. Antipsychiatry activist Thomas S. Szasz was one of them. A "human being, whether a philosopher or a murderer, has certain rights and dignities that remain his as a man awaiting execution," Szasz wrote in the *New Republic* in 1977, when the state of Utah was preparing to execute Gary Gilmore. Having dropped his appeals, Gilmore was poised to become the first condemned inmate to be executed since the *Gregg* decision. Szasz was critical of the unbidden efforts organizations like the ACLU were making to stop the execution. Gilmore, Szasz sympathetically explained, thought death was preferable to a lifetime of emasculating indignities in prison. "Despite Gilmore's crimes," Szasz wrote, "society is in his debt for dramatizing the fact that there are fates worse than death."[79]

As perspectives like Szasz's illustrate, in the late 1960s and early 1970s, a civil libertarian concern with protecting offenders' mental autonomy worked, often unwittingly, alongside a reactionary concern with asserting their blameworthiness. The demands for psychological freedom and moral clarity that different sets of actors made on the criminal justice system could be satisfied, ideologically, by retributive punishment in general and the death penalty in particular. With its ancient pedigree, capital punishment symbolized an alternative to the modern, institutional approaches to punishment that conservative and civil libertarian critics alike found problematic. But while the ideology supporting capital punishment was anti-institutional, the courts and prisons that implemented it were not. In the decades that lay ahead, we shall see, a contradiction between rhetoric and reality would become evident in Americans' images of those they put to death and of the state that did the killing. Rather than eroding support for capital punishment, however, these contradictions would initially work to strengthen it.

# PART II
# Executable Subjects

## CHAPTER THREE

# Fixed Risks and Free Souls

*Judging and Executing Capital Defendants
after* Gregg v. Georgia

During their lonely and barren confinement, the condemned die a slow psychic death; numb submission to the executioner has become the norm in the death house.[1] — Robert Johnson, criminologist (1990)

It's a good day to die. I walked in here like a man, and I am leaving here like a man.[2] — Last statement of Earl Behringer, executed by the state of Texas (June 11, 1997)

Fourteen years after reading Truman Capote's account of two of the last executions to happen before the Supreme Court shuttered the nation's execution chambers in 1972, Americans flocked to bookstores to buy another true crime novel about the very first man to be executed when it reopened them four years later. In Norman Mailer's *The Executioner's Song*, they found a very different kind of condemned man and a very different sort of execution. Gary Gilmore, convicted of killing a gas station attendant and a motel manager in Provo, Utah, could not have been less like Perry Smith. If Smith was pathetic—the "walking wounded," as Capote memorably described him at his execution—Gilmore was swaggering.[3] He was unapologetic for what he had done. "I was always capable of murder," he told an interviewer before his execution in 1977, rejecting the suggestion that something must have happened to turn him into a killer. "There's a side of me that I don't like. I can become totally devoid of feelings for others, unemotional. I know I'm going to do something grossly fucking wrong. I can still go ahead and do it."[4] It was simple, he said: he had evil instincts, he knew he should curb them, and he freely chose to follow them instead. Indeed, Gilmore's execution by firing squad gave him one last opportunity to insist on his free will. Staring at four shotgun barrels peeking out from a narrow slot in a wall, he said, "Let's do it," reminding the witnesses that he was, like them, a full-fledged signatory of a social contract that prescribed the death penalty for murder.[5]

Mailer ultimately made Gilmore seem delusional in his over-the-top bravado, but the condemned man's performance of swaggering manhood contained a deeper cultural truth. Between Capote's *In Cold Blood* and Mailer's tome, a new vision of capital punishment had taken hold in the United States, one that sought to use the lawful violence of an execution to abolish the existential anxiety generated by the insecurities of the age.

In some ways Gilmore's execution in 1977 lived up to the reactionary values that ideologically underwrote the death penalty's revival. His execution did not exactly have the local, public, and makeshift qualities of a nineteenth-century hanging, but in Mailer's account it was anything but sophisticated. Utah officials held the execution in a prison factory, a cavernous cannery that they had converted to an execution chamber, pushing to the side empty paint cans, old tires, and discarded machinery to make room for the firing range. At one end of the room they strapped Gilmore loosely into an office chair. When witnesses filed in, Mailer wrote, "Gary was still in control. He was carrying on conversations, not loud enough to hear, but saying something to the guards strapping him, to the Warden, and to the priest."[6] This was no technocratic act of neutralization, and until the end Gilmore was able to perform his brand of swaggering manhood.[7]

The frontierlike quality of Gilmore's execution, though, would prove atypical in the new era of executions it had initiated. In May 1979, John Spenkelink became the first person in the United States to be executed *involuntarily* since the Supreme Court reauthorized the death penalty in 1976. The thirty-two men and women who watched Spenkelink die in the Florida electric chair saw something quite different from those who witnessed Gilmore presiding over his own death. When officials opened the blinds on the window separating the execution chamber from the observation room, witnesses felt as if they were staring not at a man about to die but at a blinking corpse. H. G. Davis, an editorial writer from the *Gainesville Sun*, recalled being shocked at the tableau that appeared in front of him: "I somehow thought he would say something," he reflected in the immediate aftermath of the execution, "but what we saw was like a wax figure, something you might see on display. He was strapped so tightly as to be almost motionless."[8] In just twenty seconds, guards unceremoniously dropped a face mask over Spenkelink's eyes and electricity abruptly began shooting through his body.

In its impersonal, detached qualities, Spenkelink's execution offered a more accurate preview of the kinds of deaths officials in prisons across the nation would strive to engineer in the decades to come: highly controlled events that ended life as efficiently and unceremoniously as possible. After 1976, in what I will refer to as the modern era of the American death penalty, executions became a sanction exacted in a manner that, in some important respects, treated the condemned more like indistinguishable objects than like unique moral beings. With the introduction of lethal injection as a mode of execution in 1983, state killing would move even more dramatically in that direction. As this quiet method[9] gradually spread to all states, including Utah and Florida, executions came to seem increasingly like the clinical removal of a cancer from the population and less like a spectacle of moral reckoning. The offender's blameworthiness in the moment of punishment was simply more difficult to convey if he was lying on a gurney like a patient awaiting surgery.[10]

The aesthetic differences between Gilmore's and Spenkelink's executions were symptomatic of the conflicting ideological demands that accompanied the revival of capital punishment. A death sentence needed to be simultaneously a public assessment of a unique individual and a sober-minded application of objective criteria to the facts of a crime. Similarly, in the nation's prisons, executions needed to simultaneously recognize the condemned as unique individuals and treat them, as prisoners, in a standardized manner. A delicate balance would arise to manage the demands of the public's retributive desire and its belief that the nation's vigilante past had been transcended. In this chapter I show how, in courtrooms and execution chambers of the post-*Gregg* era, government officials maintained that balance.

In courtrooms, the sentencing phases of capital trials introduced—in structured form—an unprecedented degree of individuation of capital defendants, ensuring that a death sentence was a community's referendum on a person rather than the mere output of a legal formula. In *Gregg v. Georgia*, Supreme Court justices had settled on procedures aimed at making death sentences seem less arbitrary, but they nonetheless maintained spaces of unpredictability in the sentencing process.

As we will see in this chapter, prosecutorial rhetoric portrayed capital defendants as unique, blameworthy citizens who deserved punishment even as sentencing statutes also pushed jurors to see offenders as members of a particularly monstrous class of criminals who required permanent incapacitation.

In execution chambers, meanwhile, the preservation of ancient execution customs applied a retributive veneer to an increasingly technocratic process. As states gradually adopted lethal injection, a mode of execution that risked presenting the condemned as sick animals being euthanized, administrators retained moments for idiosyncratic input by inmates that was common in public execution spectacles of the past. They continued to solicit final meal requests and last statements from inmates. In so doing, the state maintained an image of the offenders that was consonant with the retributive purpose of their deaths; in media accounts of their executions, they appeared as living, choosing persons, even as the procedure for killing them treated them like objects being acted upon in an assembly-line fashion.

In a culture that craved security but was distrustful of government, carefully curated moments of discretion and unpredictability, built into the sentencing and execution process, maintained an image of condemned inmates as individuals whose uniqueness the state acknowledged, rather than elided, in the act of punishment. At the moment of sentencing and execution, condemned inmates could appear, paradoxically, both highly controlled and psychologically free.

Capital proceedings and execution protocols in Texas in the 1990s and early 2000s, the focus of this chapter, illustrated this paradox. By most measures, Texas was an outlier among the thirty-nine states that reinstated the death penalty in the aftermath of *Furman v. Georgia* in 1972. By the end of 2014, the Lone Star State was responsible for killing 37 percent of the 1,394 men and 13 women put to death nationally since executions resumed in 1977.[11] Nearly everything about its use of capital punishment is exceptional. Texas uses a capital sentencing statute that is, as we shall see, uncommon among death penalty states. Its Department of Criminal Justice not only executes the most inmates of any state, it broadcasts its work to an extraordinary degree. Launched in 1997, the state's death row website is notably grander than that of any other state and packed with information about condemned inmates past and present. Texas may be an exceptional case, but its representation of its condemned inmates exemplifies, in spirit if not in magnitude, how the death

penalty everywhere has required balancing a technocratic logic of incapacitation with the individualized purpose of retribution. To keep the
death penalty meaningful in a modern age, states still needed to recognize offenders' humanity at the moments of sentencing and execution.


## Broadcasting Death

If nobody claims the body of an executed inmate in Texas, the state buries it in Captain Joe Byrd Cemetery, a plot of land near its Huntsville execution chamber. There, in a grave marked only by a date of death and
an inmate identification number, the deceased's body is placed alongside
the unclaimed remains of other prisoners who died while incarcerated.

While only the unclaimed are literally buried by Texas, every executed inmate is interred in a virtual graveyard maintained by the state's
Department of Criminal Justice. On a web page titled "Executed Offenders," visitors will find over five hundred neatly arranged rows of
data, one for each execution the state has conducted since December 7,
1982, when it executed Charlie Brooks Jr. for killing an auto mechanic.
Executions appear on the table in reverse chronological order, with the
most recent at the top of the page. Reading from left to right, readers
will find basic information about each person the state has executed,
such as name, race, or the county in which the trial occurred (see fig. 3).[12]
The department began posting information about its death row inmates
when the website was launched in 1997 and in 2000 expanded it to include links to offenders' last statements and last meal requests.[13]

At first glance the page looks like a dispassionate addendum to a bureaucratic report. Embedded in each row of data, however, are links that
take viewers to content reminiscent of the published accounts of crime
and punishment sold to crowds on execution day in colonial America.[14]
Executed inmate Jonathan Green, for instance, occupies row 487 of the
state's online list of executed offenders. He is, viewers learn, Inmate
999421, a forty-four-year-old black male sentenced to death by a Montgomery County jury and executed on October 10, 2012.[15] Clicking on the
"offender information" link, though, leads visitors to a picture of Green
and an account of his crime. "On 06/21/2000, in Montgomery County,
Texas, Green kidnapped a 12 year old white female from a private residence," an employee of the Department of Criminal Justice has written
under the euphemistic heading "Summary of Incident." "Green took the

## Executed Offenders

| Execution | Link | Link | Last Name | First Name | TDCJ Number | Age | Date | Race | County |
|---|---|---|---|---|---|---|---|---|---|
| 501 | Offender Information | Last Statement | Quintanilla | John | 999491 | 36 | 07/16/2013 | Hispanic | Victoria |
| 500 | Offender Information | Last Statement | McCarthy | Kimberly | 999287 | 52 | 06/26/2013 | Black | Dallas |
| 499 | Offender Information | Last Statement | Chester | Elroy | 999280 | 43 | 06/12/2013 | Black | Jefferson |
| 498 | Offender Information | Last Statement | Williams | Jeffrey | 999350 | 37 | 05/15/2013 | Black | Harris |
| 497 | Offender Information | Last Statement | Parr | Carroll | 999479 | 35 | 05/07/2013 | Black | McLennan |
| 496 | Offender Information | Last Statement | Cobb | Richard | 999467 | 29 | 04/26/2013 | White | Cherokee |
| 495 | Offender Information | Last Statement | Threadgill | Ronnie | 999424 | 40 | 04/16/2013 | Black | Navarro |
| 494 | Offender Information | Last Statement | Lewis | Ricky | 999097 | 50 | 04/09/2013 | Black | Smith |
| 493 | Offender Information | Last Statement | Blue | Carl | 999151 | 48 | 02/21/2013 | Black | Brazos |
| 492 | Offender Information | Last Statement | Hughes | Preston | 939 | 46 | 11/15/2012 | Black | Harris |
| 491 | Offender Information | Last Statement | Hernandez | Ramon | 999431 | 41 | 11/14/2012 | Hispanic | Bexar |

FIGURE 3. The Texas Department of Criminal Justice "Executed Offenders" page on July 18, 2013.

victim to his residence, where he killed her by strangling her to death. The victim was also sexually assaulted. Green buried the victim in his backyard, then dug up the body and placed it inside the residence, behind a chair."[16] Clicking on the "last statement" link in the adjacent column, viewers travel to a different page where they can read a transcription of the words Green spoke to witnesses in the moments before his death. "I'm an innocent man," he said. "I did not kill anyone. Y'all are killing an innocent man. My left arm is killing me. It hurts bad."[17]

The structured mix of clinical detachment and vivid details on the state's website presents a dual impression of Green and the hundreds of other condemned inmates whose executions are remembered there. The account of Green's "incident" has the diction of a laboratory report, yet it also provides salacious details about the crime that turn it from an "incident" into a scene of horror: a burial of his victim, a subsequent exhumation of her body, a puzzling placing of it behind a chair. Green's last words, moreover, communicate his subjective experience of execution.[18] Like Green, each offender is both an abstract point of data—one row among over five hundred—and a distinctive individual who responded uniquely when the time came to suffer the consequence for his (or in six cases her) crime. The state's online presentation of condemned inmates like Jonathan Green is symptomatic of a broader ambiguity about the meaning of death sentences and executions in the contemporary era. Are they, as social theorist Émile Durkheim would understand them, sacred occasions in which members of an aggrieved community reaffirm their commitment to a moral order that an offender has violated in a particularly egregious way?[19] Or, in a world that has abandoned punitive spectacles, are they as Michel Foucault imagines them, acts of neutralizing a class of offenders who are "biological dangers" to the rest of the population?[20] The answer is that their capacity to be both has allowed death sentences and executions to fulfill their retributive purpose while containing the excesses that characterized a racist, uncivilized past. Support for the death penalty has thrived in the post-*Gregg* United States through, rather than in spite of, contradictory understandings of the executable subject.

## Paradox in the Courtroom

The development of Texas's capital sentencing statute demonstrates how federal death penalty jurisprudence preserved the retributive meaning of death sentences even as it demanded more consistency in sentencing outcomes. After *Furman*, Texas legislators created a new sentencing law that preserved jurors' discretion but differed from the scheme adopted by Georgia and other states. Instead of weighing aggravating factors against mitigating ones, jurors in Texas determined a defendant's sentence by answering yes-or-no questions in a particular order. In the statute Texas legislators devised, jurors were first asked to look into the future and consider whether, beyond a reasonable doubt, there was a "probability that the defendant would commit criminal acts of violence that would constitute a continuing threat to society." A no answer would result in a life sentence. A yes answer would prompt jurors to consider two more questions. They would have to consider "whether the conduct of the defendant that caused the death of the deceased was committed deliberately and with the reasonable expectation that the death of the deceased or another would result." Then they would determine "whether the conduct of the defendant in killing the deceased was unreasonable in response to the provocation, if any, by the deceased." A yes to the second and third questions would result in a death sentence.[21]

Those latter two questions only minimally called jurors' attention to the defendant's state of mind in the immediate context in which he committed his crime, suggesting that legislators wanted them to contemplate moral responsibility in narrow terms. Indeed, it is difficult to see how jurors answering no to the second and third questions would have found the defendant guilty of capital murder in the first place.

On its surface, the Texas sentencing statute was initially much more focused on reducing risk than on assigning blame. In *Penry v. Lynaugh* (1989), though, the US Supreme Court found that narrow focus unacceptable. It denied a jury, the majority said, "a vehicle for expressing its 'reasoned moral response'" to mitigating evidence such as abuse the defendant suffered during childhood.[22] A death sentence was to be a moral judgment of a person rather than simply a risk calculation.

To bring its statute into line with the Court's requirements, legislators replaced those second and third questions with one that put moral culpability at the center of the sentencing decision. Jurors still had to predict whether the defendant would pose a continuing danger to society, but they then had to answer a new question:

> Do you find from the evidence, taking into consideration all of the evidence, including the circumstances of the offense, the defendant's character and background, and the personal moral culpability of the defendant . . . that there is a sufficient mitigating circumstance or circumstances to warrant that a sentence of life imprisonment without parole rather than a death sentence be imposed?

A yes answer resulted in a life sentence. A no answer resulted in a death sentence.[23]

By making the question of moral blameworthiness central to the sentencing decision, the Court tempered the state's focus on managing risk with a requirement that juries also contemplate capital defendants as moral beings endowed with greater or lesser degrees of free will. The addition of a blameworthiness standard had the potential to create confusion, in jury deliberations, about the purpose of the death penalty. On one hand, the first question asked jurors to set aside the question of blameworthiness—and with it the question of free will—and instead view a death sentence as eliminating a risk to public safety. On the other hand, by taking up the question of the defendant's blameworthiness, the law asked jurors to base their judgment not on public safety in the future but on moral culpability in the past. The revised statute fixed the defendant as a data point, a probability, in question one, then revivified him as a moral being in question two.

Nowhere was the tension between these two goals more evident than in the closing arguments prosecutors in Texas made to juries during the penalty phase of capital trials in the 1990s and 2000s. Take, for instance, the prosecution's closing argument in the penalty phase of Herman Addison's 1997 trial. Days before they began hearing testimony about Addison's life, jurors had convicted him of the murder of William Johnson, the son of his ex-girlfriend. According to prosecutors, Addison had talked his way into the Houston apartment of Paula Ely, his estranged girlfriend, and tried to kiss her. When she rebuffed him, he stabbed her once in the abdomen and dragged her upstairs to the bedroom. As he shoved Ely onto the bed, he heard someone shut off the water in the apartment's bathroom and realized that Ely's son, William Johnson, was home. Having incapacitated Ely, Addison took Johnson by surprise and stabbed him repeatedly. As Johnson lay dying on the floor next to the bed, Addison sodomized Ely with a broomstick and raped her.

To make the case that Addison was blameworthy, prosecutor Marie Munier took the jury through the series of events that led to Paula Ely's horrifying rape and her son's brutal death. She singled out four particular points in time for the jury to contemplate: the moment when Ely rebuffed Addison, the moment when he stabbed her in the abdomen, the moment when he heard the water turned off in the bathroom, and the moment when he stabbed her son. At each of these junctures, she argued, Addison made a choice. When he was initially rebuffed, the prosecutor suggested, Addison had two options: "He could walk away, or he could stay and fight." When Ely continued to rebuff him, he took his knife out and at that point, according to the prosecutor, made yet another choice: "He could have held it to her, he could have said, 'All right. Are you going to listen to me or not? . . . That's not the choice he made, though. He didn't just threaten her with the knife. He came up to her and immediately attacked her with it."[24] When he saw Ely bleeding from the abdomen, the prosecutor suggested to jurors, "He could have said, 'My God, what have I done? Look at the results of what I have done here. I didn't intend for this to happen.' [He] could have left. He could have walked out the door. He could have grabbed his bag, walked out the door, and walked away."[25] When he heard the water turned off, the prosecutor rhetorically asked the jurors, "Does he choose to leave at that point in time, to flee because Will is there? Huh-uh. Huh-uh. No, he doesn't. . . . The defendant made his choice that he was going to eliminate the problem."[26] Finally, when Ely's son hit the ground, Addison had one final choice to make:

> He could have walked away. He could have done anything. He could have done a lot of things in that circumstance, but what he chose to do was stay and repeatedly rape this young woman in every way imaginable and to humiliate her in every way imaginable and to terrorize her in any way imaginable that night. As her son lay dying on the side of the bed, on the floor dying, he made those choices.[27]

Choice was a word prosecutors used frequently in their efforts to persuade jurors that a capital defendant deserved death.[28] By emphasizing the numerous opportunities the defendant had to reflect on his actions, the prosecutor heightened Addison's culpability for the crime. This was not an impulsive act, she said. Nor was it the product of some physiological or social pathology. Threatening Ely with a knife, remaining after he saw the blood he had shed with it, sodomizing her, raping her, killing her son—these were all isolated, free choices. They had nothing to do with the social disadvantages the defendant had suffered in the decades preceding the attack. They were unrelated to evidence of brain damage the defense had presented to jurors in an effort to convince them that Addison did not deserve a death sentence. Addison's crimes were choices made from a position of freedom: "When you understand the circumstances of this offense, you understand who was in control. He wasn't uncontrollable. He wasn't in a rage. He wasn't some madman, crazy. He was in control of what he did, of who he did it to, and how he did it," the prosecutor argued.[29]

But to make the case that there was a probability Addison would commit a future act of violence, the prosecutor had to abandon the rhetoric of choice and argue that he lacked self-control. Minutes after she discounted the mitigating evidence presented by Addison's defense team, Munier began a dramatically different line of argument. Pointing to the same evidence of brain damage she had moments earlier denied as relevant, she argued that Addison's physiological deficits made the death penalty even more necessary. The brain damage, she said, had to become "part of the equation": "He's just predestined to be [a violent person] because of his physical condition. That's who Herman Addison is. He can't control himself. He has violent responses which he does not have the ability to control. That makes him a violent man. That makes him a dangerous man. That makes him the man that you have to judge today."[30] In less than two minutes, Addison's prosecutor went from saying that Addison "was in control of what he did" to asserting that he "[couldn't] control himself."

This kind of paradoxical portrayal of a capital defendant became common in prosecutors' closing arguments in Texas in the aftermath of the Court's 1989 *Penry* decision. Defendants, prosecutors suggested, were dangerous because some ungovernable inner force compelled them to hurt others or because they lacked the capacity to know right from wrong. The prosecutor in Danny Dean Thomas's trial informed his jury that the defendant could not be "socialized. He has no care for others. Complete disregard for others. No conscience. He doesn't care about others. He cares about himself."[31] In Derrick Leon Jackson's case, the jury heard that the defendant "doesn't have a moral compass that would prevent other people from committing those kinds of acts."[32] To keep the jury in Jeffrey Williams's case from thinking he had the potential for rehabilitation, his prosecutor argued, "It's human nature for us to want to think that people can be fixed, that there is a reason that people do things, because we don't go out and do things like the defendant. Because we have a conscience, unlike the defendant. Because we have those little moral compasses that tell us what's right and wrong."[33] Similarly, the prosecutor in Eric Cathey's case argued, "This is a man without a conscience, something that can't be taught and learned."[34]

The language the prosecutors used here is, importantly, the language of capacity rather than will. Danny Dean Thomas does not refuse to be socialized; he lacks the capacity to be socialized. Derrick Leon Jackson and Jeffrey Williams do not have a moral compass that they willfully ignore; they simply have no internal apparatus for determining which action is right and which is wrong. Eric Cathey does not reject moral instruction; he cannot be taught. A consequentialist rationale for capital punishment thus remained a crucial component of prosecutors' arguments for death: juries ought to sentence the defendant to death because he will kill again unless incapacitated.

Questions of will, though, returned when prosecutors shifted their sights to the question of a defendant's moral blameworthiness. To counter the defense's claim that a history of poverty or abuse diminished an offender's blameworthiness, prosecutors had to depict the offender as a man who *does* have a moral compass, who knows good from evil and chooses to do evil. Less than a minute before he called Eric Cathey "a man without a conscience," Cathey's prosecutor told jurors, "He's capable of knowing the truth, good, right from wrong, and he knows and has the ability to make choices and make decisions on his own."[35]

The contradictory representations of capital defendants in prosecutors' rhetoric were the natural result of the philosophical contradictions built into the death penalty statute after *Penry*. The defendant who was, at one point in a closing argument, an out-of-control animal was, at other points, endowed with the same capacity for self-control as other victims of deprivation. Such incoherent visions of the capital defendant did not, however, work against juries' willingness to sentence capital defendants to death. The inclusion of much more mitigating evidence in the penalty phase of capital trials did not appear to slow death sentences. From 1977 to 1989, when *Penry* was decided, an average of nearly twenty-nine capital defendants were sentenced to death in Texas each year. From 1990, after the decision went into effect, until 2002, an average of nearly thirty-four capital defendants were sentenced to death each year.[36]

If anything, the *Penry* decision added punitiveness to the meaning of a death sentence in Texas. This was ironic, as the outcome of the case was understood to help capital defendants present evidence to juries of their diminished culpability. *Penry* was part of a larger group of post-*Furman* decisions that derived from a "civilizing" imperative on the part of the Supreme Court.[37] In an enlightened society, the Court insisted, only competent adults could face execution—a principle the justices would uphold in subsequent cases forbidding the executions of juveniles,[38] the mentally disabled,[39] and the mentally ill.[40] By giving defendants the opportunity to challenge the idea of free will and by requiring that jury instructions prioritize the question of blameworthiness, however, the Court incited the very debate over moral responsibility that undergirded the punitive turn. Undoubtedly *Penry* saved some lives by giving skilled defense attorneys the ability to put in front of juries mitigating evidence they otherwise would not have had the chance to hear. But each death sentence after *Penry* broadcast, in a way that previous capital sentences had not, the degree to which capital jurors in Texas saw capital defendants as endowed with a responsibility for their actions that was not easily compromised.[41] A juror's vote for death after *Penry* would become a vote against excuses, against the idea that people were the products of their environments—votes that, in a culture that had recommitted itself to a negative understanding of freedom, were not hard to come by. Instead of giving defense attorneys a fighting chance, the weight that the revamped statute placed on a killer's blameworthiness often made their work more challenging.

## Rationalizing Death: The Technocratic Overhaul of Execution Procedures

I have argued that an initial demand that death sentences be made more objective spurred second thoughts in Supreme Court justices who insisted that juries evaluate defendants as unique human beings rather than figures on an actuarial table. By approving new guidelines that promised to reduce the arbitrariness with which juries meted out death sentences while also preserving jurors' ability to grant mercy, the Court unwittingly balanced a legal desire for fairness with an equally compelling cultural desire for a death sentence to be an individualized referendum on a person's blameworthiness.

A similar balancing act occurred in the nation's execution chambers. The fear that a soulless state would treat defendants as a "faceless, undifferentiated mass" posed challenges not only to states' efforts to standardize sentencing protocols,[42] but also to prisons' efforts to standardize execution protocols. As executions resumed in the late 1970s and early 1980s, so too did a much longer process of changing them into professional operations.[43] As early as the 1830s, elite reformers in the northeastern United States had begun transforming executions from communal, ad hoc events played out in public to technically sophisticated, routine operations that occurred within the confines of jail yards and, eventually, the bowels of large state prisons. By the end of the twentieth century, this process had permanently altered the character of execution ceremonies.[44] Writing in 2000, political theorist Timothy V. Kaufman-Osborn observed, "Distinctively modern executions, precisely because they are not ritualized affairs whose time-consuming purpose is to evoke and reinforce substantive collective norms, seek to extinguish life as rapidly as possible or, in the best of all possible worlds, instantaneously."[45]

Consonant with this argument, anthropological studies of executions in the modern era have drawn a connection between execution protocols and a loss of agency of both the condemned and the state actors engaged in "death work."[46] After studying and witnessing a southern state's execution routine in the 1980s, criminologist Robert Johnson noted that "the point of the modern bureaucratic execution procedure is to suppress any real-life human reactions on the part of the prisoners or their executioners. Human reactions—displays of character or faith—would interfere with the efficient administration of the death penalty and indeed draw unwanted attention to the violence of the proceedings."[47]

The techniques the state used to kill its condemned prisoners were perhaps the most obvious manifestation of these principles. Executions after *Gregg* increasingly left nearly no mark on the body, thereby reducing the legibility of its experience of pain and cultivating an image of the execution as humane. Lethal injection, the most common mode of execution in the United States since 1977, appeared simply to put the prisoner to sleep, reducing the opportunities for drama that lethal gas, hanging, and electrocution provided.

The mode of execution was but the most visible element of a protocol that encompassed everything from the arrangement of furniture in the execution chamber to the arrival time of witnesses. As executions occurred more and more frequently in the 1980s and 1990s, scholars and journalists noted how antiseptic they had become.[48] Before the execution, guards followed institutional procedures to manipulate the prisoners into remaining calm. Though methods varied across states, the goal was the same: to reduce the likelihood of resistance or uncomfortable emotional outbursts. Thus prisons offered sedatives to the condemned. Prison personnel reassured them that the execution would not hurt.[49] The execution device's control panel, an avoidable source of anxiety for the condemned, was kept out of sight. On the day before their execution, policies in some states kept the condemned from listening to music or visiting in person with family members or friends.[50] In other states, prison personnel strapped inmates to the gurney ahead of time and wheeled them into the execution room, eliminating the drama of a "last walk."[51]

The toll that long-term institutionalization took on offenders also played a key role in producing docile offenders. In the post-*Gregg* era, inmates have been executed on average nearly eleven years after they were sentenced to death.[52] Time spent in isolation on death row has often made the person hooked up to the execution device unrecognizably different from the person who entered the prison a decade earlier. Writing in 1990, when executions happened an average of 7.9 years after sentencing,[53] Johnson wrote that "worn down in small and almost imperceptible ways, [inmates] gradually but inexorably become less than fully human. At the end, the prisoners are helpless pawns of the modern execution drill. They give in, give up, and submit; yielding themselves to the execution team and the machinery of death."[54]

The incongruity of pacifying practices with the retributive rationale for the death penalty created a tension between the values of order and individuation similar to the one I discussed earlier in my analysis of the Supreme Court's capital jurisprudence. The punitive rhetoric of prosecutors and politicians described offenders as self-made human enemies who were responsible for their actions. The practices outlined in execution manuals, however, treated them as faceless members of a high-risk population who were being permanently incapacitated.[55]

This contradiction had the potential to diminish a sense of clarity about who the targets of capital punishment were. On his back, strapped to a gurney, the offender might not live up to his reputation in criminological and political discourse as a "dangerous other" to be feared or as a morally responsible person to be punished.[56] Popular, retributive justifications for severe punishment could become difficult to believe in those final moments. Condemned men were supposed to be threatening menaces who deserved what was coming to them, but given the clinical nature of executions that came years after their crimes, they were more likely to appear like docile automatons.

In the midst of practices that discourage pathos, though, two historical traditions persisted in the modern period that invited just the opposite response: the opportunities for the condemned to request a special "last meal" and to make a speech to those assembled to witness the execution. At first glance these custom-made meals and final speeches served no immediately recognizable, rational purpose.[57] Nourishing those who were about to die was obviously unnecessary and, unless they were directed toward helping prison staff find veins suitable for the lethal injection, offenders' words were not needed to end their lives.[58] These ancient traditions, however, sustained the retributive spirit of executions in a technocratic age. The practice or pretense of allowing the condemned to say and eat whatever they chose before death, and the subsequent dissemination of information about their "choices" to the general public, individualized those the state killed. Offenders' last words and last meal requests countered potential perceptions of them as docile automatons, instead cultivating an image of unique individuals whose personalities remained unencumbered even at the moment of death. By showing that offenders were still capable of making their own decisions, the state and the media reinforced a retributive understanding of the individual as acting freely in the world, unfettered by circumstance or social condition.

At the same time, through other procedures designed to pacify offenders, the state also displayed its ability to maintain order and satisfy the public's retributive urges humanely. In so doing, it cultivated an understanding of offenders as self-made monsters endowed with both agency and intrinsic evil.[59] Ultimately, this paradoxical representation made executions seem both necessary and deserved, rational and sacred.[60]

The retributive role of last statements and, until very recently, last meals have been especially obvious in Texas. While many states have continued to let the condemned make final statements and choose last meals before execution, Texas has emphasized these protocols in ways that have called attention to their significance. Indeed, as Kevin Francis O'Neill has noted, administrative protocols in Texas have required the warden to solicit final words from the condemned, stipulate that their speech must be made audible to witnesses, and abstain from limiting their time and content.[61] Only two of the other top ten states that executed the most prisoners, Louisiana and Florida, have had policies as deferential to the offender as Texas's policy.[62] In the early 2000s, Texas went even further. Within a day or two of the execution, a state employee began posting the offender's final words on the website of the Texas Department of Criminal Justice, a practice that continues to this day. No other state has gone to such elaborate lengths to ensure that the public hears the offender's voice beyond the prison walls.[63]

## Last Words

The diversity of inmates' final statements is striking. Final statements in Texas can be bawdy or contrite, submissive or defiant. In most of these statements readers find not a numbed, institutionalized voice, but a dramatic, emotionally laden expression of defiance, pain, reconciliation, or identity. Some offenders have apologized to the victims' families: William Davis went to his death contrite for his criminal behavior, saying, "I would like to say to the Lang family how truly sorry I am in my soul and in my heart of hearts for the pain and misery that I have caused from my actions. I am truly sorry."[64] Charles Bass told witnesses, "I deserve this. Tell everyone I said goodbye."[65] Others have attempted to subvert the intended meaning of their executions through displays of righteousness and deviance, strategies popular among the condemned in the Western world of the seventeenth and eighteenth centuries.[66] In Texas, a self-righteous Garry Miller used his last statement to pray, saying, "Lord, be merciful with those who are actively involved with the taking of my life, forgive them as I am forgiving them." Robert Atworth and Brian Roberson, by contrast, told witnesses at their executions to kiss, respectively, their "proud white Irish ass" and "black ass." Through their final statements, all three men rejected the moral authority of the state.[67]

Other statements, by contrast, have been directly critical of the state. Some have proclaimed their innocence or suggested that the government had denied them justice in some way or other.[68] Still others have commented on the death penalty, usually expressing disapproval. Before going to his death, James Beathard attacked his country's foreign policy:

Couple of matters that I want to talk about since this is one of the few times people will listen to what I have to say. The Unite[d] States has gotten to a [point] now where they [have] zero respect for human life. My death is just a symptom of a bigger illness. At some point the government has got to wake up and stop doing things to destroy other countries and killing innocent children. The ongoing embargo and sanctions against places like Iran and Iraq, Cuba and other places. They are not doing anything to change the world, but they are harming innocent children.[69]

Still other inmates in Texas have attacked government officials as corrupt, as Anthony Fuentes did when he said, before his execution, "It is wrong for the prosecutors to lie and make witnesses say what they need them to say."[70]

Examining last statements, some scholars have argued that they offer inmates the opportunity to shape the meaning of their executions and, in doing so, have often made their punishments seem unjust.[71] Undoubtedly, the final statements of aggrieved or remorseful inmates have strengthened the resolve of dyed-in-the-wool opponents of the death penalty. But encountering a public that has been overwhelmingly in favor of the death penalty since the 1970s, subversive last words have had little effect at changing minds about the death penalty. Readers of news accounts of an execution may feel sympathy for an inmate when they "hear" that the lethal injection "hurts bad" or that the condemned thanked the warden or asked for forgiveness from the victim's kin.[72] They may wonder whether a defendant's vehement declaration that the state was killing the wrong man was true, especially in the 2000s, as the media increasingly covered exonerations of condemned inmates.[73] But divorced from the realities of the criminal justice system, most Americans have encountered inmates' dying declarations fleetingly.[74] In such a context, last statements serve a limited, but crucial, function: they simply but powerfully reinforce the perception that the condemned die as unique human beings, people whose mental freedom remained unencumbered at the time of execution.

This has been most evident when prisoners contest the notion that they have been dehumanized by their stay on death row.[75] When Texas executed Jamie McCoskey in November 2013 after over twenty years on death row, he told the witnesses, "The best time in my life is during this period. If I had to do [it] again, I would not change a thing. . . . I appreciate the people that helped me out."[76] McCoskey's statement implicitly disputes the characterization of life on death row as the experience of being "suspended" in "timeless time," spiritually frozen while awaiting execution.[77] In a similar interpretation, legal studies scholar Linda Ross Meyer has interpreted some condemned inmates' use of their final statement to thank their appellate lawyers, fellow inmates, and prison officials as a way for inmates to make clear "that the formation of relationships does not end with prison."[78] Indeed, many inmates seem to want to appear psychologically free in their final moments.

Still, the substance of what condemned inmates say has ultimately been less important than the act of speaking. Whether inmates protested their innocence or pleaded for forgiveness, offered an indictment of civil authorities or a tribute to them, each final statement has left witnesses near and far with a final image of the offender as a human being making a choice. So strong has this appearance of control been that almost one-third of the prisoners have given a verbal cue—often in the form of permission or even command—to begin the execution. "Do what you do, Warden," one said; "Let's ride"; "All right, Warden, let's do it"; "I'm ready"; "Warden, take me home"; "Set me free, Warden"; "I am ready to go home and be with my Lord"; "I'm done. Let's do it"; "Do what you have to do"; "Let's do it; Lock and load"; and "Warden, just give me parole and let me go home to be with the Lord."[79] By addressing the warden, the official ultimately responsible for inflicting the punishment, inmates have conveyed a semblance of control over their own deaths. For many years, after the inmate completed his speech, the warden's signal to begin the lethal flow of drugs was nonverbal: he would take off his glasses, thus giving the prisoner, in effect, the last word.[80] The irony here is striking: inmates tied tightly to a gurney appeared, in their final few seconds of life, to be making the choice to die.

## Last Meals

The final meal requests of Texas inmates, which the state released to the media or reported online, revealed more than just their appetites. They invited the public to contemplate personality, to perceive gluttony or ascetic restraint, fearlessness or abject terror, from orders for T-bone steaks and ice cream. Jessy San Miguel asked for "pizza (beef, bacon bits, and multiple types of cheese), 10 quesadillas (5 mozzarella cheese, 5 cheddar cheese), 5 strips of open-flame grilled beef, 5 strips of stir-fried beef, chocolate peanut butter ice cream, sweet tea, double fudge chocolate cake, broccoli, and grapes." His precision revealed an exacting temperament or, perhaps, an abiding distrust of an institution that would shortchange him if given the chance. Charles Tuttle ordered "four fried eggs sunny side up, four sausage patties, one chicken fried steak patty, one bowl of white country gravy, five pieces of white toast, five tacos with meat and cheese only, four Dr. Peppers with ice [on] the side & five mint sticks," expressing a capacious appetite, not to mention idiosyncratic tastes. A fastidious Frank McFarland ordered a "heaping portion of lettuce, a sliced tomato, a sliced cucumber, four celery stalks, four sticks of American or Cheddar cheese, two bananas and two cold half pints of milk." He "asked that all vegetables be washed prior to serving. Also asked that the cheese sticks be clean," perhaps believing that the food served to him was often unsanitary. Some requests, on the other hand, were notable for their simplicity: Stacey Lawton requested "1 jar of dill pickles"; Benjamin Stone and Patrick Rogers just wanted "a Coke"; Chester Wicker sought lettuce and tomatoes; James Russell asked for an apple; and Gerald Mitchell wanted "1 bag of assorted Jolly Ranchers."[81]

Other inmates used their meal requests to convey political and religious beliefs or to demonstrate social consciousness. Odell Barnes Jr. ordered helpings of "Justice, Equality, World Peace." Jonathan Nobles asked for the Eucharist. Carlos Santana asked for "Justice, Temperance, with Mercy." Danny Harris wanted "God's saving grace, love, truth, peace and freedom." Robert Madden "asked that final meal be provided to a homeless person."[82] Some inmates, conscious perhaps that the final meal is often mentioned in execution reporting, refused it and, through their refusal, called attention to the death penalty or contemporary public issues. In North Carolina, a state that has also published final meal requests and final statements, Ricky Sanderson used his last statement to explain the significance of his last meal:

> I didn't take [a last meal] because I have very strong convictions about abortion and with thirty-three million babies that have been aborted in this country, died for no reason, I'm dying for a deed I did and I deserve death for it and I'm glad Christ forgave me. Those babies never got a first meal and that's why I didn't take the last, in their memory. I'm just thankful God has been gracious to me. That's it.[83]

And so the final meal request became far more than simply a choice of food. Everything about it—the type and quantity of food specified, the instructions on how kitchen staff should arrange or prepare it, the assertion of its political and religious meaning—revealed the individuality of the offenders.

Importantly, Texas reported offenders' final meal requests even when they went unfulfilled. Former prison cook Brian Price notes that the state did not meet all requests. All food had to come from the prison's existing supplies, so to those who requested lobster, for instance, the institution served a filet of processed fish. The state would automatically pare down large quantities of items. Instead of the twenty-four tacos he requested in 1998, David Allen Castillo got four.[84] The public relations team for the prison only sometimes made the public aware of these limits. For instance, the entry for Ruben Cantu read, "Barbecue chicken, refried beans, brown rice, sweet tea and bubble gum (bubble gum is not permitted under TDCJ regulations)."[85] In publishing the prisoners' orders, not the content of their actual meals, Texas revealed that its purpose was not democratic transparency about the punishment, as department spokesperson Michelle Lyons claimed. It served, instead, as a state-sponsored individuation of offenders.[86] The selection of a final meal was one of two moments during the deathwatch and execution when the state could ask the offender to differentiate himself from those who came before him and those who would come after.[87] As law and technology made the legitimate taking of life a more standardized affair, final words and final meal requests became symbolic indicators of offenders' agency, reminding observers of their status as human beings who deserved to suffer for acts they willed on their own. The death penalty appeared not simply as incapacitation, but as retributive incapacitation: offenders needed to be executed because they willed themselves into uncontrollable beings who were not just incapable of reform but unworthy of it.

Texas's "executed offenders" web page presents this balanced picture of condemned inmates. Reminders of their agency appear in the final statements. Reminders of their incorrigibility, though, fill the dossiers posted about them (See fig. 4). The state's profile of executed offender Carlos Santana, for instance, describes him in ways that cast doubt on his capacity for reform. While he had no prior prison record, the state tells readers, "In June 1981, Santana was found to have been involved in an escape attempt from the Harris Co. Jail. The escape attempt was aborted when a pistol, tear-gas canister, two homemade knives, and a handcuff key were found in a maximum security cell." He is a man, we are told, who cannot be incapacitated, even by imprisonment. He is irredeemable, part of an elite class of offenders for whom the only management strategy is death.

Other offenders appear sadistic in the state's online accounts of their crimes. Troy Kunkle's dossier reads, "After the killing, Kunkle reportedly said, 'another day, another death, another sorrow, another breath.' Later, he reportedly said the murder was 'beautiful.'" Portraying Kunkle as someone who finds murder both banal and beautiful, the state presents a specimen of monstrosity rather than a rational human being.[88] And yet, by soliciting last words and last meal requests from men like Santana and Kunkle while describing them as irredeemable, Texas allows the public to see them simultaneously as monsters and as human beings facing punishment.

Indeed, executions could not deliver the experience of catharsis unless they were able to communicate this vision of the offender as both self-controlled and out of control, calculating and calculable, agentic and inert. The average person does not, as Walter Berns notes, take pleasure in euthanizing animals, even rabid ones, so executions in the post-*Gregg* period have had to present offenders as humans who chose to be rabid, who willed themselves into an irredeemable condition.[89] The retributive satisfaction that punishment promised depended on the

**Name**: Troy Albert Kunkle      **D.R. #** 784

**DOB**: 05/27/66    **Received**: 03/02/85    **Age**: 18   (when received)

**County**: Nueces      **Date of Offense**: 08/12/84

**Age at time of offense**: 18      **Race**: white   **Height**: 6-1

**Weight**: 163    **Eyes**: blue    **Hair**: brown

**Native County**: Nurenburg      **State**: Germany

**Prior Occupation**: student      **Education Level**: 11 years

**Prior Prison Record**:

None

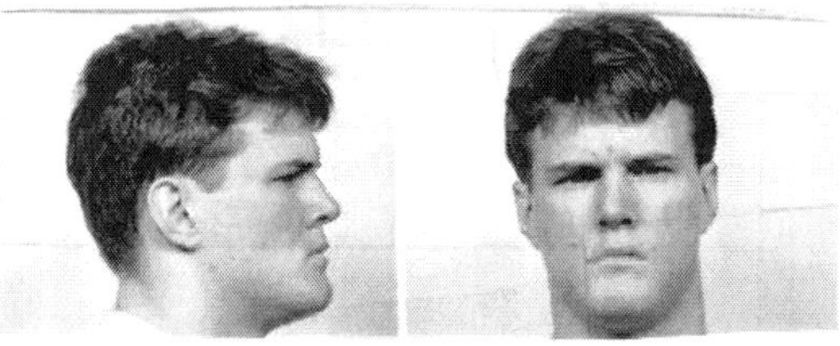

**Summary:**

Convicted in the abduction, robbery and shooting death of Steven Wayne Horton, 31, in Corpus Christi. After driving from San Antonio and visiting the beach in Corpus Christi, Kunkle and three co-defendants drove around town looking for someone to rob. They saw Horton walking near the 1600 block of Paul Jones Road and induced him into the car by offering him a ride home. Once in the car, co-defendant Russell Stanley put a gun to Horton's head and demanded his wallet. When Horton refused, Kunkle told Stanley to kill him, but Stanley said it wasn't necessary. Kunkle then took the .22 caliber pistol from Stanley and told accomplice Aaron Adkins to drive behind a nearby skating rink, where he shot Horton once in the back of the head. Accomplice Lora Lee Zaiontz, Kunkel's girlfriend, then pushed Horton's body from the car and took his wallet, which contained $13. After the killing, Kunkle reportedly said, "another day, another death, another sorrow, another breath." Later, he reportedly said the murder was "beautiful."

**Co-Defendants:**

Lora Lee Zaiontz #392303, H/F, DOB: 1/16/66, rec. 2/21/85, life, capital murder. Russell Stanley #394109, W/M, DOB: 10/18/66, rec. 3/20/85, 30 years, murder. Aaron Adkins #394104, W/M, DOB: 9/24/64, rec. 3/20/85, 30 yrs., murder.

**Race of Victim(s):**

White male

FIGURE 4. The Texas Department of Criminal Justice posts, on its website, a dossier on each of the inmates it has executed or is planning to execute.

public's capacity to imagine the condemned inmate as a human rather than an animal. Thus, the transformation of executions into efficient acts of incapacitation had to remain slightly incomplete; executions had to retain unpredictable elements that called attention to the condemned person's humanity in the period immediately preceding his death.

## Conclusion

In a 2003 article in the *Atlanta Journal-Constitution* that examined the public's "curious" desire to know about the last meals of condemned inmates, renowned capital defense attorney Stephen Bright interpreted this interest as a sign of just how shallow the American public's understanding of the death penalty was: "So often, these cases have very compelling issues—questions of justice, questions of mental capabilities, questions of age and maturity at the time of the crime—and here we are, dealing with the most awesome and enormous kind of thing that human beings can do, which is to take a human life, and we're focused on the trivial."[90]

While inmates' last meals may be "trivial" from the perspective of a defense attorney, the role that differentiating details have played in maintaining the retributive purpose of the death penalty in the 1990s and 2000s is decidedly not. By maintaining small spaces for the unpredictable in executions, elite actors have kept a humanistic buffer around an increasingly mechanical practice.

In this and in the court ordered retention of jurors' discretion in sentencing, we can perceive a fundamental cultural uneasiness with an approach to capital punishment that justified itself solely in terms of the cold logic of incapacitation. In the contemporary era of the death penalty, ideals of freedom were just as important as the need for order in making a punishment satisfying. What was attractive about incapacitation—the security it promised, the appearance it created of passionless distance from a barbaric past—threatened to undermine the humanity of the condemned individual. In soliciting last meals and last words from him, the state demonstrated that he had retained his psychological freedom. By preserving a token amount of space for individualization in the act of sentencing a person to death and executing him, Supreme Court justices, state legislators, and prison personnel curbed the potentially undesirable excesses of bureaucratic rationalization.

In addition, the birth of individualized sentencing hearings and the retention of ancient execution-day customs in the modern era of the American death penalty illustrate an important principle about retribution. Retribution degrades the punished, reducing him to a lower social, economic, physical, or political status. As such, the candidate for punishment must initially appear to have something to lose. He needs to be, before the punishment, "a sacred subject capable of being profaned."[91] As managerial science and evolving understandings of due process brought more reason to bear on death sentences and executions, the retention of spaces for the exercise of discretion on the part of various parties to the punishment was necessary to preserve its retributive character. Juries retained the discretion to condemn some while showing mercy to others. Offenders retained the discretion to use words and food to make meaning out of their deaths. And journalists, as a result, used the unpredictable consequences of the exercise of discretion to maintain the pathos of punishment in a technocratic age.

Popular culture, as we shall see in the next chapter, took this principle one step further. In Hollywood renderings of the death penalty in the 1980s and 1990s, moviemakers would depict the condemned as human not only to make their punishment retributive, but also to make it into a personal and social good.

## CHAPTER FOUR

# Shock Therapy

## *The Rehabilitation of Capital Punishment*

"What profit him to bleed? Shall the dust praise him? Shall the worms declare his truth?"[1]
— Arthur Miller, *The Crucible* (1953)

In colonial New England, public executions were dramas of sin and redemption played out in front of attentive crowds. On hanging day, clergy delivered moralizing sermons to the assembled community, the crowd sang hymns, and the condemned, following an unofficial script, spoke of her hope for God's grace.[2] The early American murderer, facing execution, was not a monster or a democratic political subject but an embodiment of the sinful humanity that resided within everyone.[3] Clergy often recounted the penitent spiritual journey the condemned had undertaken since their conviction for the capital crime, expressing hope that God's grace had saved them from hell.[4] Indeed, until at least the nineteenth century, defenders of capital punishment would argue that a death sentence was more likely to rehabilitate a person than was a penitentiary.[5]

In our comparatively secular age, this understanding of a death sentence as a soul saver seems strange. That may explain why, as Supreme Court justices sorted through the various historical rationales for capital punishment in their 1972 *Furman* ruling, none mentioned it. Justice Warren Burger, for instance, made no mention of the religious relation between retribution and redemption in upholding the constitutionality of the sanction. Instead, he wrote of the "severe emotional stress" of awaiting an execution. He saw nothing beneficial about the mental anguish the condemned experienced; that pain was, he admitted, "cruel in the sense that all suffering is thought cruel."[6]

When rehabilitation did appear in the *Furman* opinions, it was part of liberal justices' arguments against the death penalty. Thurgood Marshall and William Brennan, the two justices who found death a cruel and unusual punishment, saw cruelty in the way death, by ending a person's existence forever, foreclosed on the possibility of their capacity to flourish in the future. Arguing that the death penalty was an affront to human dignity, Justice Brennan described an execution as irrevocable exile from the human race:

> Although death, like expatriation, destroys the individual's "political existence" and his "status in organized society," it does more, for, unlike expatriation, death also destroys "his very existence." There is, too, at least the possibility that the expatriate will in the future regain "the right to have rights." Death forecloses even that possibility. Death is a truly awesome punishment. The calculated killing of a human being by the State involves, by its very nature, a denial of the executed person's humanity.[7]

In his own concurring opinion, Justice Marshall expressed this idea much more succinctly: "Death is irrevocable; life imprisonment is not. Death, of course, makes rehabilitation impossible; life imprisonment does not."[8] In many ways Marshall and Brennan articulated the commonsense, secular assumption of mainstream criminology in the 1950s and 1960s: capital punishment ended lives rather than transformed them for the better. What better way to express hopelessness about an individual's capacity for change than to execute him?

Writing in the early 1970s, however, the justices of the Burger Court did not anticipate how popular representations of capital punishment would turn that logic on its head in the decades to come. In the 1980s and 1990s, as death row populations were growing considerably and executions were becoming an increasingly regular occurrence, fictional films about the death penalty became an important vehicle through which punitive, retributive ideology gained power. Rather than pandering to Americans' resentment of the criminal, though, they crafted a vision of the death penalty as spiritually beneficial to the condemned as well as the community his crime had harmed.

While they demonstrated the redemptive power of a death sentence, these films also sought to purge capital punishment of its historical associations with white supremacy. At times only the condemned would benefit from their spiritual transformation in the shadow of the execution chamber. But at other times the inmate would stand in, as he did in colonial New England, for members of a society worried about its sinful history. In the hands of filmmakers, executions were more than acts of retribution and incapacitation. They were opportunities for personal, and sometimes cultural, redemption.

## Whitewashing the Death Penalty

The historical use of the death penalty as a tool of white supremacy made its revival in the aftermath of the civil rights movement politically precarious. The death penalty had a long history of disproportionate use on African Americans, predating the Civil War.[9] Furthermore, its lopsided use in the early and mid-twentieth century as a punishment for black men accused of raping white women connected it to a horrifying history of public torture lynchings in the South.[10] In a culture that was now professing to be race blind, the death penalty stood out, to many, as a particularly potent symbol of a racist past.

Sexism had also shaped the use of the death penalty in the past. Lynch mobs and district attorneys had presented women as the beneficiaries of lethal punishment, its use on their alleged attackers a sign that the community recognized their vulnerability. A paternalistic attitude toward women also shaped, conversely, their perceived capacity for criminal agency. Executions ascribed to the condemned a degree of dangerousness and blameworthiness that few women were thought to have. As a result, states rarely executed women, even when one accounts for their much lower homicide commission rates.[11]

Racism and sexism in the administration of the death penalty—evident in the disproportionately high execution rates of those who killed white people and the disproportionately low execution rates of women—continued into the modern era of the American death penalty.[12] In some ways this reflected the rightward political drift of white Americans. As violent crime rates doubled in the 1960s, so too did coded demands for law and order that were built on long-standing racist representations of African Americans as savage.[13] Indeed, *Gregg* was decided in 1976 at the beginning of an incarceration boom that would so disproportionately affect African American men that legal studies scholar Michelle Alexander has famously called it "the new Jim Crow."[14]

Still, the appearance of race and gender relations had shifted considerably by the 1980s. The death penalty reemerged in a world where the rules of mainstream political discourse no longer permitted open avowal of the principles of white supremacy and patriarchy.

The sheer volume of studies focused on the role of racial bias following the resumption of executions in 1977 was itself an indicator of a heightened public sensitivity to race. While some studies questioned the existence of bias in meting out death sentences,[15] a substantial number confirmed the enduring salience of race in Americans' support for and states' use of the death penalty. States that have the death penalty, scholars found, were likely to be those with the greatest number of black residents.[16] Support for capital punishment in a given locale was associated with levels of black presence and racial prejudice.[17] Some white capital jurors still conceived of themselves as embattled moral insiders whose duty it was to punish racial outsiders, even as they actively disavowed the role race played in their decision making.[18] Perhaps most damning of all, the death penalty was disproportionately applied in cases where the victim was white. "Our data strongly suggests that Georgia is operating a dual system, based on the race of the victim, for processing homicide cases," legal scholar David Baldus and his colleagues wrote in a study of capital punishment after Georgia had overhauled its statutes to meet the demands for sentencing fairness in *Furman v. Georgia*. All other factors being equal, they found that those convicted of killing whites were four times as likely to receive a death sentence as those convicted of killing nonwhites. The murder of a black person had to be much more heinous than that of a white person for prosecutors to seek, and juries to impose, a death sentence.[19]

All this evidence, however, was for naught. In 1987 lawyers for Warren McCleskey, a black death row inmate in Georgia, presented the Supreme Court with Baldus's statistical evidence that, despite the new standards of "guided discretion," juries were returning sentences that reflected the influence of unlawful bias. The Court nonetheless refused to overturn McCleskey's death sentence. Statistical patterns were not enough, it said, to prove discriminatory intent. "We decline to assume that what is unexplained is invidious," the Court wrote, backing away from the commitment it had made in *Furman* to ensuring fair outcomes in capital cases.[20]

Thus, in the law, race-based arguments against the death penalty went nowhere. In the cultural life of capital punishment, however, they were periodically given a public hearing. The result, though, was the same. Over the course of the 1980s and 1990s, Hollywood films assured audiences that antiblack racism no longer infected the practice of capital punishment in the United States.[21] State killing, they showed, was an act that primarily targeted white people and was carried out by racially diverse prison personnel.[22] Racist white men, not the black victims of racism, were the objects of punishment in these films. The death penalty might be objectionable for a whole host of reasons, these films collectively suggested, but racism was not among them.

One of the simplest changes in modern death penalty films was the visual alignment of people of color with the killing state. Films of this era differed from their predecessors in their frequent portrayals of African Americans as wardens, guards, and prosecutors. In *The Execution of Raymond Graham*, a 1985 ABC made for television movie that was filmed live for audiences, African American actor Morgan Freeman portrayed a compassionate, professional prison warden who, in the teleplay's final scene, somberly gives the signal to start the lethal injection that kills Raymond Graham, a white inmate.[23] *Last Light*, a 1993 television movie starring Kiefer Sutherland and Forest Whitaker, depicted the unlikely friendship that flourishes between a black prison guard (Whitaker) and his poor white ward (Sutherland) on death row.[24] Toward the end of *The Chamber*, a 1996 film version of the John Grisham novel, a white death row inmate apologizes for his racism to a black guard, who sympathetically accepts his apology.[25] Finally, in *Better Off Dead*, a 1993 made for television movie produced by Gloria Steinem for the Lifetime cable television network, Tyra Ferrell played Cutter Dubuque, an African American prosecutor who is upset that "nobody in this country gets the death penalty for killing a black man."[26] When Kit Kellner (Mare Winningham), a poor white woman, kills a black man, Dubuque gets her chance to right this wrong.

Conscious efforts to avoid racial stereotypes may have contributed to the inverted racial dynamics of some of these films.[27] Writing about *The Execution of Raymond Graham* in 1986, the *New York Times* quoted a producer from ABC who acknowledged that Raymond Graham was white when "the great majority of convicts on death row are black."[28] "There are almost no ethnic villains on television," he claimed. "Almost every villain you see is a WASP," the result of network censors anxious to avoid the ire of "pressure groups" concerned with negative stereotyping.[29]

However noble or politically calculating the reason for making Graham and the condemned inmates in other death penalty films white, the effect was a whitewashing of the death penalty. By portraying African Americans as both decision makers and dutiful civil servants whose work involved them in the execution of white men and women, these films inverted the racial lines that had long divided those operating the machinery of the killing state and those subjected to it. The effect was a tacit cultural denial that racism still underlay the death penalty in America.

Some films went further and depicted white death row inmates as the literal and metaphorical victims of African American men. In *Better Off Dead*, the made for television movie, a poor white woman is sentenced to death for killing a black man who had attempted to rape her.[30] Kit, the protagonist, is a con artist; she runs an elaborate extortion scheme in which she seduces men and then cries rape when her boyfriend arrives upon the scene posing as a police officer. In this encounter, however, the boyfriend does not show up on time, and her would-be victim actually does become an attacker, overpowering her when she tries to leave. In the scuffle that follows, she gets hold of the man's gun and shoots him dead. He was, we learn, an undercover police officer, and his murder is thus a capital crime.

In showing a white victim of an attempted rape sentenced to death for killing her would-be rapist, the film reversed the roles that black men and white women have historically occupied in capital cases. Rather than a punishment levied against a black man convicted of raping a white woman, the death penalty is here used on a white woman who kills her black would-be rapist. The film cultivates sympathy for Kit—and takes its broader stand against the death penalty—by presenting the condemned white woman as the victim of black sexual predation. The film's strategy—opposing the death penalty while earnestly evoking one of the most common conceits in the racist white imagination—illustrates just how bizarrely Freudian the racial politics of death penalty films in the modern era could be.

Tapping into contemporary white anxiety about white disadvantage in an age of pluralism, the 1996 film *Last Dance* told a story of "reverse racism" on death row. Sharon Stone played Cindy Liggett, a condemned white woman who murdered a white teenage couple while under the influence of drugs. She has changed in the years since her death sentence and is haunted by her past. As Liggett's execution draws near, she develops a relationship with Rick Hayes, a young lawyer working for the state's clemency commission who finds in Cindy an excellent candidate for commutation. Threatening Liggett's case, however, is a black death row inmate, John Henry Reese, who is also up for execution. Reese, we learn, is a trickster who has shrewdly manipulated white guilt to his advantage. A black version of Caryl Chessman, he has written a bestselling book that has drawn A-list Americans to his cause. Both the "top cardiovascular surgeon in New York City" and the dean of Yale Law School have made pleas for clemency on his behalf. He brags to Hayes,

> I've strategized all my appeals, you know. I taught myself. I've taken control of the killing machine. Look at me. . . . What is the smart money saying, huh? I mean, who's gonna live, me or the white girl? Who's he gonna forgive? A man of color who earned a law degree, who wrote a best-seller and won the admiration of some of our best people, or a white trash girl who bludgeoned two people to pulp without blinking an eye? They will be diminished by my death 'cause I represent everything they love and admire. How they gonna go and kill a man who has been on the *New York Times* best-seller list?[51]

The question, of course, is rhetorical, and in his quest to save Liggett, Hayes learns an unexpected lesson about the politics of the death penalty. Turning the race-based justice system on its head, the governor grants clemency to Reese and signs Liggett's death warrant—all, conveniently, on the same day. Liggett becomes a sacrificial lamb to a powerful black electorate demanding racial parity in punishment. Rather than depicting the killing state as an expression of racially charged anxieties about crime, *Last Dance* portrayed African Americans as the beneficiaries—and even manipulators—of death penalty politics.

While most death penalty films grappled with race in stories set in the present, two films of the period tackled the racist history of the death penalty directly in stories set in the past. These films, too, ultimately worked to weaken the perception of the death penalty as a tool of racial repression. Perversely, one of them, the top-grossing death penalty film of all time, presented execution as a source of black liberation. In Frank Darabont's 1999 blockbuster *The Green Mile*, John Coffey (Michael Clarke Duncan), a towering developmentally disabled black man, is sent to Louisiana's death row—the "green mile"—in 1935 after being wrongly convicted of the prototypical lynching crime, the rape and murder of two blonde six-year-old sisters. He was, in fact, with the girls at the time of their deaths, but he had come upon them after they had been left for dead and was caught attempting to bring them back to life. Coffey, the film shows us, has a Christlike power that enables him to heal the suffering by (literally) sucking out of them the evil that torments them—disease, injury, hatred. His actions are misinterpreted by the white posse that discovers him trying to help the girls, and Coffey is swiftly sentenced to death after a sham trial. His own defense attorney refers to him as a "mongrel dog."[32] A black man facing execution in a southern state during the 1930s, Coffey embodies the pain of the nation's history of racial injustice.

The film presents itself as enlightened—sensitive to the racism of a bygone world in which white Americans saw black subordination as both a prerequisite to white freedom and the gravest threat to it. In demonstrating just how wrong the image of Coffey as a menacing predator is, the film depicts him, in a no less problematic way, as a happy subordinate. In healing white people in pain, the saintly Coffey magically and lovingly does what enslaved African Americans literally did for white Americans, taking on, in their unpaid labor, the physical and emotional burdens of white existence. He also alleviates fears of black threats to white freedom. His gigantic stature (a point made when he must duck his head to enter his cell) suggests that he could overcome his captors, but we watch as he submits easily to them (see fig. 5). Indeed, he initially scares, but then brings relief to, Paul Edgecomb (Tom Hanks), the well-meaning guard in charge of death row who has been suffering from a urinary tract infection. Coffey unexpectedly grabs Edgecomb's crotch through the bars of his cell, sucking the evil of the infection out of Edgecomb's body and restoring, we see in a subsequent scene, Edgecomb's ability to have sex with his wife. Coffey, in short, is the antithesis of the physical and sexual threat to white supremacy that black men have occupied in the racist imagination. In him we find a gentle giant who wants to enable, not threaten, white freedom; to restore, not usurp, white virility; to take away, not create, white pain.[33] Edgecomb soon becomes convinced of Coffey's innocence.

Coffey, though, has grown tired of his role as a repository for the world's pain. Death by execution, he says, will allow him to escape his Christlike role as a black sufferer of white sins. And most important, it will give white Americans—embodied by Edgecomb—the opportunity

FIGURE 5. In *The Green Mile* (1999), John Coffey initially embodies the menacing black man of the racist imagination, only to subvert the stereotype.

to redeem themselves by taking back the pain they had historically off loaded onto African Americans. As his execution day draws near, Coffey declines Edgecomb's offer to help him escape from the prison. Edgecomb pleads with him, anticipating the unbearable guilt he will feel for Coffey's death: "When I stand before God and he asks me why did I kill one of his true miracles, what am I going to say?" he asks Coffey. Coffey replies,

> You tell God the father it was a kindness you done. I know you're hurting and worrying. I can feel it on you. But you ought to quit on it now. I want it to be over and done with. I do. I'm tired, boss. Tired of being on the road, lonely as a sparrow in the rain. I'm tired of never having me a buddy to be with, to tell me where we's going to, coming from, or why. Mostly, I'm tired of people being ugly to each other. I'm tired of all the pain I feel and hear in the world every day. There's too much of it. It's like pieces of glass in my head all the time. Can you understand?[34]

Edgecomb acquiesces to Coffey's wish to die, and with the black Christ figure's execution, the film seems to complete the allegorical narrative it has set up. But John Coffey's death is not a sacrifice that relieves white humanity of its sins; it is a mechanism for allowing whites to expiate their racial sins in a new way. Because he presided over Coffey's execu-

tion, the audience learns, Edgecomb has taken on the sins of a white supremacist world. He expiates white sin not through dying, but through
living. Edgecomb, the film's final scene reveals, has lived well past one
hundred, his extended stay on the planet a kind of stay in purgatory that
is cleansing him—and the white humanity he embodies—of the sins of a
white supremacist past.[35]

*The Green Mile*, then, makes capital punishment the crucial catalyst
in a story about the expiation of white sin. The film depicts a rabidly
racist South in order to reassure us of its place in a backward past from
which black and white Americans have fled. Execution in the Louisiana
execution chair serves, perversely, as a mechanism of black relief from
a racist world. The assumption of guilt for white supremacy by a fault-
less, enlightened white southerner, meanwhile, represents a sacrifice for
white humanity, a working off of a collective white debt for a racist past
that is, like Edgecomb's anticipated death, mercifully on the horizon.

*A Lesson Before Dying*, a 1999 television movie based on Ernest J.
Gaines's best-selling 1993 novel, presented a different vision of the death
penalty as a vehicle for black liberation. In the film Jefferson, a poor
young black man played by Mekhi Phifer, is accidentally present at the
scene of a murder of a white shopkeeper and is caught with his hand in
the cash register when the police arrive. His trial is grossly unfair: Jefferson's defense attorney compares his client to a hog, arguing that he ought
not be punished because he does not have a conscience. The defense attorney's belittling rhetoric is meant to illustrate the depths of southern
injustice. Nonetheless, the film initially presents Jefferson in a similar,
albeit kinder, light, as childlike. He cannot read. He does not speak. He
seems indifferent to the imminence of his execution. Jefferson's mother
enlists a local black schoolteacher, Grant Wiggins (Don Cheadle), to
"turn him into a man" before his execution, and the bulk of the film depicts Wiggins's efforts to reach Jefferson. His efforts are ultimately successful. By the end of the film, Jefferson has transformed from a docile,
weak "boy" into a literate critical thinker.[36]

While the film seems to depict the death penalty as a tool of racist repression, it presents the imposition of a death sentence as an occasion
for the empowerment of a young black man, a transformation of his self-
image that would not otherwise have happened. From the education system to the prison system, the state has treated Jefferson as if he were a
hog. Death at the hands of the state, we are shown, becomes a means for
Jefferson to transcend the state's racist treatment of him, to reject the

racist appraisal of his value that he had internalized. Men like Jefferson may well die as the result of racist inequality, the film seems to say, but they can at least die as men and undercut the racism of the system. In what the film presents as a tragic trade, dignity compensates Jefferson for his loss of life. From a contemporary perspective, such compensation is absurd—Who cares if you have dignity if you're dead?—but the film's point is that in a world governed by intractable racial hierarchies, resistance is still possible. The manhood Jefferson achieves as his execution approaches renders illegitimate the racist logic underlying southern hierarchies. In truth, though, the material consequence of the execution, which the film tellingly does not depict on-screen, is still a dead black man.

From casting decisions that showed African Americans as representatives of the killing state to the portrayal of whiteness as a liability for condemned inmates to a self-actualization execution narrative about an illiterate black man on death row, Hollywood worked, in the post-*Gregg* period, to distance the death penalty from its racist past or to distort the severity of that past. Yet at the same time it tried to atone for that past. In the character of Paul Edgecomb, viewers of *The Green Mile* encountered a carrier of white guilt whose burden, the film reassured them, would soon be lifted. Collectively, these films raised the anxieties created by historical memory—but they did so to reconstruct, rather than dismantle, the killing state. Through on-screen exorcisms of a racist past, the cultural life of capital punishment made the new American death penalty consonant with a society that had, once and for all, dismantled old hierarchies.

## The Martyr as Sinner: New Directions in Existential Execution Narratives

In the modern era of capital punishment, death penalty films distinguished themselves from their early- and mid-twentieth century predecessors not only through their thematic engagement with race but also through their portrayal of the condemned.

Whereas films in earlier periods depicted the condemned as innocent or their crimes as excusable, films of the post-*Gregg* period featured men and women who were guilty of inexcusable crimes that had destroyed the lives of innocents. With a seventeenth-century religious sensibility, these films showed how a death sentence transformed the condemned from a reckless, sinful wretch into a self-disciplined, morally grounded adult. *Dead Man Walking* (1995), *The Chamber* (1996),[37] *Last Dance* (1996),[38] and *Last Light* (1993)[39] all depicted dispossessed, guilty white people who found in their executions the opportunity to expiate their sins and gain release from a sinful past.

In some ways this was a surprising development. In our backlash-centered accounts of a nation that repurposed its criminal justice system in the late twentieth century, retribution and incapacitation displaced rehabilitation as the primary purpose of criminal punishment.[40] In these explanations, the state gave up an ambitious goal of rehabilitating prisoners and replaced it with a more modest but accomplishable one: delivering to offenders the pain they deserved for their wicked acts and preventing them, through confinement or death, from harming others. The return of the death penalty symbolized a newfound consensus against redemption.

The gallows conversions these films depicted, and the compassionate feelings they cultivated for their condemned protagonists, do not fit into this narrative easily. They do fit, however, into a slightly different story about the rise of a punitiveness that effectively manipulated sympathy as well as antipathy for criminals. These films engineered a positive image of the death penalty by subtly acknowledging and assuaging two anxieties that capital punishment, and the broader political culture that supported it, could inspire.

The first was a humanist anxiety that the death penalty was an intolerable affront to human dignity. Indeed, its revival in the United States represented a significant cultural break with the rest of the Western world. Since the end of World War II, Western European states had gradually been abolishing the death penalty, a process that was completed with France's abandonment of capital punishment in 1981. In European human rights discourse, it became axiomatic that the death penalty was a gross violation of human rights. The Charter of Fundamental Rights of the European Union in 2000 codified a right to life that explicitly forbade the death penalty. As abolitionism spread across Europe, a vocal abolitionist minority in the United States pointed to the European break with the death penalty as evidence that the United States had become a shameful exception to a rising respect for human dignity among Western states.

The second anxiety was inchoate. A broader contraction of the welfare state had generated new psychological and economic pressures on many Americans. By the mid-1980s, a new political-economic perspective, adopted by Republicans and Democrats alike, was becoming dominant in the United States. Neoliberalism—a revival of the classical economic liberalism of the eighteenth century—justified the deregulation of industries and the adoption of free trade agreements that accelerated the movement of industrial production to countries with cheaper labor costs. It offered, moreover, a harsh assessment of the welfare state, arguing that the free market was a better supplier of many of the social goods the state had secured since the 1930s. Ideologically, neoliberalism reflected and reinforced the retributive criminal justice policies that were expanding the size of the nation's prison and death row populations. Both neoliberalism and retributivism extolled individual responsibility and denied structural explanations for poverty or crime. Together, they formed the foundation of a political culture that blamed people for their bad acts (criminal justice) or their economic failures (neoliberal policy) and justified the consequences they incurred when they failed to abide by the law or maintain economic solvency.

Those who had prospered most from the welfare state—working-class white Americans—felt its retrenchment keenly. As automation and deindustrialization put many industrial workers out of jobs and trade unions lost political power, a downward pressure on real wages for unskilled and low-skilled labor was felt across the working class, even as productivity and gross domestic product rose.[41] A faith in personal responsibility, so integral to retributive and neoliberal ideologies, often contradicted their own lived experiences as their manufacturing jobs migrated overseas. Having been born into a world in which living wage jobs for those with a high school education felt like a birthright, many now watched anxiously as their economic horizons receded through no fault of their own.[42]

Two anxieties, then—one rooted in doubts about the humaneness of capital punishment, the other rooted in doubts about the foundations of a culture of responsibility—surfaced, at times, in death penalty films of the modern era. Two films in particular worked through these anxieties in notable ways. *Dead Man Walking* (1995) and *The Chamber* (1996) wrestled explicitly with the fear that the death penalty was an intolerable affront to human dignity. Implicitly, they portrayed anxieties about working-class white men's solvency in an era of wealth polarization and downward pressure on wages. In both cases, punishment perversely provides relief from these anxieties. Both films revealed how sympathy for the condemned could be mobilized in ways that ultimately made the death penalty seem morally appropriate.

*Dead Man Walking*, Tim Robbins's 1995 feature film starring Sean Penn and Susan Sarandon, is the best known and most discussed of the spate of death penalty movies released in the mid-1990s.[43] Penn played Matthew Poncelet, a white death row inmate convicted of participating in the rape and murder of a white teenage couple. Sarandon played Helen Prejean, a nun who works with the poor in New Orleans and agrees to write to Poncelet as a favor to a friend. Their correspondence leads to a meeting at Angola State Penitentiary, where Prejean encounters a bitter, angry racist who complains about welfare-entitled "niggers" while insisting that he has truly been wronged by the state. He refuses to take responsibility for his part in the murders, insisting that he was a bystander.

But if Poncelet seems to be in deep denial, he also seems somewhat amenable to change. Prejean challenges him when he complains about "welfare-taking coloreds sucking up tax dollars" who "make themselves out as victims." "I don't know any victims," she says of the black people in her life. "I know a lot of cool people, hardworking." Poncelet eventually is moved to admit that he likes rebels and that some black people can be good rebels: "Martin Luther King led people to DC, kicked the white man's butt," Poncelet says. "He put up a fight, wasn't lazy." "So it's lazy people you don't like," Prejean suggests, not black people. "Can we talk about something else?" Poncelet responds, backed into a corner, the wheels in his brain spinning with this new idea.

Poncelet's obsession with strength, with kicking butt, Prejean soon realizes, issues from his own internalized sense of impotence. When she visits Poncelet's mother, who does not have money for food, let alone a funeral for her soon to be executed son, we see the poverty Poncelet experienced as a child. "Life's plowed them over," Prejean later tells her family. Impotence, rather than evil, is the source of Poncelet's swastika tattoos, his delusions of grandeur, and his plan to use his last words to excoriate the families of his victims.[44] Understanding the etiology of Poncelet's bullish pride allows her to intervene effectively in his thought processes. She disarms and seduces him, espousing a theology that is more evangelical than Catholic. Breaking ranks with the prison's orthodox chaplain, Prejean tells Poncelet that the mindless parroting of doctrine is insufficient to gain salvation. "Redemption isn't some kind of free admission ticket you get because Jesus paid the price," she tells him. "You gotta participate in your own redemption. You got some work to do."[45] Poncelet's problem, we have learned by this point, is that he had fallen under the influence of misguided peers because he had never learned to think for himself.

As the execution draws near and Poncelet's appeals are exhausted, the film turns from the question of whether he will die to whether he will die redeemed. Will Poncelet leave the world a hateful, remorseless, bitter man? Or will he take responsibility for his crimes, find goodness in himself, and leave the world as a spiritually transformed man? In the final, climactic moments of the film, as Poncelet waits in the holding cell that is his final stop before the execution chamber, the audience gets its answer. Spouting his anger at the situation that led him to the scene of the crime, where he still maintains he did nothing to instigate the violence, Poncelet is interrupted by Prejean. "Don't blame the drugs," she says to him, cutting him off. "You could have walked away. Don't blame [your accomplice]. You blame him. You blame drugs. You blame the government. You blame blacks. You blame the [victim's family]. You blame the kids for being there. What about Matthew Poncelet? Is he just an innocent, a victim?" With the clock ticking toward execution time, this moment of tough love finally does the trick. He confesses his involvement in the crime to Prejean in an emotional outpouring. "Do you take responsibility for both of their deaths?" she asks him. "Yes ma'am," he responds. "When the lights dimmed last night I kneeled and prayed for them kids. I never done that before." As he confesses, Poncelet breaks down into tears, his voice trembling as he speaks (see fig. 6). The scene is intensely erotic; indeed, Prejean lets out an orgasmic exhale when Poncelet confesses, her spiritual seduction of Poncelet having finally achieved its goal. "Oh, Matt," she breathily responds. "There are spaces of sorrow only God can touch. You did a terrible thing, Matt, a terrible thing. But you have dignity now. Nobody can take that from you. You are a son of God, Matthew Poncelet."[46]

Self-abasement becomes, for Poncelet, the way to spiritual wealth. His confession elicits an outpouring of love from Prejean, escalating their intimacy and providing him a security he had never felt before. As if to underscore the point, the film repeats the trope moments later. When Poncelet learns he cannot wear his boots to the execution chamber, he breaks down again and begins to have a childish tantrum of frustrated masculinity. Prejean, though, quickly intervenes, telling him, "Look, I want the last thing you see in this world to be a face of love. So you look at me . . . when they do this thing. You look at me. I'll be the

FIGURE 6. Moments before his execution in *Dead Man Walking* (1995), Matthew Poncelet confesses his crime to Helen Prejean and, in admitting his vulnerability, is freed from the hateful mental schemas that had dominated him.

face of love for you." With Prejean offering him loving support, Poncelet delivers his final words with grace in the execution chamber. The gurney standing upright and his arms outstretched as in a crucifixion, he says, trembling, to his victim's family, "I don't want to leave this world with any hate in my heart. I ask your forgiveness for what I done. It was a terrible thing I done in taking your son away from you. . . . I hope my death gives you some relief." His death offers a relief for him as well; it is a liberating testament to his escape from the harmful mental schemas that had dominated him for so long. The man who shocked Prejean earlier in the film by blithely comparing himself to Jesus dies in a Christlike posture, a "son of God," as Prejean puts it. Poncelet martyrs his body for his spirit—a Christ figure dying not for the sins of humanity, but for the sins of his former self.[47]

*Dead Man Walking* had a political-economic subtext that provides insight into the welfare-oriented meaning that retributive punishment could have in a libertarian culture. Interestingly, the film's psychological analysis of Poncelet resembles the liberal explanation for black criminality most famously voiced in Senator Daniel Moynihan's 1967 report, "The Negro Family."[48] Moynihan had explained black criminality as one of a host of social problems that stemmed from a lack of access to well-paid jobs. Unable to provide for their families, he theorized, black men abandoned their fatherly obligations. The absence of fathers earning breadwinner wages had resulted in a pathological black culture mired in social problems like crime. *Dead Man Walking* applied that logic to its poor white protagonist. The fatherless, impoverished Poncelet, Prejean learns, has adopted a racist, bullish identity in an effort to overcome his feelings of economic dispossession. That swaggering masculinity, masking profound insecurity and impressionability, lead him to commit his depraved act of violence. Taking a cue from "The Negro Family," the proper response, the film suggests, is a sympathetic recognition of the offender's vulnerability and a commitment to investing him with the dignity he has lacked. That, however, is where the similarity ends. Whereas Moynihan argued that the state ennobled undisciplined men by expanding their economic horizons, *Dead Man Walking* suggested that punishment, not provision, catalyzes moral maturation. Dignity could not be bought for men by the state; they had to earn it.

Poncelet's achievement of dignity through suffering reflected and reinforced the broader role that pain has played in neoliberal thought.[49] In antiwelfare rhetoric, pain or the threat of pain creates incentives for human beings to develop themselves into people worthy of recognition. *Dead Man Walking* carried that logic from the marketplace to the prison. The pain of his impending execution breaks Matthew Poncelet. It makes him receptive to Prejean's influence, prompts him to abandon the corrosive ideologies that have dominated him, and enables his transformation into a man worthy of love. In return for his apology, Poncelet gains from Prejean positive recognition of his vulnerability. Her authentic love dissolves his false pride; the comforts of loving interdependence replace the pressures of performing a cartoonish, Gary Gilmore–like version of the convict-cowboy. Yet the love is consummated by a "manning up," by taking full responsibility for his crimes. The endurance of harsh punishment becomes a way of achieving recognition that Poncelet and those like him never found in the political or labor marketplace.[50]

Studying these final scenes, abolitionist critics of *Dead Man Walking* have written that, despite the liberal viewpoint of its director, Tim Robbins, the film ultimately endorses a "conservative cultural sensibility" by making Poncelet's acceptance of responsibility its climactic moment.[51] It does so, however, in a nuanced way. "Personal responsibility" in the film is more than a glib justification for harsh punishment; it is instead a spiritual destination. The process of holding Poncelet responsible reveals his profound sense of dispossession, locates it in his race, gender, and class position, and offers a compensatory recognition of his goodness in exchange for his penitence.

In this way the film reconciled the rehabilitative concerns of the welfare state with the violence of the killing state and the austerity of the neoliberal state. Indeed, the death penalty functions here, as Caryl Chessman once put it, as a kind of "shock therapy."[52] The setting of the execution date provides the shock, and Prejean provides the therapy. Poncelet is penetrated, finally, not by representatives of the paternalistic state or the hierarchical church, but by an irreverent outsider who, by tempering a conservative commitment to accountability with a liberal recognition of his vulnerability, opens him up to a divine understanding of right and wrong and reconstitutes him as a responsible member of the moral community. He adopts, in the end, a moral vision of the world that aligns with conservative politics—one in which deprivation is no excuse for immoral behavior. He does so, though, not as the result of some forced, paternalistic adjustment to social norms, but through a spiritual rebirth facilitated by a woman.

A similar spiritual reconstitution occurs in *The Chamber* (1996). Based on the best-selling novel by John Grisham, *The Chamber* told the story of Sam Cayhall (Gene Hackman), an aging white supremacist about to be executed, decades after the fact, for the death of two little girls in a 1960s bombing of a Jewish civil rights lawyer's office in Mississippi. Belatedly sentenced to death for the bombing, Cayhall is unrepentant. He protects the white elites who cravenly manipulated him into committing the crime by maintaining that he acted alone. Like Poncelet, he is a white man whose racism is a response to an internal self-loathing that made him easily manipulated by those who convinced him that his value lay in his skin color. That shallow basis for his self-worth has had devastating consequences. His crime, we learn, has shattered his own children; his son killed himself in shame, and his daughter became an alcoholic.

Over the course of the film, though, an ongoing dialogue with his grandson Adam Hall (Chris O'Donnell), a northern lawyer working on his appeal, softens Cayhall, prompting his maturation. Cayhall reestablishes contact with his alcoholic daughter Lee Bowen, who is haunted not only by the bombing but also by a childhood spent watching her father lash out in criminal acts of racist violence. As a little girl she had watched helplessly while her father shot and killed an African American man in a petty dispute. Reconciling with her father in a death row visiting room, Bowen finally gets some relief. His voice cracking in sorrow, Cayhall reassures his daughter that she bore no responsibility for his crimes. Seeing the devastation he has caused his daughter, Cayhall exhibits sorrow for his sins

As in *Dead Man Walking*, the film suggests that self-loathing underlies white violence and that harsh punishment offered the chance for condemned white men to abandon their false pride, acknowledge their vulnerability, and accept responsibility for their violence. Through his execution, Cayhall takes on his shoulders the sins of moderate white southerners, personified by his daughter, who witnessed racial violence during the classical phase of the civil rights movement but did nothing to stop it. Right before his execution, Cayhall expresses to Hall, just as Poncelet did to Prejean, full-fledged remorse for his acts, admitting to his grandson, "Of all the people and things I hated my whole life, the one that I hated the most was me. I was given free entry into this world to make of it whatever I could. I've been sitting here for sixteen years, just thinking about how I never did anybody any good. Then you came down." He renounces his attitude toward his son, Hall's father, whose suicide he had earlier called a sign of weakness. "See, if I'm gonna be proud of you I gotta be proud of your daddy," he says. "He wasn't weak; he was strong—strong enough to give you whatever you got."[53] In giving his grandson the love he withheld from his son, Cayhall abandons a conception of strength as impenetrability. As his final act before walking into the gas chamber, he removes a leather bracelet adorned with symbols of white supremacy and hurls it against the wall. White racism is, in the end, a symptom of personal insecurity that Cayhall has finally overcome.

The credit for this breakthrough, and for the racial reconciliation that follows, goes to the death penalty. Cayhall's proximity to death ultimately catalyzes his penitence and releases him from the corrosive racism that has ruined his life. It is not until the eleventh hour, when death is imminent, that he decides to sign the affidavit that implicates prominent white citizens in the bombing. As he goes to his death, the audience gets the satisfaction of seeing a montage of the arrests of the white elites Cayhall had been been protecting.[54] He apologizes, too, to a black guard who had treated him kindly, making personal as well as political amends for his crimes.

*The Chamber* demonstrates the virtue of the death penalty by pushing its audience to see that Cayhall's death does more than satisfy the vulgar bloodlust of a public hell-bent on his destruction. While the film disapprovingly depicts the Mississippi governor whipping a crowd into a frenzy outside the penitentiary, it imagines its own audience as a second, more enlightened execution crowd that appreciates the therapeutic benefit of execution for the penitent Cayhall and his sympathetic family.[55] Capital punishment has done what imprisonment did not: it has liberated Cayhall from his pride and transformed his soul.[56] Indeed, responding to the film, a reviewer for the *New York Times* observed, somewhat nonplussed, that "although Mr. Grisham is evidently no friend of the death penalty, 'The Chamber' may be read as a tribute to the redemptive value of being sentenced to be gassed."[57]

In *Dead Man Walking* and *The Chamber*, audiences found two white men whose violent crimes were symptomatic of an entitled, bullish temperament. Over the course of the films, though, they learned that the men's crimes were in reality an overcompensating response to feelings of insecurity. Like the imagined criminal in mid-twentieth-century criminology, the films ascribed horrifying violence not to an excess of freedom but to a deficit of it. Cayhall's and Poncelet's violence resulted, audiences saw, from a deep-seated class- and race-based sense of impotence. Unlike their midcentury predecessors, though, the therapeutic response these films prescribed was not counseling alone but counseling in the shadow of the execution chamber. Preparing to die became a liberating experience of letting go of stubborn pride, admitting a vulnerability one has fought so long to conceal, and finding intimacy with another person. These men experience true freedom when they come to see themselves as part of a moral community that they betrayed.

By depicting the condemned as white men who achieved redemption by preparing for their executions, *Dead Man Walking* and *The Chamber* fantasized that capital punishment, and the retributive ideology that underlay it, did not simply recognize a criminal's moral agency (as the last words traditions do) but catalyzed its emergence in him.

## Beyond the Box Office

While fictional narratives of redemption flourished on-screen, real-life claims of redemption by condemned inmates got little response from

governors and pardon boards.[58] Efforts on behalf of two condemned inmates whose claims of rehabilitation made them causes célèbres captured the nation's attention in the 1990s and 2000s. In 1998, thousands of
Americans rallied to save the life of Karla Faye Tucker, a white woman
Texas planned to execute for murdering a man and his girlfriend with a
pickax while they slept. Tucker had become a born-again Christian on
death row and had impressed community leaders and prison officials
alike with the depth of her repentance and the genuineness of her transformation. Although they are normally more likely to support harsh, retributive forms of punishment than members of other branches of Christianity,[59] evangelical Christians wrote thousands of letters to Governor
Ann Richards in 1992, urging her to commute Tucker's sentence.[60] Her
story so moved evangelical minister Pat Robertson that he changed his
opinion on capital punishment and said he thought mercy should be
shown to those who, like Tucker, had demonstrated "a genuine change
of heart."[61]

Redemption was also at the heart of the efforts to save the life of Stanley "Tookie" Williams, a black former gang leader who was executed in
California in 2005. Williams had apologized for his role in founding the
Crips, renounced gang violence, written a series of children's books with
antigang messages, and been nominated for the Nobel Peace Prize. He
too had amassed a host of supporters, including Jamie Foxx, who played
Williams in *Redemption*, a made for television movie that aired in 2004.

Despite massive media attention to their cases, both Tucker and Williams failed to win clemency. A number of factors explain their fates.
Critics of Williams imputed to him some of the darker qualities of individualism. He was, some said, a manipulative swindler, and his claims of
redemption were only a calculated ruse. "I don't think a murderer like
Stanley Williams can be reformed," Nancy Ruhe-Much, executive director of the victims' rights organization Parents of Murdered Children,
told the *New York Times*. "I think he's just writing these books because
he wants to get off death row."[62] Governor Arnold Schwarzenegger,
meanwhile, perceived a toxic pride in Williams's refusal to acknowledge his guilt for the crime that had landed him on death row. "Is Williams' redemption complete and sincere, or is it just a hollow promise?"
he asked near the end of a statement explaining his decision to deny Williams clemency. "Stanley Williams insists he is innocent, and that he will
not and should not apologize or otherwise atone for the murders of the
four victims in this case. Without an apology and atonement for these

senseless and brutal killings there can be no redemption. In this case, the one thing that would be the clearest indication of complete remorse and full redemption is the one thing Williams will not do."[63]

But even when most observers were convinced that redemption was real, as they were in Tucker's case, clemency was not compatible with a larger commitment to equality. For many, it was clear that support for Tucker was linked to her gender; she was to become the first woman executed in Texas since the Civil War.[64] To some concerned with gender parity, granting Tucker clemency would affirm an older paternalistic way of thinking that treated women as juveniles who could never be as responsible for a heinous crime as a man could be. One feminist abolitionist publicly chose death for Tucker over the sexist paternalism that clemency would represent: "As much as I am opposed to the death penalty, it should show no gender bias," argued Robyn Blumer in the *St. Petersburg Times*. "Faux Victorian notions that women are defenseless beings who need to be protected from harm and who lack the physical or mental capabilities to do harm themselves" still plagued the nation, she wrote. Those notions were "the last vestige of institutionalized sexism that needs to be rubbed out. Ironically, as Texas will soon discover, gal murderers may be perfect for the task."[65] That logic seems to have played a role in Governor George W. Bush's denial of clemency for Tucker. His spokesperson Karen Hughes took up the question of gender in explaining his refusal to grant a stay of execution. "The gender of the murderer did not make any difference to the victims," she said, echoing nearly word for word a line spoken two years earlier by the fictional governor in the film *Last Dance*.[66]

Hollywood films, however, may also offer an additional reason that the redeemed so often failed to earn clemency in the modern era of capital punishment. In a more modern, secular form, Hollywood brought back into popular consciousness a comforting, antiquated, and religious view of an execution as a wayward soul's reentry into the moral community—or, as a guard in *The Green Mile* put it, becoming "square with the house again."[67] Death, moreover, provided the ultimate test of the claim that rehabilitation had occurred. Being on the brink of death, we like to think, acts as a kind of truth serum. At the moment of execution, Linda Ross Meyer writes, describing this myth, "earthly incentives to lie or dissemble are presumed to be gone. . . . It is an almost-perfectly Kantian moment, when one has the chance to act without concern for consequences, when the pressures of finitude are lifted and our position almost resembles the perfect being of reason who has no inclinations contrary to reason."[68] It is in this moment, and this moment only, that we might discern the truthfulness of a rehabilitation claim. Redemption, Hollywood suggested, cannot excuse one from execution because execution is the very thing that makes redemption possible, and the only thing that makes it verifiable.

## Conclusion

Writing thirty-five years and 1,057 executions after Justice Thurgood Marshall asserted in *Furman v. Georgia* that "death, of course, makes rehabilitation impossible," Justice Anthony Kennedy, in a 2007 opinion, articulated philosophically what popular texts had taught Americans over the course of the post *Gregg* era: retribution was, in the end, compatible with redemption. "It might be said that capital punishment is imposed," Kennedy wrote, "because it has the potential to make the offender recognize at last the gravity of his crime."[69]

Kennedy's observation reflects just how dramatically the relation between capital punishment and human freedom had changed in the thirty-five years since retribution moved toward the center of public policy about punishment. In the punitive imagination, the death penalty was not simply an expression of backlash but a generative kind of violence. Through execution stories, filmmakers affirmed the nation's aspirational values: in on-screen execution chambers, the face of justice became black and brown as well as white, punishment oddly helped a nation transcend its racist past, and sinners found their goodness. All this, it must be noted, redounded to the benefit of a dominant white culture. In an age of pluralism, fictional executions became therapeutic experiences for white men and white audiences, opportunities for them to fantasize, both culturally and individually, about escaping the psychic burdens of personal responsibility for the past and the present. Indeed, in stoking fantasies and resolving anxieties about the freedom of the poor and nonwhite, films about capital punishment made it easier for retribution to take hold in post-*Gregg* America. Watching the experience of condemned inmates on the silver screen or on television, Americans found not racist and soul-crushing repression, but rather soul-elevating justice. Through its newly rediscovered capacity to rehabilitate, capital punishment was itself rehabilitated.

The legal and cultural imaginings of executable subjects, however, were only one way capital punishment reflected and reinforced the return of negative freedom to the center of American political culture. In the chapters to come, I turn to constructions of the killing state and its cultural proxies.

# PART III
# The Killing State

## CHAPTER FIVE

# "A Country Worthy of Heroes"

## The Old West and the New American Death Penalty

There was a code in the Old West hardly noticed today. Back then a man's word was his bond whether outlaw or lawman. Marshal Tilghman once arrested [Bill] Doolin down in Eureka Springs, Ark., and brought him back to Guthrie. Tilghman didn't handcuff him when Doolin gave his word he wouldn't try to escape. They rode the train together back to Guthrie without incident. Down Oklahoma County way there is an administrator of the law who is cut from the same fabric. . . . This administrator always wears a black string tie. Personally I'd like to see him wearing a black frock coat with a matched pair of pearl-handled Colts. Friends, I'm talking about District Attorney Bob Macy, one of the last vestiges of the Old West.[1] — Letter to the editor, the *Oklahoman* (1997)

In an 1893 speech to the American Historical Association, Frederick Jackson Turner famously contemplated the role the frontier had played in forming American identity. The individualism, buoyancy, and practical know-how it cultivated, he argued, had existed in productive tension with the civilization of eastern life. The existence of land not yet settled by European Americans had made masculine individualism the defining quality of American life, Turner said in his elegy for western expansion: "That coarseness and strength combined with acuteness and inquisitiveness; that practical, inventive turn of mind, quick to find expedients; that masterful grasp of material things, lacking in the artistic but powerful to effect great ends; that restless, nervous energy . . . and withal that buoyancy and exuberance which comes with freedom—these are traits of the frontier, or traits called out elsewhere because of the existence of the frontier."[2]

Historians have long challenged Turner's historical claims about the nature and meaning of European Americans' settlement of the West.[3] Nonetheless, the prototypical frontiersman at the heart of his analysis— a white man who uses righteous violence to carve civilization out of the wild—maintains an abiding hold on the American popular imagination. Writing about our frontier myth, philosopher Robert B. Pippin suggests that it has operated to legitimate our modern civilization, one that late modern political theorists from Marx to Nietzsche have criticized as requiring a "conformism and social dependence" that is "psychologically unsatisfying or even psychologically unworthy of human beings."[4] Without legends, Pippin writes, "a pretty prosaic world would come to look even more prosaic, raising psychological questions about its sustainability as a political enterprise."[5] From Buffalo Bill's Wild West shows in the late nineteenth century to John Ford's midcentury westerns to crime vigilante films of the 1970s, the performance of legends about men who use violence to create civilization has allowed audiences to experience a world where it was still possible for men to be great. In the popular imagination, that greatness has long been, as American studies scholar Richard Slotkin has shown, white and masculine. White men's violent repression of "savage" racial others—from Native Americans on the frontier to freed African Americans in the postbellum South to immigrant laborers in industrial cities to nonwhite peoples in foreign war zones— has been the occasion for the collective experience of white spiritual regeneration.[6]

In this chapter I argue that, at the end of the twentieth century, frontier myth played an integral role in representing capital punishment as a virtuous practice in two of the communities responsible for the largest number of executions in the modern era. Those who study the revival of the death penalty and the broader punitive turn the nation took in the 1970s have long been sensitive to the racial insecurities underlying the demand for harsh punishment.[7] With few exceptions, however, they have not been attentive to the image of district attorneys, those men and women vested with the power to seek or not seek the death penalty in capital cases. In what follows, I study journalists' portrayals of district attorneys in two exceptionally punitive counties. Mapping out the substance of their public identities allows us to see how, for some, the pursuit of capital punishment was a pleasurable enactment of a mythical, racially charged vision of American freedom, one in which white men use violence for noble purposes while showcasing their own capacity for self-control. As lethal injection masked the violence of executions and a complex federal jurisprudence governing capital cases lengthened appeals times and kept capital defendants on death row for long periods, district attorneys like Johnny Holmes and Bob Macy embodied the kind of killing state many Americans wished they had—one in which the punishment of capital offenders revealed the negative freedom of the men charged with bringing them to justice.

## The Criminal Frontier

Out of the 453 counties that had executed at least one person between 1977 and 2010, Bob Macy (fig. 7) and Johnny Holmes (fig. 8) presided over two—Oklahoma County, Oklahoma, and Harris County, Texas, respectively—that have together been responsible for over 12 percent of all executions.[8] The two generated plenty of support: from 1980 to 2000,

FIGURE 7. Bob Macy, district attorney of Oklahoma County, Oklahoma, from 1980 to 2001. Photo by Paul Hellstern. The *Oklahoman*.

voters consistently signaled their approval of these two district attorneys, electing them over and over again by significant margins.[9] Capital punishment formed the core of these men's public identities. Its existence was the basis for their reputations, its imposition the occasion for explicating their values, and its violence the tangible evidence of their power. When Macy died in 2011, the *Oklahoman* mentioned the death penalty in the very first sentence of its front-page obituary: "Former Oklahoma County District Attorney Bob Macy, who sent dozens of murderers to death row, died Friday night at his ranch home in Newalla." The article went on to note that Macy "kept count of how many he put on death row—54 in the end."[10] In a similar vein, one postretirement profile of Holmes in the *Houston Chronicle* was headlined, "Former DA Ran Powerful Death Penalty Machine: Mr. Law and Order."[11] As men known nationally not just for their support of the death penalty but for their demonstrated willingness to seek its imposition, Holmes and Macy provided decades of fodder for journalists in Houston and Oklahoma City.

In mostly admiring coverage, the *Oklahoman* and the *Houston Chronicle* represented Holmes and Macy as mythic frontiersmen. In its obituary of Macy in 2011, the *Oklahoman* emphasized his attachment to images of frontier life: "Macy was well-known for his look, like he belonged in a movie about the Old West. He almost always wore cowboy boots, a big cowboy hat, a black string tie, a Western-cut suit and a white shirt. He sometimes took his gun with him to court," the article noted. "He decorated his office from the beginning with drawings of cowboys. Later, he put up the movie poster from the popular Western, 'Tombstone.' 'Justice Is Coming,' it said at the top. Away from the courthouse, he liked to be on a horse roping calves and steers. He lived on ranches."[12]

Holmes got similar treatment from the *Chronicle*. In a story covering his retirement, reporter Armando Villafranca wrote, "Step into his office today and the law-enforcement influence is unmistakable. His office is like an East Texas roadstop filled with bits of Texana, Old West bric-a-brac and law-enforcement mementos collected over the years. Down to his handlebar mustache, Holmes appears the embodiment of the frontier lawman. . . . [T]he mustache also symbolizes Holmes' image as someone with little regard for those who disagree with him."[13]

Over the years, journalists portrayed Holmes and Macy as larger-than-life figures whose willingness to mobilize violence against threatening enemies distinguished them from men who had been tamed by

FIGURE 8. Johnny Holmes, district attorney of Harris County, Texas, from 1980 to 1999. Larry Reese / © *Houston Chronicle*. Used with permission.

life in the modern world. Sometimes duty required them to violate the ideal of peace in order to avoid its enervating side effects. Yet, as in frontier myth, the whole point of these displays of individual might was to preserve the rule of law. Because they were district attorneys acting in official capacities, there was never any real danger that their behavior signaled an actual return to the Wild West. Instead, in marshaling the violence of punishment, they were reinvigorating civilization.

Ultimately, the presence of frontier myth in the charismatic media portrayals of these death-seeking district attorneys suggests that the meaning of capital punishment in the late twentieth century, like the meaning of the frontiersman in imaginings of the West, was caught up in racially charged questions about the effects of bureaucratic states on white people's freedom. When linked to the personas of Holmes and Macy, the death penalty was part of a worldview that safely reconciled white men's violence with their nobility. Macy and Holmes—and the death penalty they stood for—were popular, I argue, because they embodied the possibility that feudal virtues—masculine honor, radical independence, patriarchal clannishness, raw physical strength—could still flourish in a technologically advanced, civilized world.

## "Whoever Said I Was an Acceptable Statistic?"
## The "System" as Enemy

To understand how Macy's and Holmes's pursuit of the death penalty was a vehicle for articulating frontier freedom, we must first understand how elements of late twentieth-century life were seen as imprisoning. In pro–death penalty discourse, conservatives frequently criticized two decision-making logics: the cost-benefit rationality of executive bureaucracy and the formal rationality of the judiciary. In the minds of some death penalty advocates, parole boards and judges took advantage of these logics to advance a liberal agenda and made good, law-abiding Americans vulnerable to criminal predation. To others, the system itself was to blame: it was an amoral machine producing outputs that no longer reflected the values of its architects. Whatever the source of the problem, the death penalty became a necessary alternative to a broken criminal justice system.

Ann Scott's testimony at a congressional hearing on the death penalty in 2006 exemplifies the distrust of the bureaucratic state that was at the heart of many Americans' support of capital punishment. Scott's daughter Elaine had been murdered in Oklahoma City in 1991, and Bob Macy had supervised the prosecution of Alfred Brian Mitchell, who was sentenced to death for the crime. Scott began her testimony by showing a photograph of her daughter to members of the committee. She explained that when her daughter was in the sixth grade, her husband received a job transfer from their northern California town to Oklahoma, a move she welcomed: "With all the crime and violence that was up and coming in California, we thought that Oklahoma would be a quiet, drug-free State and a great place to raise kids." She presented her daughter as a model citizen: "Elaine graduated from Jenks High School with good grades. She played both the flute and the piccolo in the high school marching band and orchestra, and she was a good kid. She attended the University of Oklahoma, majoring in elementary education and minoring in music. She worked part-time at Pilot Recreation Center in Oklahoma City with children from poor families."[14]

Scott then turned her attention to Elaine's killer, Alfred Brian Mitchell. Whereas Elaine was, by Scott's account, a flourishing young woman who embodied traditional ideals, Mitchell was a noncitizen, a mistake, a "bad seed that never should have been born." Throughout the trial and appeals process, she noted, Mitchell had laughed at the family at every opportunity he could. "Through all of this, Mitchell has never shown any remorse for his actions. If you ask if we seek retribution, yes, we do. I, me, I want this bully gone. I want him to disappear off the face of this Earth. I want him to rot in Hell for all of eternity."[15]

Scott blamed the welfare state for her daughter's death. Years before Mitchell killed her daughter, the state of Oklahoma had locked him up for raping a child. But the juvenile justice system had released him when he turned eighteen, Scott explained: "The Department of Human Services, DHS, could've kept him for another year but chose not to because they couldn't help him. They needed his bed, and they needed it for someone they thought that they could help. And so he came home."[16] Although the explanation for Mitchell's release could have been the basis for a cautionary tale about the dangers that arise when underfunded social service agencies cannot meet the demand for services, Scott spoke of it in the context of death penalty advocacy. She laid the blame not on the legislature's underfunding of the Department of Human Services, but on bureaucrats who cared more about rehabilitating salvageable juveniles than incapacitating known predators.

Scott implicitly cast the death penalty as a necessary remedy not only for hardened criminals but also for the state's own misguided attachment to rehabilitation. "I think that my husband and I would possibly consider a life-without-parole sentence, if it truly meant life without parole," she told Kansas senator Sam Brownback. It did not, however. Scott explained, "In the State of Oklahoma, you can become eligible to have your sentence downgraded from life without parole to a life sentence after serving 15 years." Bureaucrats and judges within the system had made her distrustful of the state, and the death penalty was a punishment that, in its finality, would prevent the social engineering experiments with probation that put innocent lives on the line. Brownback repeated back to Scott what he thought was the gist of her testimony: "You don't trust the system and you don't believe the system can keep people safe from a known murderer in it." "That's correct," she confirmed.[17]

Anxiety about parole was, to a certain extent, anxiety about justifications for lenient treatment that relied on actuarial logic and cost-benefit analyses. In 1988, Republican vice president George H. W. Bush swayed voters in the presidential race away from Democratic Massachusetts governor Michael Dukakis by linking Dukakis to a rehabilitative program in Massachusetts that gave weekend furloughs to first-degree murderers serving life sentences. Furlough, the temporary release of an offender into the community while he is serving his sentence, fit into the larger utilitarian goal of the welfare state: securing the greatest good for the greatest number through evidence-based practice. Offenders who used furloughs to maintain ties to the community during their prison sentence were statistically less likely to offend again when the state released them for good. In Bush's view, however, furloughs were a reckless social experiment. In a now famous attack ad that touted Bush's support for the death penalty, the Bush campaign frightened voters with the specter of Willie Horton, a black man serving a life sentence for murder in Massachusetts whom state corrections officials had furloughed for a weekend on Dukakis's watch. Horton did not return, at the end of the weekend, to the prison. A year later he invaded a home in Maryland, raped a white woman, and stabbed her husband.

To defend Dukakis, district attorneys, sheriffs, academics, and his campaign staff tried to put the incident in broader perspective. The president of the Massachusetts Sheriffs' Association reported that the furlough program had a 0.5 percent escape rate.[18] In a letter to the *Wall Street Journal*, John J. Larivee of the Crime and Justice Foundation noted that of 5,554 furloughs for inmates serving life sentences for first-degree crimes in Massachusetts, eleven had failed to return from a furlough in the past sixteen years, an escape rate 0.2 percent—better than the 0.6 percent rate for all furloughed inmates.[19] The Dukakis campaign noted that crime in Massachusetts had declined 13 percent during Dukakis's governorship and that the state had the lowest homicide rate of any "industrialized state."[20] Dukakis himself pointed out that those who participated in furlough programs were statistically less likely to commit crimes when they were released from prison for good. "The real test is whether or not someone in my position has really made progress in doing the kinds of things you have to do to make life safer for your citizens. And that we have done," Dukakis said,[21] embracing an actuarial view of governance—one in which the state manages risk rather than trying to eliminate it altogether. The very words Dukakis used belied a technocratic acknowledgment that no public policy could create perfect results. The state might not be able to make people totally safe, but it could make them safer.

The Horton incident has become shorthand for the racial subtext of crime politics in the 1980s and 1990s, but it also revealed a broader discomforting sense that modern risk management strategies devalued individual lives. To many, the use of cost-benefit analyses to justify soft treatment of criminal offenders was not just wrongheaded, it was an insult. "Whoever said I was an acceptable statistic?" Horton's stabbing victim, Clifford Barnes, rhetorically asked a reporter from the *New York Times* when he heard Dukakis's defense of the furlough program.[22] The implication here was that policymakers should not quantify the value of innocent lives harmed by violent crime and compare it with another value, the low recidivism created by furlough programs. To do so was to adopt a callous, soulless view of the world in which the suffering of innocent victims was "acceptable" collateral damage.[23] A vote for Bush became, for many, a vote against the utilitarian logic of the welfare state. It was a vote for protecting the individual lives of innocent people at all costs. Draconian punishment like the death penalty, which Bush favored in cases of first-degree murder, was a rejection of a utilitarian approach to the common good. Bush went on to win the election, the effectiveness of the Horton campaign a significant component of his victory. Indeed, having learned the lesson of Dukakis's defeat, four years later Democratic governor of Arkansas Bill Clinton interrupted his presidential campaign and returned to his home state to pointedly refuse clemency to Ricky Ray Rector, a mentally disabled African American man who was executed shortly before the New Hampshire primary.[24]

Pro–death penalty discourse did not just target technocratic approaches to government. It also attacked what criminologist Steven Kohm calls the "liberal-legal model of law," which emphasizes "the primacy of atomistic, individual legal rights and due process."[25] Within this framework, law ought to be equally available to all citizens, with the understanding that "sometimes the innocent suffer while the guilty are able to capitalize upon their misdeeds."[26] By the 1990s, the capital appeals process was inspiring impassioned critiques of liberal legalism. Since the resumption of the death penalty in 1978, the average time a condemned inmate spent on death row during the appeals process had grown to an unprecedented ten years. One source of this growth was the federal judiciary's receptivity to habeas corpus appeals from death row inmates who had been convicted and sentenced in state courts. Historically, habeas appeals have offered imprisoned persons access to judges who could evaluate the legality of their confinement on broader grounds than those available during the direct appeals phase, when the legality of their convictions is assessed primarily based on issues raised by defense counsel during the trial. Conservative members of Congress began to cry foul, arguing that many federal judges had abused their power, unilaterally deciding that the death penalty was wrong, indulging frivolous appeals by death row inmates, and manipulating rules to keep defendants from execution. To tie the hands of federal judges, Congress passed sweeping changes to the law governing habeas corpus relief in the 1996 Antiterrorism and Effective Death Penalty Act. The act, which followed the terrorist attack on the Alfred P. Murrah Federal Building in Oklahoma City, sought to use procedural rules to limit the number and substance of habeas corpus petitions in federal courts. Under the terms of the act, defendants were given just one bite at the apple—they had to make all their claims up front and file a single habeas petition within a narrow period after their claims were rejected in state court.

The act also sought to tie the hands of federal judges by prohibiting them from granting relief based on claims applicants raised unless state courts had resolved the claim in a way that was "contrary to, or involved an unreasonable application of, clearly established Federal law, as determined by the Supreme Court of the United States" or if the state court's decision was based on "an unreasonable determination of the facts in light of the evidence presented in the State court proceeding." These were both extraordinarily high standards.[27] If federal judges disagreed with how the state court had interpreted a point of federal constitutional law, but the Supreme Court had not weighed in on the issue, they were powerless to intervene. Likewise, if federal judges thought that a defendant was "probably" innocent but that the evidence presented to them was not "clear and convincing," they could not act on the defendant's behalf.

Debating the merits of the legislation, Senator Orrin Hatch pointed to a chart on the floor of the Senate that compared the 2,976 convicted murderers then on the nation's death rows with the 281 executions that had happened since *Gregg*:

> There are multiple frivolous appeals in almost every one of these almost 3,000 death row cases. If they lose on one, they conjure up another one, and then they conjure up another one, and they conjure up another one. . . . There is no finality, no way of solving these problems. It is a farce. Why is it? Because liberal judges—and I have to say active defense lawyers who are doing their jobs under a system that allows this charade to go on and on—continue to allow this to happen because they do not like the death penalty.[28]

The consequence, Hatch argued, was that the law appeared to be simultaneously weak-willed and cruel, or at least cruel in its weakness.

Hatch related the story of William Andrews, who forced his victims to drink Drano and drove pencils through their eardrums before killing them. Andrews sat on death row for eighteen years and launched thirty appeals during that time. The result, in Hatch's view, was a legitimation crisis for the state: "You wonder why people in this country are worried about the laws and do not believe in them," Hatch said, disgusted. "Every time [Andrews] brought up a habeas corpus petition, the victims and their families had to relive the whole murder situation again."[29] If the Willie Horton campaign ad presented the death penalty as an effective antidote to complex bureaucratic prison systems that were run according to a technocratic logic most Americans did not understand, the demand for habeas reform revealed the alienating effects of a different kind of logic—that of procedural justice. Capital punishment had promised unadulterated justice, but its supporters found it had become just as mired in technobabble as the rest of the criminal justice system.

## Crime Warriors: Bob Macy, Johnny Holmes, and the Frontier Mentality

In this cultural climate, district attorneys Bob Macy and Johnny Holmes appeared, in local media, as state officials who rebelled against a technocratic bureaucracy and a due process judiciary. With their trademark symbols, the string tie and the handlebar mustache, the two satisfied, in the popular imagination, a desire to fuse heroic individualism to the rule of law. Over the years, their pursuit of the death penalty became part of a larger statement that the criminal justice system had not suppressed the expression of masculine, frontier qualities but was still dependent on them. In admiring depictions of these men as law-enforcing outsiders, their hometown newspapers and biographers portrayed them as the embodiment of sovereign power *and* as a vigilante alternative to it.

### Embodying Sovereign Power

Sovereignty is notoriously faceless in democracies.[30] Agents of the state who have no personal stake in a punishment are supposed to mete out the penalty according to administrative protocols. By depersonalizing the use of legitimate force, modern legal systems reduce opportunities for individual expressions of political authority. In Harris and Oklahoma Counties, however, depictions of Holmes and Macy worked to reverse the anonymizing tendencies of the rule of law. In depicting the two men, the *Chronicle* and the *Oklahoman* often rhetorically collapsed the distinctions between prosecutor, sentencer, and executioner; they nominally occupied just one of these roles, that of the prosecutor, but symbolically they inhabited all three.[31]

Portrayals of Holmes sometimes cast him as a street cop—expected, unlike prosecutors, to exert violent physical force over other persons in the name of the state. In a tribute to Holmes published in the *Chronicle* when he retired, Harris County criminal court judge Jan Krocker told readers that Holmes was exceptional because he was really a police officer at heart, ready to intervene physically when innocents were endangered. "My all-time favorite Johnny Holmes story, first reported in the *Chronicle* in 1989," Krocker wrote,

> is about how the DA convinced a little girl who was terrified of the defendant to take his hand and go into the courtroom to testify. He told her that if the bad man tried to hurt her he'd beat him up. I like that story because it is vintage Johnny Holmes. I like it because I observed it. But mostly I like it because it is about the wisdom of children. That child knew instinctively what the people of Harris County learned over two decades—that Holmes was telling them the truth. His legacy to Harris County is that he was never afraid of the bad guy.[32]

Krocker's tribute reinforced an idea of Holmes as a man who was unique not only for his willingness to ask the state to impose harsh punishment on criminals, but for his willingness to impose that violence himself at a moment's notice. At the dedication of Houston's new criminal courthouse, he addressed the audience wearing a SWAT team jacket, identifying himself with the special police force used to apprehend suspects violently and without warning. Holmes also kept a police radio in his car, she noted, and occasionally got to crime scenes before police investigators did. "Every fiber of Holmes' being—down to the tips of his handlebar moustache—has been devoted to taking the street officer's war on crime into the courtroom," she wrote. In expanding the domain of the "street officer's war on crime," Holmes served as a charismatic figure in which the disparate elements of the criminal justice system were united. He was a welcome reversal of the elaborate division of labor that characterizes bureaucratic law enforcement.[33]

The *Oklahoman* represented Bob Macy similarly. In coverage of Macy's 2011 death, the newspaper noted that Macy thought of himself as a police officer long after his 1950s stint as an Oklahoma City patrolman had ended. The obituary quoted Oklahoma City police chief Bill Citty: "He believed in his country, his community and especially the cops on the street. He dedicated a lot of his career to provide justice to a lot of victims of crime. . . . He loved police officers probably more than anyone I know. I think he was a true law enforcer at heart who just happened to be our DA." The more intellectual work of the prosecutor, the newspaper insisted, was secondary to Macy's self-identification as a "true law enforcer."[34]

Several years after Macy retired, an appellate court vacated a conviction in a death penalty case Macy had originally prosecuted and ordered a new trial. The court reversed Bigler Jobe Stouffer II's capital murder conviction and death sentence because it found that Stouffer's trial attorney had provided him with an inadequate defense. Prosecutors subsequently retried Stouffer, won a conviction, and persuaded a new jury to send him back to death row. Wes Lane, Macy's successor, arranged for Macy to be appointed a special prosecutor for the sentencing so that he could stand in the courtroom (and in front of the press) as an official participant in the proceeding. Macy had no legal reason to stand in front of the bar with the prosecution; he had not participated in any part of the recent trial. Explaining the former district attorney's official presence at the sentencing, the paper quoted Stouffer's actual prosecutor, Richard Wintory: "I thought it was very appropriate for [Macy] to assist in representing the state to send Mr. Stouffer back to where he belongs. If there's a message, it's nothing more than we're not going to wear out and we're not going to wear down."[35]

Indeed, Macy's physical presence was at the center of the *Oklahoman*'s coverage of the sentencing. While prosecutors' bodies are irrelevant to the role they play in the enforcement of law, the *Oklahoman* took pains to note Macy's physical vitality. The story began,

Retired Oklahoma County District Attorney Bob Macy stood Thursday beside convicted murderer Bigler Jobe "Bud" Stouffer II, just as he did almost 18 years ago, while a judge sentenced the defendant to death. It was Macy's

first time in the courtroom since he retired June 30, 2001, after 21 years as the
county's chief prosecutor. Macy, 72, was appointed by District Attorney Wes
Lane as a special assistant district attorney so he could stand at the bench
with prosecutors Richard Wintory and Christy Reid as Stouffer received a
death sentence for the second time.

The story that followed was focused as much on Macy's physical condition as it was on Stouffer's case: "Since Macy retired, he has been di-
agnosed with Parkinson's Disease," the newspaper reported before re-
assuring readers that "the disease is under control with medication,
which allows him to still ride his horses and rope." As if to prove the
point, the story went on to note that Macy, "wearing the string tie by
which he was known for more than two decades," believed he had in-
timidated Stouffer. Stouffer would not make eye contact with the former
DA, Macy told the newspaper, a detail that suggested how intimidating
Macy's presence still was.[36]

The *Oklahoman*'s coverage of Stouffer's sentencing burnished Macy's
tough public image as a living rebuke to legal-rational ideals. Under a ra-
tionalized approach to legal authority, Macy and Wintory should have
been interchangeable actors occupying the role of the prosecutor at
Stouffer's trial and retrial, respectively, and Macy's presence at the retrial sentencing would have been superfluous. By spending so much time
discussing Macy's presence at the resentencing, however, the *Oklahoman* suggested that there was an identifiable man meting out Oklahoma
County's death penalty.

### Reconciling Ego and Duty

Newspaper presentations of Holmes and Macy did more than identify
them with sovereign power. They tapped into the contradictions inherent
in frontier myth. Specifically, Holmes and Macy both embodied an oxymoronic ideal of the frontier hero as an arrogant ascetic. In their decision to pursue the death penalty, they often seemed to disdain the will of
others. And yet, as we will see, descriptions of their vigorous pursuit of
harsh punishment were frequently accompanied by a discussion of their
voluntary submission to a larger, awe-inspiring, sacred authority—an exacting code of honor (Macy) or democratically created laws (Holmes)—
that would sometimes cause them to suffer.

In its depictions of Holmes, the *Chronicle* suggested that personal in-

terest rather than public duty motivated him. In announcing his retirement, reporter Steve Brewer wrote, "Holmes said he still loves the job
and still comes in every day between 5:15 and 5:30 a.m. and doesn't leave
until around 6 p.m. 'And it's not because of some loyal government service bull[shit],' Holmes said Tuesday. 'I enjoy being part of it and take
a great deal of pride in what I do.' . . . 'I've enjoyed the ego satisfaction of being a trial lawyer doing what's right. You can't buy that kind
of satisfaction.'"[37] Holmes's attachment to government, his words suggested, was merely instrumental; it lent legitimacy to his self-serving, yet
moral, impulses. A kind of impatience with the broader enterprise of
law as a complex system of rules informed his career path, he implied.
"I never wanted to be a lawyer," he said. "I wanted to be a prosecutor."[38]
Prosecutors, unlike other kinds of lawyers, wielded the law for very specific purposes that happened to align with Holmes's own vision of the
moral good.

Stylistically, Holmes presented himself as unwilling to bow to convention. In one profile he talked about the response his handlebar mustache
provoked when he was an up-and-coming young assistant district attorney: "Everybody said I looked like a dope dealer. I was hard-headed and
said: 'You have some objection to facial hair? Well, how about the color
of my skin or my surname? Why don't you just leave [me] alone because
my mustache stays.'"[39] In a culture that connects unconventional appearance to personal permissiveness, Holmes's facial hair represented a conservative appropriation of a dissident identity. He was a punitive rebel.
Reports connected his unconventional personal appearance to a defiant
refusal to go easy on those his office prosecuted. Early in his career he
asked a jury to sentence to life imprisonment a twenty-five-year-old sub-
stitute teacher who had sold a marijuana cigarette to a high school student. The teacher received probation instead, and in his later years the
paper held up Holmes's zealousness as an example of his draconian approach to law and order. Looking back on the incident, he rejected the
notion that community norms should have tempered his judgment: "You
know, it doesn't make any difference [to me] what people think about
that. I did what I thought was appropriate. The jury saw it differently,
and I think the reason they saw it differently is because the guy had tes-
ticular cancer."[40] Although he always acted within the prescribed legal
boundaries, Holmes insisted that his decisions were free from the influence of everything but his own moral instincts.

His approach to the death penalty was no different. When deciding whether to seek it in murder cases, "that decision is mine unilaterally," he said to the press. "Every chief prosecutor who handles a capital case comes to me for formalization for whether or not they're seeking death and I either agree with them or I disagree with them."[41] Coverage of Holmes, then, tended to depict him as defiantly individualistic. Whether exercising discretion over his personal grooming or the fate of capital murder defendants, he would defer to nothing but his own moral intuition. Indeed, when the *Chronicle* wrote a piece in 2008 about the Bible that Harris County district attorneys had inscribed and passed on to one another for moral wisdom since 1951, Holmes dismissed its importance: "I held that office longer than anyone ever has," he said. "And I never opened it. I didn't need it."[42]

At the same time, *the Chronicle* made sure to note that Holmes's self-interest aligned with an uncompromising allegiance to the rule of law. In media profiles, reporters portrayed Holmes as an enforcer of laws who would bend them for no one—not even himself. He "religiously kept his speedometer" at fifty-five miles per hour on highways, the *Chronicle* reported, to avoid breaking the law.[43] "The saying about Johnny is that he would indict his own grandmother," Houston defense attorney Dick DeGuerin joked. "I don't think he's ever been tested on his grandmother."[44] Holmes appeared to revel in this reputation: "Maybe I shouldn't call down an assistant DA because open and obviously in front of me they turn illegally or they jaywalk or they commit some other, maybe to everybody else, seemingly minor offense. But we live in a glass house. How can we go in justice court and prosecute people who aren't displaying a license plate on their vehicle and then choose to drive down the street without one on ours? I just don't think that's right."[45] Holmes, in short, took pains to communicate his disdain for the hypocrisy of those in power.

Challenged in 1992 by a Democratic opponent who suggested that the district attorney ought to focus his prosecutions on suppliers of drugs rather than street-level buyers (whose cases were clogging the system), Holmes was indignant. For him the uniformly harsh prosecution of criminal offenders without regard to the social consequences—like a rising incarceration rate's disparate impact on minority populations—constituted a refusal to exercise more power than he had been given by the electorate. "We don't do social engineering here," he responded. "We enforce the law, and if people don't like the laws we're enforcing, they need to go and have those laws changed and that's in the hands of the

Texas Legislature."[46] For Holmes, the prosecutorial discretion he sometimes boasted was "his alone" was at other times nonexistent. As he explained to the *Dallas Morning News,*

> What I think doesn't make a . . . bit of difference. Prosecutors don't have the
> right to pick and choose which laws they'll enforce. I hated licensing Texans
> to carry guns. I thought it was stupid, and I still do. But in a democracy, the
> people have the right to be wrong. I hate all this Common Cause crap about
> campaign finance disclosure. I think it deters good citizens from seeking pub-
> lic office. But I'm the only prosecutor in the state who's ever put someone in
> jail for violating it.[47]

Indeed, when a reporter told him that 739 people per 100,000 in Houston's population were incarcerated (compared with a national rate at the
time of 530 per 100,000) and asked when the massive growth in incarcer
ated inmates might end, his glib response was "when people follow the
rules."[48]

Ironically, by endorsing the limits on his authority, Holmes was in a
way transcending them. The very act of pronouncing himself subordinate to the Texas legislature suggests that there could be a doubt that he
was not, like all civil servants, governed by the rule of law. Holmes's pronouncements of radical fidelity to the rule of law, in other words, could
be interpreted as expressions of personal preference rather than a sense
of duty. The distinction is purely stylistic, to be sure, but Holmes's dramatic profession of self-restraint is also a profession of self-awareness
and choice that distinguish him from uncritical rule followers.

In a very different way, portrayals of Bob Macy featured a tension
between his own ego and the law. While the *Oklahoman* was sympathetic to the popular prosecutor, it reported on times when his refusal
to abide by rules governing prosecutorial conduct got him into trouble.
Macy was frequently in trouble with appellate courts for circumventing
rules pertaining to inflammatory rhetoric during capital trials. In one
case he made audible side comments during voir dire that informed prospective jurors of the defendant's extensive criminal history. During
the penalty phase's closing arguments, moreover, he told the jury that
it would be unjust to "send this man to prison, let him have clean sheets
to sleep on every night, three good meals a day, visits by his friends and
family, while [victim] John Howard lies cold in his grave." John Howard's family, he reminded the jury, could only visit a tombstone.[49] Noting

a track record of striking "foul blows" and acting deceitfully in court-room oratory, the tenth circuit wrote, "Macy's persistent misconduct, though it has not legally harmed the defendant in the present case, has without doubt harmed the reputation of Oklahoma's criminal justice system and left the unenviable legacy of an indelibly tarnished legal career." Even more damning, the court went on to write, "our past experiences with this prosecutor leave us convinced that his 'inappropriate' commentary (to jurors) at trial was intentional and calculated."[50]

Macy's decisions while in office put him at odds not only with courts but also, sometimes, with his constituents. In the aftermath of the Oklahoma City bombing, a federal jury had convicted Terry Nichols of conspiring with Timothy McVeigh to carry out the terrorist attack and sentenced him to life imprisonment, forgoing the death penalty. Dissatisfied with that outcome, Macy decided to pursue a death sentence for Nichols in state court. The decision incurred substantial opposition from the public, the state legislature, the victims of the bombing, and the *Oklahoman*'s editorial board. Polls showed that the majority of Oklahomans did not think a state trial for Nichols was necessary, particularly because a federal jury had given him a life sentence and the cost of such a trial would be so high.[51]

Macy's defense of his decision was unabashedly personal. In an interview with CBS News about why he wanted a state trial for Nichols, Macy claimed direct responsibility for the death sentences his office procured and suggested they were motivated by personal, rather than public, interest: "I've sent several people to death row for killing one person. I certainly feel that death would be the appropriate punishment for killing 19 babies."[52] He ("I"), not juries or judges, sent death row inmates to their fates, he had said. Indeed, Macy linked his judgment not to legal standards for prosecutors, but to his own presence at the scene of the crime. In an editorial in the *Oklahoman* defending his decision to try Nichols in state court, Macy said he was fulfilling a promise he made to the dead and their families at the scene of the attack: "Standing in the rubble the morning of April 19, 1995, watching men, women, and children brought out one by one, I knew that only the death penalty would bring justice to the perpetrators of this crime. . . . I found myself trying to comfort the living by promising to see justice done for the dead. I hope you will understand why I will keep my word," he wrote.[53] His decision to proceed with the prosecution against public opinion was a stand for personal honor. It was a rebuke to utilitarian calculations of the greatest good for the greatest number, calculations that subordinate the duty we owe to victims to larger policy goals like fiscal responsibility or a return to normality in the aftermath of collective trauma.

Macy's public defense of his behavior and his repeated proclamations that Terry Nichols needed to be prosecuted in Oklahoma so that he could be executed eventually led the district court to remove him from the case. The state supreme court upheld that decision. "I have never seen such a blatant open violation of the rules of professional conduct," district judge Ray Dean Linder told the *Oklahoman*. "There is no doubt in my mind that Mr. Macy is too closely involved."[54] In a follow-up article, the *Oklahoman* explained the legal principles behind the decision to remove Macy from the case. It summarized interviews with legal ethics experts who explained that prosecutors "must stay professionally detached from their cases so their judgment on how to proceed is not clouded" and that Macy's incendiary comments might taint a jury pool.[55] On the whole, however, the newspaper defended Macy against the criticism: "Surely many residents of Oklahoma County who have supported Macy through the years have done so for precisely the reasons that landed him in legal trouble: He is a committed crime fighter, honed by years as a policeman on a beat, who takes murder and other serious crimes in a personal, passionate way—and doesn't mind saying so."[56]

In its defense of Macy's conduct, the newspaper imagined the district attorney as a figure who refused to be constrained by rules that, it complained, demanded that legal actors leave their personal experience at the courthouse door. The law's intolerance of a man who intended to exert "every ounce of his very being into bringing the perpetrators to justice" was, the paper suggested, evidence of its soullessness. The courtroom was not a forum but a battlefield, and the law ought to permit a man who was "touched personally by the worst act of terrorism in American history" to fight upon it.[57] This aversion to the law's transcendent aspirations was at the core of the vigilante ethos Macy maintained about his work. Despite Macy's numerous instances of prosecutorial misconduct, the *Oklahoman* reconstructed him as a crusader who heroically disregarded technical rules when they conflicted with own sense of justice.

Compared with Holmes, whose zealousness was not haunted by a reputation for misconduct, Macy was more critical of the federal courts.[58] He balanced his arrogance not with a radical fidelity to the rule of law, but with obedience to an extralegal moral code of honor imbued with practical "homespun cowboy wisdom" and prescriptive hierarchical values.[59] For Macy, judges did not always inspire deference. In response to being chastised by the tenth circuit in a 2002 decision, he shook off the criticism, remarking, "When you spend 21 years trying to make Oklahoma County a safer place, I'm sure I offended people along the way. . . . It is very clear the appellate courts are opposed to the death penalty."[60] Macy's fidelity to a moral conscience rooted in traditional values shared by the citizens he served was the standard against which he judged his work as prosecutor. If positive media coverage of him was any indicator, it was one he easily met in the eyes of many of his constituents.

While important differences distinguished the media portrayals of Holmes and Macy, both men embodied the paradoxical relationship that the frontier hero has with civilization, reminding their constituents of the violent and egotistical underpinnings of the democratic political order. At times, both men proudly rebuffed criticism that their decisions to seek harsh punishment—or the means they used to pursue those ends— were incompatible with legal and social norms. Indeed, their exercise of power became the triumphant exercise of individual will against the constraints of civilization. "I will keep my word [to the victims' families]," Bob Macy retorted to critics of his decision to prosecute Terry Nichols. "It doesn't make any difference what people think," Holmes said of his decision to seek an unusually stiff sentence against a defendant. Defiant assertions of ego were, in these moments, reminders of the unequal distribution of power that enables the democratic order to function. Yet while Holmes and Macy called attention to the fact that their discretion allowed them to make sometimes unpopular decisions and reveled in their image as iconoclasts, they simultaneously insisted that their behavior was bound by a code. Like judges who perform judicial restraint with rhetorical flourish in opinions, they would carry out the will of Texans and Oklahomans even if their constituents became, in particular cases, paralyzed by timidity or distracted by utilitarian concerns like the financial or emotional cost of a capital trial.[61]

In portrayals of these men, harshness became proof that they remained uncorrupted by a legal and technocratic culture that sought to separate morality from law, emotion from punishment, strength from individual bodies. Through punishment, these men seemed to reverse the neutral indifference with which the law responded to gross injustice. Part of their appeal was the sense that they were, like mythic frontiersmen, more comfortable with shotguns than with law books. Yet in their decision to channel their violent impulses for the common good, they demonstrated a willingness to restrain themselves, to keep from indulging in the antisocial violence that all strong men are capable of. In the collective imagination of Harris and Oklahoma Counties, Johnny Holmes and Bob Macy found a niche—and earned iconic stature—by rejecting a civilized status quo in the name of protecting civilization. In so doing, they exhibited a kind of freedom that too often seemed missing in the lives of law-abiding Americans.

## Maintaining a Vigilante Ethos

I have argued that throughout their tenures as district attorneys of Harris and Oklahoma Counties, Johnny Holmes and Bob Macy embodied the fantasies and tensions that Americans have long found in the popular myth of frontier heroes. In that myth, strong, honorable men are untouched by society yet act heroically on its behalf. Civilizing, righteous egotism triumphs over a savage, criminal egotism that sows disorder.

The pursuit of death sentences became the most obvious way that these two men embodied that mythology, but it was not the only way. Both Holmes and Macy identified with a kind of vigilante ethos even as they cautioned regular citizens against taking the law into their own hands. In 1996 the *Chronicle* regaled readers with an account of Holmes's decision to intervene personally at the scene of a crime. Holmes was at home one morning finishing his daily workout when he heard a loud clunking noise outside. Peering out his window, he saw a man suspiciously loading materials from a construction site into a pickup truck. He sprang into action. The response in his household, as the *Chronicle* reported it, fell along traditional gender lines: while his wife called 911, Holmes ran downstairs, blocked the man's truck with his car, and, in the district attorney's words, "threw down on him with a shotgun." "Don't think about going anywhere," he told the man. Holmes then held the man at gunpoint until police arrived and arrested him. This story, which reporter Lisa Teachey recounted in the next day's *Houston Chronicle* under the headline, "D.A. Reached for a Shotgun, Not a Law Book," presented the district attorney as a man with vigilante instincts.[62] "I did not do it for any other reason than the guy was stealing and I think that's wrong," Holmes later explained. Later in the interview, though, he seemed to contradict himself by qualifying his account of what happened: "I'm not sure it's a good idea for the average Joe to do [what I did]," he said, referring to his vigilante response to the burglary. "Understand, I am a peace officer."

A few years into his retirement, the *Oklahoman* ran an article on Macy that portrayed him as similarly capable of defending himself with violence:

> Macy angered a lot of criminals in his 21 years as district attorney but he said he doesn't worry about his safety. He did think a recently released former death row inmate might seek him out. He said he decided "I'm not going to change my lifestyle for some punk . . . who should have been executed. I've got a rifle upstairs that has a good powerful scope on it. I've got several weapons. If anybody tries to get in here, they may get in but they may have a hell of a time getting out," Macy said. "I figure all the time they've been in prison they haven't been shooting and I shoot . . . several times a year."[63]

After his death in 2011, Macy's biographers likewise cultivated an image of him as a man willing to engage in and tolerate occasional lawlessness in order to do justice. "Some of the best crime fighting never resulted in an arrest," the biographers noted of Macy's tenure as a police officer and district attorney.[64] Instead, in Macy's career as a police officer, there "was a lot of street corner justice dispensed."[65] The text presented Macy as a man whose vigilante impulses were sometimes so strong he could not resist them—especially when provoked by men who threatened women and children. Remembering his days as a beat cop, Macy's biographers wrote that "domestic cases were a particular problem and sometimes challenged his sense of peacefulness. If a wife or child was battered or beaten, and the drunken abuser was still there, the fellow 'stood an excellent chance of getting his rear kicked before being put in jail.'"[66] In his career as district attorney, the biographers noted, sympathy for police officers often tempered his response to allegations of police brutality. Macy understood, they said, that the adrenaline involved in protecting innocent citizens occasionally morphs into excessive force that we must accept if we are to have the security that rough men provide. That philosophy was one reason why, Macy confessed, he "would have had little mercy for Rodney King."[67]

In these stories, portrayals of vigilante violence were the occasion for an invigorating assertion of the power that individuals using physical force (or the threat of physical force) retain even after they have entered into the social contract. The state's monopoly on violence requires the subordination of our egotistical desire for total control to a larger system of social control. Portrayals of both Holmes and Macy approvingly noted limits on their ability to abide by that subordination. "Some would suggest it's probably good business to turn the other cheek," Holmes admitted in the article covering his apprehension of the thief. "I just can't do that."[68] Likewise, Macy's refusal to change his lifestyle "for some punk" depended on his ability to defend his home with guns. Preparing for the former death row inmate who might show up on his doorstep, Macy maintained, in spite of the law's monopoly on violence, a small arsenal. The "punk" posed no threat because Macy refused to rely on the state alone for his protection.[69]

## Conclusion: The Racial Underpinnings of Liberation

In the 1890s, the same decade that Frederick Jackson Turner famously announced the closing of the American frontier, some white men began enacting what it meant to be white and male in a new way. In response to economic, technological, and demographic change, historian Gail Bederman has argued, middle-class white men adopted a newer, more accessible ideal of white manhood based on physical prowess. A Victorian ideal of manliness rooted in self-restraint gave way to a more vigorous, unapologetic, unconstrained masculinity, justified as necessary for maintaining civilization against nonwhite savages.[70] Spectacle lynchings in the South most dramatically enacted this "civilizing" white violence, as white men saw themselves as duty-bound to deploy barbaric violence to protect white women from the primitive, uncontrolled sexual desires of black men.[71] As he entered into mythology, the frontiersman, too, represented a figure whose righteous violence, often against people of color, had liberating and purifying effects.

In their depictions of Johnny Holmes and Bob Macy as modern-day frontiersmen, journalistic mythmakers of the late twentieth century tapped into an iconography that conveyed, in its critics' eyes, nostalgia for this past. In a nation with death rows disproportionately populated by members of racial minorities, punitive figureheads with cowboy personas inevitably reminded some of the historical connections between racial anxiety and lethal punishment.[72] Others, of course, would disclaim the relevance of that history in a world that had legally dismantled Jim Crow. The meaning of symbols evolves, they would argue.

The demographics of death row are not prima facie evidence of discrimination; studies showing evidence of racial bias can be—and have been—criticized by those suggesting that the racism of the past has been transcended.[73]

Macy and Holmes would likely count themselves among that latter group. For the most part, the two outwardly acquiesced to the gradual development, after World War II, of a political culture in which explicit expressions of white supremacy were no longer acceptable in mainstream political discourse.[74] Holmes had an anti-integrationist past, the *Chronicle* noted upon his retirement: in 1961 he led a petition drive at the University of Texas to stop the integration of the university's athletic programs, fraternities, and sororities. The paper reassured readers, however, that he was "clearly uncomfortable" discussing this part of his past.[75] Macy, meanwhile, worked to distance himself from any hint of racism or sexism. His authorized biography awkwardly documents numerous exposures to African Americans who admired his work. The biographers quote him expressing antiracist humility while reminiscing about his undergraduate years at Earlham College: "The school recruited blacks, and the fellows they got were stellar. . . . [S]omeone once told me that black men were my inferior. I retorted that they were smarter than me in class, could kick my butt on the field, and were the darlings of the parties. I was only a wallflower, so if they are inferior, then I'm in a heck of a mess," he told them.[76]

Indeed, the public personas of Macy and Holmes fit into a more modern expression of white manhood in the 1980s and 1990s. In a world that was increasingly committed rhetorically, if not materially, to racial and gender equality, idealized depictions of white men focused on them as warriors while deemphasizing the racial nationalism that had traditionally underlain American imperialism. Like militaristic celebrations of white men in *Top Gun* or *Rambo* or self-help movements that encouraged men to get in touch with their primal side, depictions of Macy and Holmes—and the death sentences they pursued—presented them as heroic, colorblind men battling for a vision of the good.[77]

Nonetheless, a more critical interpretation of this iconography, one that holds that it is not race neutral, is reflected in and reinforced by recent findings about the counties that have used capital punishment the most since the 1970s. Legal studies scholars James S. Liebman and Peter Clarke have argued that, on a number of measures, death-prone counties exhibit high degrees of libertarianism and parochialism. The presence of these two ideologies, they argue, creates an atmosphere conducive to the use of capital punishment. A libertarian refusal to use taxes to adequately fund a criminal justice infrastructure, combined with a parochial sense that outside forces are threatening to undermine local values, makes the death penalty an attractive sanction. Race, as a variable, enters their model through parochialism: in communities most likely to seek the death penalty, African Americans are seen as one of a number of outside forces, like cosmopolitanism or permissiveness, that threaten to destroy traditional values.[78]

In their analysis, Liebman and Clarke treat libertarianism and parochialism as discrete variables. Given the historical context from which they draw their data, though, the two ideologies may not simply be *interacting* in counties that seek capital punishment the most; parochialism may be partly *constitutive* of, and thus conceptually inseparable from, the libertarianism present in these counties. As we have seen in earlier chapters, middle-class white anxiety about modern life, with its iron cage of bureaucracies, rules, and procedures, emerged in postwar America well before the social upheavals of the 1960s. In that decade, growing unease about race relations lent new urgency to concerns about the effects of institutions and mass culture on personal autonomy in a modern age. For white Americans anxious about the rising profile of racial others in their world, the legal dismantling of Jim Crow and the bureaucratic initiation of a war on poverty added a new, racial dimension to a broader wariness of technocracy. In many eyes, the primary beneficiaries of the welfare state were now urban-dwelling nonwhites; the federal government had abandoned its commitment to supporting white freedom and grown estranged from traditional arrangements of power. As part of a racially charged aversion to a bureaucratic welfare state, parochialism in these places may have fueled libertarian policymaking. Libertarian distrust of government, in other words, was the product of parochial anxieties about race.

Libertarian ideology offered a powerful and colorblind way to manage racial anxiety in an age of racial pluralism. Small-government nostalgia in the 1980s and 1990s may have been born out of a recent history thoroughly suffused with white resentment of African American demands for redistribution and a federal government that seemed to be meeting those demands. On its surface, though, it was detached from these racial underpinnings; its ideal of negative, libertarian freedom could seem utterly unrelated to anxieties about threats to white

supremacy and white autonomy posed by taxpayer-funded welfare programs, affirmative action, and Warren Court jurisprudence.

Indeed, the public images of Johnny Holmes and Bob Macy help us
to see how deeply intertwined libertarianism and parochialism, freedom
and hierarchy became in conservative American discourse. For twenty
years they presided over powerful death penalty machines that disproportionately killed men of color, the media linking their personas to a
frontier freedom that was historically premised on the subjugation of racial minorities. As political actors at the end of the twentieth century,
however, they disavowed explicit articulations of white male supremacy,
instead tapping into an ostensibly race-neutral nostalgia for a frontierlike world in which good, powerful individuals used their mental and
physical prowess to solve problems rather than depending on a bloated,
inefficient state. In a world in which libertarianism and parochialism
were so intertwined, it could easily be seen as a coincidence that the evidence of the proposition Johnny Holmes and Bob Macy stood for—that
the power of untamed, yet morally right individuals still could flourish in
chaotic, modern times—so often came in the form of condemned black
bodies.

## CHAPTER SIX

# Father Knows Best

*Capital Punishment as a Family Value*

It's all about sacrifice—for the good of the family.[1] — Dexter Morgan (Michael C. Hall) to one of his victims on *Dexter* (2009)

In 2001, shortly after Johnny Holmes left the Harris County District Attorney's Office, a death penalty trial was getting under way in Houston. One by one, the clerk called prospective jurors to the witness stand for questioning by the attorneys. As the prosecutor for the state continued her interview of a prospective juror, legal fireworks went off in the courtroom. "Let me ask you a couple more questions," she began. "Obviously, we represent the family of the victim in this case." The defense attorney interrupted. "Excuse me your honor," he said. "I object. That's a misstatement of the law." The judge responded peevishly. "Can you let her finish the question? She's not done talking. Let her finish." The prosecutor then quickly added, "as well as the citizens of the State of Texas." The defense attorney again interrupted. "I renew my objection. That's a misstatement of law." A quick "overruled" ended the discussion, and the prosecutor's questioning of the prospective juror continued.[2]

Despite the judge's ruling, the prosecutor had indeed erred in referring to herself as the representative of the victim's family. In a liberal democracy, the state tries defendants for offenses committed against society; a crime incurs punishment because it is a violation of the democratically enacted law rather than an injury to a private party. Crimes harm particular persons, of course, but in the eyes of the state, victims belong to the broader category of "the people," the citizens on whose behalf a prosecutor acts.[3] Culturally speaking, however, the prosecutor was on firmer ground. Her alignment with the victim's kin captured one of the more important qualities of the contemporary killing state. To many death penalty supporters in the modern era, an execution was a punishment the state meted out on behalf of a grieving family.

Underlying this sort of thinking is a tribalism of the family that has its contemporary roots in the political history of the 1970s. As state legislatures across the nation were reviving the death penalty, a powerful branch of conservatism was spreading through the nation's evangelical Christian churches. In response to cultural changes they found intolerable, evangelical Christian leaders mobilized their flocks, urging their constituents to become more politically active. Extolling the importance of "family values," they launched a campaign to place a particular iteration of the family—middle-class, heteronormative, and nuclear—at the center of American public policymaking. As their involvement in politics grew, "family values" would become shorthand for opposition to gay rights and abortion rights. The movement, however, had a strong political philosophical foundation that this narrow political agenda did not fully capture. Family values conservatives saw the father-led family, rather than the individual, as the fundamental and sacred unit in a society. Family deserved the state's protection and deference in a way that individuals did not.

In what follows, I argue that family values provided a powerful interpretive framework through which Americans justified harsh punishment in the modern era of the American death penalty. In the previous chapter I showed how men like Johnny Holmes and Bob Macy embodied frontier fantasies about men liberated through a civilizing violence. This chapter examines the significance of a crucial dimension of that fantasy. The imagined beneficiary of their righteous violence—the foundation of the social order they protected—was the family. The death penalty protected the family not only by punishing those who harmed it with acts of murder, but also by serving as an implicit rebuke to a paternalistic state that had improperly usurped the authority of the father. To some an execution represented a return by the state to its first, most sacred (and in some ways more modest) duty: to use violence against those who threatened the social order. I call the resulting ideology of the killing state—a mixture of the frontier libertarianism that Holmes and Macy embodied with the civilizing virtues of family—"family values libertarianism." It trafficked in the fantasy that Americans could symbolically privatize the infliction of capital punishment without losing its socially regenerating qualities.

## The Rise of Family Values Conservatism

In the late 1960s the suburban, lily-white image of the United States that Americans saw on television sitcoms was coming into sharp contrast with the world they encountered on the nightly news.[4] Cities burned each summer as working-class African Americans revolted, having achieved little economic progress in the aftermath of the decade's seminal civil rights legislation. Tens of thousands of Americans gathered in 1967 to protest the Vietnam War, marching from the Jefferson Memorial to the Pentagon. Trash cans outside the Miss America Pageant in Atlantic City in 1968 filled up as women tossed in everything from beauty aids to *Playboy* magazine to protest oppressive gender norms. At the Stonewall Inn in New York City, queers rioted in 1969 in response to yet another police raid on the bar. Social movements took more radical turns as minorities and women began demanding political and cultural recognition from a nation that, they insisted, needed to respect rather than assimilate them. Black, red, and yellow power activists, difference feminists, and radical queers all demanded political equality with white, middle-class, heterosexual Americans while rejecting suburban domesticity as a cultural ideal. Indeed, at the heart of much activism on the left was the principle that the "universal ideals" of America, embodied in Cold War America by the heteronormative, middle-class family, were not universally shared at all, but an ideology that justified the oppression of outsiders.

To social conservatives, such thinking and the political and cultural fragmentation it sowed were corroding the nation's soul.[5] The traditional family was its chief casualty. Rising divorce rates, abortion on demand, pornographic displays of sex and violence in entertainment, the rising visibility of sexual minorities, and the proliferation of women in the professions—all were symptoms of a cultural relativism that encouraged a dangerous hedonistic decoupling of sexual pleasure from the bonds of marriage and child rearing. Nothing could give children the moral foundation essential for future citizens, they thought, but a childhood spent in a two-parent home with a mother and a father. But cultural changes were not just forestalling the creation of new nuclear families, they were threatening those that already existed. Parents could not give their children a moral foundation if the world outside their home was constantly undercutting traditional authority. To save the family, they organized. From Jerry Falwell's Moral Majority in the 1970s to Pat Robertson's Christian Broadcasting Network in the 1980s to Ralph Reed's Christian Coalition in the 1990s, conservative activists sought to place "family values" at the heart of American public policy.

## Family Values in a Punitive Culture

Criminal justice policy did not occupy the central place on the family values agenda that opposition to abortion, the Equal Rights Amendment, or gay rights initiatives did. Over time, though, the foundational principles of family values conservatism would grow increasingly intertwined with the punitive turn in American political culture.

One of the most celebrated and lavishly covered executions in the modern era illustrates how harsh punishment could provide unique opportunities for advancing the family values agenda. In January 1989, on the day before his execution in Florida's electric chair, condemned white serial killer Theodore Bundy sat down for a final interview with James Dobson, evangelical founder of the family values organization Focus on the Family. He told Dobson and the listeners of Dobson's radio show, which reached people across the world on 1,300 stations, that exposure to pornography as a teenager sparked in him the desires and inclinations that eventually resulted in the violent rapes and murders of dozens of women. "As an adolescent, he wanted ever-more-violent and hard-core material," Dobson explained. "It came to a point where nothing else he could see visually could give him the same high."[6] Bundy's narcissism and emotional hollowness were precisely the deficits that social conservatives feared would emerge in a world that detached sex from meaningful human relationships.

As an example of how social conservatives understood crime, Dobson's interview with Bundy challenged the liberal criminology of the recent past, which placed great weight on economic and educational opportunity in explaining why people turned to crime. For Dobson and like-minded conservatives, crime was instead a symptom of a culture that encouraged immoral behavior. The problem, conservatives argued, lay not in lack of economic opportunity, but in cultural attitudes. De-industrialization, for instance, was not the "root cause" of a crack epidemic and the violence it generated in the 1980s—an oppositional culture was.[7] Psychological abnormalities were not what led a man like Bundy to serially abduct, rape, and kill women—a culture that permitted adolescents easy access to hard-core pornography was. It was morality, not money or mental health, that was missing in offenders' lives. Bundy and other white psychopaths became extreme examples of the consequences of a world in which government had failed to preserve the conditions necessary for families to transmit moral values to their children effectively.

This interpretive framework demanded a different approach to punishment than government-centered, prevention- and provision-based strategies offered. Liberal, rehabilitation-oriented punishments took moral censure out of punishment, instead imagining it as a remedy for the educational, psychological, and attitudinal deficits in an offender's childhood that were not his fault. The infliction of harsh punishments on offenders, on the other hand, reasserted the importance and vitality of a traditional morality that had become marginalized by the liberal welfare state. It represented a recognition that moral accountability, rather than therapy, was what Americans needed from their government. Capital punishment was the most potent symbol of this thinking. "Reinstitution of the death penalty," social conservative Patrick Buchanan argued to readers of his syndicated column in 1976, was "less the mark of a society sinking into barbarism than the symptom of a society regaining its health, a society no longer absorbed in self-analysis or paralyzed by self-doubt."[8] Buchanan's choice of psychotherapeutic language was telling. Capital punishment represented a reversal of a corrosive cultural tendency to sympathetically explore the psyche of the criminal while regarding with suspicion the desire to hold people accountable to a fixed, sacred moral order.

As family values conservatives brought morality to bear on explanations of crime and justifications for punishment, a nascent and politically powerful Victims' Rights Movement became a chief outlet through which many of their views could be put into action. Cultural studies scholar Raphael Ginsberg traces the movement's birth to 1972. That year, just months before the Supreme Court would declare the process of capital sentencing unconstitutionally unfair, activist lawyer Frank Carrington testified before Congress in favor of the death penalty. In his testimony he articulated the logic that would come to shape victim-centered criminal justice policy: "Perhaps the rights of potential victims and actual victims . . . should be weighed much more heavily in the balance than the rights of the convicted killers," he said.[9] Three years later, with support from the conservative Heritage Foundation, Carrington wrote *The Victims*, a book that decried a criminal justice system that excluded victims and their family members from participation in criminal proceedings. Its impact was substantial. Activists founded nongovernmental organizations like the National Organization for Victim Assistance (1975) and the Parents of Murdered Children (1978) and set out to get legislation passed that would expand the rights of victims and their family members.[10] Much of that legislation centered on expanding the rights of victims and their families to participate in the process of assessing punishment. Punishment, the movement held, was a mechanism for providing psychological closure for victims and their family members; it released them from the trauma of the past or, at the very least, allowed them to begin healing.[11]

The movement's successes were remarkable. The election of Ronald Reagan to the presidency significantly bolstered its visibility and impact. In 1982 Reagan appointed Carrington to the President's Task Force on Victims of Crime, which produced a series of recommendations that Congress incorporated into the Victim and Witness Protection Act of 1982. Among other policy changes, the act "established the right of victims to present their views on sentencing to judges and required prosecutors to solicit victims' views before plea deals."[12] States, too, started passing legislation. Some explicitly permitted homicide victims' family members to testify about the impact of their loss during the sentencing phases of capital and noncapital trials. District attorney's offices across the country created positions for liaisons to victims and their family members, who would keep them apprised of the progress of cases and provide emotional support during the trial. Starting in 1984 with Louisiana, twenty-three states passed laws guaranteeing a victim's family members access to the execution of their loved one's killer.[13]

In federal public policymaking, meanwhile, lawmakers increasingly considered capital punishment in terms of the healing it made possible for aggrieved families. From 1926 to 2009, the Senate and House Judiciary Committees and the Senate's Committee on the District of Columbia held dozens of hearings on various matters related to the death penalty. Judges, attorneys, professors, and representatives of police and abolitionist organizations consistently testified about the sanction throughout this period. In 1993, however, a committee heard the testimony of the family member of a murder victim for the first time.[14] That year, Miriam Shehane pleaded with legislators not to support proposed legislation that would expand capital defendants' appellate rights. Explaining the devastating effect the murder of her daughter Quenette had had on her, Shehane entreated the committee to pay attention to the needs of families: "I implore you, please search your hearts and consider the impact it will have on— this bill will have on us. Another extension of the appeals process will mean a longer timeframe before we can bury our loved ones. Please hear my cry for healing."[15] Too often, she said, judges delayed executions to examine fraudulent claims of innocence. Just as important as ensuring that no innocent person was executed was the obligation Congress owed to "those innocent victims of murder whose lives were taken so abruptly and viciously without any provocation, and yet, without *any* right to appeal," Shehane said in her prepared statement; "consideration of the innocence of the victim is imperative."[16]

Family members of murder victims went on to testify or submit letters that were entered into the record at Senate hearings conducted in 1997, 2001, and 2006. At the heart of this testimony was the documentation of the pain of a capital crime in terms of its devastating effect on the family. Take, for instance, the testimony I examined in the previous chapter of Ann Scott, whose daughter Elaine was murdered in Oklahoma in 1991 by Alfred Brian Mitchell. In explaining the pain she, her husband, and her sons had endured, Scott appealed to a sentimental vision of the nuclear family, one of strong fathers and caring mothers raising responsible children who, in turn, reproduced and carried on the family tradition. Before Elaine's murder, she said, her family experienced that sense of family-based security. Now, she testified,

> I have had my husband break down and sob in my arms, and I have watched his health, both mental and physical, deteriorate over the years. I have seen Elaine's two brothers struggle with life. David, the oldest, has gone through panic attacks and at times thought that he should be dead because he has outlived his sister and that is not the way it should be. I have watched Elaine's little brother clam up. To this day, Robert still cannot talk about his most favorite person in the whole wide world. His big sister is gone, taken violently from him, and he still can't deal with it. The rest of us, my husband and I, have closed ranks with our children. Even though they have grown and David is married now, we still have become more protective and we are frightened every time that they are out of sight or we don't hear from them.[17]

Scott presented the family's pain by pointing to the gap between how their life is and how "it should be." Were it not for Mitchell, she suggested, Elaine would have outlived her brother David because she was younger. Were it not for Mitchell, Scott's husband would not have lost his masculine composure. Were it not for Mitchell, the Scotts would have gradually given their children more freedom as they grew older, allowing them to become responsible, autonomous citizens. Mitchell's death would offer redress not simply for the death of Elaine, but for the psychological crippling of a family.

Scott's testimony was remarkable not for its genuinely heartbreaking content, which is all too tragically common, but for its presence in official deliberations by federal legislators over the merits of the death penalty. Undoubtedly, sympathy for a victim's grieving loved ones had long motivated many death sentences and shaped the local responses to many executions.[18] Still, until the 1990s, family members of murder victims did not authenticate the value of capital punishment in front of congressional committees the way Scott did here.

Before the modern period, victims' families had also been less visible in fictional and journalistic representations of executions. Before World War II, cinematic dramatizations of capital punishment almost never portrayed the stake victims' family members had in executions; those in the post-*Gregg* period, by contrast, often pushed audiences to think about their needs.[19] Likewise, between World War I and World War II, coverage of executions in major metropolitan newspapers rarely mentioned the reaction of victims' family members to the executions of their loved ones' assailants. Indeed, they often did the opposite: nearly half the time, they mentioned the family members of the condemned, calling attention to the loved ones that he was leaving behind.[20]

A pre- and post-1970s comparison of the coverage of two seminal cases in one of the nation's most sober-minded newspapers illustrates how prominent the family members of victims became in the modern period of capital punishment. While the *New York Times* covered spree killer Charles Starkweather's 1958 capture in a story that began on the front page and included photographs and a map,[21] it buried news of his 1959 execution on page 58 in an account of fewer than one hundred words and made no mention of the response of his victims' families to his punishment.[22] The newspaper's coverage of serial killer Ted Bundy's execution, however, made the front page.[23] Several weeks later, moreover, the paper ran a second front-page story on the family members of Bundy's victims and their response to his execution. The *Times* reporter had visited with family members in their homes to capture how the loss had engulfed them. "For some families . . . it seems as though the clock stopped with the death and never started ticking again," the article read. "The bedroom of Denise Maslund, with her guitar, her teddy bear, her first doll, remains much as she left it on July 14, 1974. Her mother, Eleanore Rose, lingers in that bedroom even now. When the sense of loss becomes unbearable she buries her face in Denise's shirts or sweaters, and breathes deeply in the hope that she can capture the scent of the loved and lost."[24] This kind of melodramatic evocation of loss did not appear in the *Times*'s execution coverage before the Victims' Rights Movement began reshaping the meaning of the death penalty. By the late 1980s, it reflected an increasingly commonsense view that a central function of capital punishment was its potential as a palliative for grief. A broader family values conservatism, filtered through an effective Victims' Rights Movement, had added a new and pressing dimension to the retributive function of capital punishment.

## Family Values Libertarianism

I have argued that, directly and indirectly, family values conservatism lent moral purpose and urgency to the death penalty. For social conservatives, executions expressed intolerance for the most depraved kinds of crime, which they linked to a decadent culture that devalued the importance of family. Less directly, the Victims' Rights Movement invoked sympathetic conservative constructions of the embattled, innocent family into its own powerful defense of the death penalty. Executions, they argued, offered much-needed closure to the grieving families homicide victims left behind.

A victim-centered death penalty also reflected a less prominent dimension of family values conservatism: its suspicion of big government. "Family values," after all, had its genesis in a sense that the state had betrayed traditional families. Indeed, in contrast to what their critics said about them, some social conservatives saw themselves less as imposing their traditionalist way of life on the public and more as reviving a government that vested moral education in the family and minimized children's exposure to messages that could interfere with the moral education their parents were giving them.[25] They were insisting, in other words, that the state respect the family as the only legitimate social engineer. As a result, they often presented themselves as critics of authoritarianism rather than proponents of it. A report issued by President Ronald Reagan's working group on the family in 1986, for instance, pointedly argued that freedom depended on the existence of strong families. The expansion of paternalistic state power into the private sphere, the fostering of economic dependency on the state—these were the strategies that totalitarian states used to maintain control over populations. "Every totalitarian movement of the twentieth century has tried to destroy the family," the report noted, making the independence of the family, not the individual, the touchstone of American freedom.[26]

Such rhetoric illustrated the libertarian ethos family values conservatives often incorporated into their rhetoric and their political positions. Pure libertarians, of course, represented a very distinctive constituency of the New Right who prioritized passing neoliberal policies that deregulated markets and privatized public goods. They could—and did—clash with family values conservatives over issues like legalizing drugs. Still, much of the libertarian distrust for the liberal social welfare state appealed to social conservatives. Historian Robert O. Self has explained that morality and economy were not always distinct in social conservatives' views of government: many of them came to believe that "family values could flourish only with a weak government that absented itself from both the market and the 'private' domain of family morality."[27] Why? The welfare state created a "broad social contract that socialize[d] common goods and economic costs."[28] That meant, for conservatives, that they were paying taxes that were underwriting public welfare programs that were often corrupted by "new gender and sexual values."[29] Parents, not politicians, they believed, ought to retain control over those tax dollars.

At the 1996 Republican National Convention, Kansas senator Bob Dole expressed this "family values libertarianism" in the speech he gave when he accepted the GOP's presidential nomination. Speaking to the party faithful in San Diego, Dole took aim at the collective, societal responsibility for children's well-being that had been at the heart of Hillary Clinton's 1996 book *It Takes a Village*. Pointing to a culture steeped in "crime and drugs," he inveighed against government-centered approaches to social problems:

And after the virtual devastation of the American family, the rock upon which this country was founded, we are told that it takes a village, that is collective, and thus the state, to raise a child. The state is now more involved than it ever has been in the raising of children. And children are now more neglected, more abused and more mistreated than they have been in our time. This is not a coincidence. . . . And with all due respect, I am here to tell you it does not take a village to raise a child. It takes a family to raise a child.[30]

In Dole's interpretation of the recent past, the state's usurping responsibility for disciplining children had undermined the authority of the family and damaged children.

Such logic continued into the 2000s. Laying out the case for family values in 2005, Pennsylvania senator Rick Santorum bemoaned that the nation had

wasted decades and countless lives under the direction of the village elders trying to build bureaucracies to aid the poor and marginal in our society, while ignoring the central importance of the traditional family. . . . [T]he worst part of their failure is that their welfare policies fractured families and pulled apart communities, pulverizing the foundation both of individual success and of the common good.[31]

Like Reagan's working group on the family, Santorum read a contempt for the common people into the creation of a state that engaged in illiberal social engineering experiments: having appointed themselves the "village elders," he claimed, liberals "think of society as fundamentally made up of individuals guided by elite and 'expert' organizations like government, not the antiquated, perhaps uneducated, independent family. The village elders want society to be individualistic because a society composed only of individuals responds better to 'expert' command and control."[32]

This kind of political imagining of the ideal state as a confederation of father-led nuclear families faced stubborn demographic and bureaucratic realities in the latter half of the twentieth century. Still, it was consonant with a broader trend toward civic disengagement. As measured in everything from participation in parent-teacher organizations to voter turnout rates, Americans' had become less involved in public life since the 1960s.[33] As a result, private life and relationships with kin had taken on even more importance in an age of privatization. In this context, the Victims' Rights Movement did more than make the needs of grieving families central to the purpose of the death penalty. It also reflected and reinforced the primacy of the family amid a larger retreat from public life.

The movement's achievements reflected the context in which it emerged, one in which appeals to a tribalism of the family trumped appeals to the social interdependence of the people. Take, for instance, one of the biggest achievements of the movement: the introduction of family impact testimony in the penalty phase of capital trials. In a 1991 decision, *Payne v. Tennessee*, the Supreme Court revisited earlier rulings forbidding family members to tell their stories to juries before sentencing.[34] Payne had appealed his sentence claiming that prosecutors had improperly inflamed the jury with evidence of the effect his crime had had on his victim's family. To help a Tennessee jury understand the pain that Pervis Tyrone Payne had caused her family, prosecutors had Mary Zvolanek testify about her little grandson's inability to comprehend the death of his mother and sister: "He cries for his mom. He doesn't seem to understand why she doesn't come home. And he cries for his sister Lacie. He comes to me many times during the week and asks me, Grandmama, do you miss my Lacie[?] And I tell him yes. He says, I'm worried about my Lacie," she testified.[35] Payne's lawyers argued that such testimony prejudiced the jury against him. "I can't think of anything more arbitrary than to allow a defendant's fate to depend on the opinion of the survivor," J. Brooke Lathram, Payne's counsel, argued to the Supreme Court.[36]

The Court disagreed, however, a majority of the justices asserting the state's right to authorize the inclusion of victim impact testimony. Justice Sandra Day O'Connor was taken by a point made in a brief by the victims' rights organization Justice for All. Murder, she agreed, was the "ultimate act of depersonalization." In her own words, she went on to explain why: "It transforms a living person with hopes, dreams, and fears into a corpse, thereby taking away all that is special and unique about the person. The Constitution does not preclude a State from deciding to give some of that back."[37] By providing a punitive forum in which the family members of a victim might publicly share their pain, the state could pay victims in social capital—in public recognition of their loved ones' uniqueness and specialness. The punishment they delivered to offenders, juries could increasingly imagine, was on behalf of a grieving family rather than an abstract public.

Indeed, Justice David Souter's opinion concurring with the Supreme Court's decision in *Payne* offered a glimpse of this vision of society. Victim impact statements were not opportunities for prosecutors to inflame juries, he argued. In a forum dedicated to assessing blameworthiness, they helped juries to understand exactly what the defendant was blamed for doing:

> Just as defendants know that they are not faceless human ciphers, they know that their victims are not valueless fungibles; and just as defendants appreciate the web of relationships and dependencies in which they live, they know that their victims are not human islands, but individuals with parents or children, spouses or friends or dependents. Thus, when a defendant chooses to kill, or to raise the risk of a victim's death, this choice necessarily relates to a whole human being and threatens an association of others, who may be distinctly hurt.[38]

In Souter's words, we see how capital punishment could reflect a social contract shrinking in its scope. The society for whom the state killed was no longer the nation, the state, or the city where the victim lived. It was a small "web of relationships and dependencies." By the early 1990s the death penalty was becoming a punishment meted out not on behalf of the public but on behalf of private parties who were *distinctly* hurt. Death, in other words, became the punishment of a society that saw itself not as a land containing multitudes, but as an archipelago of families.

Toward the end of the twentieth century, I have argued, pro–death penalty rhetoric often sought to root the political authority of the state in the moral authority of the father-led family. In the conservative imagination, capital punishment represented a sublime antidote to a bureaucratic criminal justice system that, like big government in general, had for too long treated ordinary Americans as "faceless ciphers."[39] As we have seen in earlier chapters, though, this cultural reimagining of the death penalty hovered above a starkly different material reality. The administration of capital punishment became more enmeshed in law, more shaped by standards of detached professionalism, than it had ever been. By the 2000s, long appeals processes and frequent reversals of death sentences and convictions meant that fewer and fewer offenders sentenced to death would be executed. The universal adoption of lethal injection as the primary method of execution meant, meanwhile, that an execution would look increasingly like a medical procedure.

These facts raised questions. Did prosaic realities threaten the sublime fantasy? Would the symbolic presence of the family in pro–death penalty discourse, in sentencing hearings, and at executions be sufficient to counteract the myriad other ways the death penalty was becoming a form of big government?

## Leave It to *Dexter*

When it debuted in 2006, *Dexter*, a new television series, seemed to be both a symptom of these questions and an answer to them.[40] In Dexter, its vigilante hero, the show initially reflected a desire for an antistatist death penalty that could deliver emotionally satisfying justice on behalf of aggrieved victims. And yet *Dexter* also embodied a fantasy that a vigilante could still maintain a degree of impartiality and restraint. In what follows I offer a close reading of the show, arguing that it may profitably be read as an allegory for the fantasies and vulnerabilities of a death penalty buttressed ideologically by family values libertarianism.

Three decades after *Dirty Harry* brought the themes of the western to the crime-addled city, Americans met a new kind of fictional vigilante: Dexter Morgan, a thirty-five-year-old forensic scientist in the Miami Police Department who moonlights as a killer. Traditionally, the writers of vigilante stories have kept a necessary distance between the vigilante and the society he protects. The rough men who do civilization's dirty work have been unmarried (Tom Doniphon, Harry Callahan) or have lost their families to violent crime (Paul Kersey, Bruce Wayne). With *Dexter*, however, Americans got a new sort of vigilante, one whose distance from the society he protects shrinks in front of their eyes.

Unlike his vigilante predecessors, Dexter began life as a cultural outsider. Traumatized by violence as a toddler (he watched members of a drug cartel kill his mother with a chainsaw), Dexter was adopted by Harry Morgan, a detective who found him sitting in a pool of his mother's blood. Harry and his wife raised Dexter alongside their biological daughter Debra. As Dexter grew, viewers learned in the show's first episodes, he exhibited signs of psychopathology, seeing hollowness in social norms, feeling no emotional response to most stimuli, and seeking relief from violent urges by killing neighborhood dogs. Recognizing that his son was destined to become a murderer, Harry channeled Dexter's dark urges, teaching him how to kill violent criminals who had escaped punishment through the loopholes of the criminal justice system. Harry is long dead when the series begins chronicling Dexter's life, but he appears frequently as a ghostlike presence Dexter consults to hash out his internal conflicts. In episode after episode, Dexter uses Harry's training and the resources available to him as a forensic scientist in the Miami Police Department to investigate, stalk, and eventually execute killers who have evaded justice. Trained in law enforcement, beholden to a code drummed into him by his father, and committed to killing the most dangerous criminal offenders, Dexter represented a fantasy of the killing state, a "one man capital punishment road show," as one television reporter put it.[41]

The show, which quickly became the Showtime cable television network's biggest hit,[42] justified Dexter's killing by articulating familiar criticisms of the state as dangerously paralyzed by bureaucracy. In almost every episode, audiences learned more about a legal system that let murderers run amok. "Florida prisons kick free 25,000 inmates a year," Dexter explains to the audience in a voiceover. "They don't do that for me, but it sure does feel like it. I search for the ones who think they've beat the system. They're not hard to find "[43] Dexter's killing is the liberating antidote to a general sense of paralysis in a world dangerously mired in complex rules. Indeed, Michael C. Hall, the actor who played Dexter, saw the character's appeal in a cultural desire for agency: "I think we live in a world where we feel a sense that we lack control," he said. Dexter was appealing because, in contrast, "he's taking some decisive control over a small part of his world."[44] For Hall, Dexter provided audiences with a vicarious sense of freedom, a liberating escape from the paralysis that, I have shown, Americans came to feel in a world that increasingly seemed to be governed by market forces, elite expertise, and arcane law.

The show fused its critique of the criminal justice system with the family values libertarianism that, I have argued, lent ideological support to the post-*Gregg* death penalty. As I have shown, in contrast to a criminal justice system that had inherited the moral softness of the welfare state, capital punishment had come to symbolize a reclaiming of the state by populists like Bob Macy or Johnny Holmes who had "heroically dismantle[d] the apparatus of the Leviathan" on behalf of the family.[45] In the show's depiction of fatherhood, *Dexter* took this ideal to its extreme, offering viewers a fantasy in which the sovereignty of the father literally replaced the sovereignty of the liberal welfare state. Yet, having entered the culture at a moment when Americans' concern about false convictions had been piqued, the show also reassured audiences that a jettisoning of the liberal state did not mean the abandonment of a sober-minded impartiality.

The father was the key figure in this balancing act. Dexter's father Harry, audiences learned, had transformed him from a psychopath destined to kill into an antihero who combined the gall of the psychopath with the discipline of the soldier. Harry gave Dexter a three-point code to follow in determining when and how to kill. While he may kill to satisfy his sadistic impulses, he must kill only when doing so will save lives. ("As a cop, I only fire my weapon to save a life," Harry instructs a young Dexter in a flashback. "That's a code I live by. Killing must serve a purpose. Otherwise it's just plain murder. You understand?")[46] Dexter must not use his violence impulsively or to settle personal scores. ("Harry's first rule was don't get emotionally involved," Dexter informs us.)[47] Finally, Dexter must ensure that those he kills are beyond all doubt guilty of murder. ("My father taught me one thing above all others: to be sure," Dexter tells us as he confirms the guilt of a prospective victim.)[48]

The show's fantasy of a killing state was thus embodied in its protagonist, a vigilante who had inherited from his father a code that permitted him to bypass the law's unsatisfying anonymity and inaccessibility while retaining its fairness and sobriety. By conferring on the son a "mythically simple system of rules,"[49] Harry ensures that Dexter's punishment is free from a corrosive self-interest. Dexter's pathological obsession with neatness and ritual, meanwhile, disciplines him in a different way. His method of killing loosely resembles the contemporary protocols states use to kill condemned inmates via lethal injection. He initially incapacitates his victims with a syringe filled with tranquilizer. While they are unconscious, Dexter disrobes them, lays them supine on a long table, and wraps them tightly in plastic wrap. When they awaken, he ritualistically cuts their cheeks, puts drops of their blood on slides, confronts them with photographs of their murder victims, then makes sure they know why they are about to be killed. Once he gives them a chance to speak, Dexter stabs them through the wrap. The ritualistic nature of the killings and the pseudo–due process Dexter offers his victims by giving them the right to speak consecrate the violence that follows, transforming it into an unofficial execution.

Dexter's method of execution may be more violent than lethal injection, but like contemporary execution protocols it aims to be as efficient and restrained as possible. The plastic wrap contains the mess of the killing, making cleanup swift. Dexter's taking of blood specimens from his victims, moreover, adds a veneer of the scientific to his executions, a reflection of the way a technocratic ethos worked to make the death penalty seem like an act of incapacitation. Dexter even puts his own spin on the modern killing state's zealous documentation of executions. Just as the state of Texas maintains a website listing its executed offenders in chronological order, Dexter maintains his slide collection, a macabre filing cabinet of sorts.

In a world where the frontier freedom of retributive pro–death penalty rhetoric had been severely undermined by a stultifying legal and technocratic killing state, *Dexter* offered a satisfying alternative: a world where order and restraint did not have to come at the expense of punitive satisfaction. With Dexter meting out justice, executions could be swift, righteous, and personalized without being error-prone and barbaric. Zealous yet self-disciplined, violent yet self-restrained, Dexter embodied the killing state many Americans wished they had.

The show also offered a world where vigilante-style executions could also be scrubbed clean of their racist past. Set in multiracial, multicultural Miami, the show presented cultural heterogeneity as a good, featuring a hero who easily navigates a pluralistic, if heteronormative, world. In contrast to crime vigilante films of the 1970s, which often targeted street thugs and cultural deviants, Dexter's victims are often hypocritical beneficiaries of the dominant culture rather than threats to it. The show often depicts its hero "punishing up," executing white men in positions with cultural, political, and economic capital who abuse the vulnerable.[50] With a bizarre equal opportunity slayer at the helm, *Dexter* worked to weaken the connection between meting out lethal punishment and maintaining hierarchies.

Despite—and sometimes through—its pluralist veneer, *Dexter* rehearsed, again and again, a conservative critique of a culture overrun by a selfish hedonism that frequently devolved into predatory violence. It embedded the critique into plots that contrasted two kinds of freedom: the ennobling freedom that Dexter gets from submission to his father's prescriptive authority, and the hedonistic freedom of those who kill without a code. In each of the first three seasons of the show, he encounters a tempter or temptress who temporarily leads him to turn away from his father's code and embrace an understanding of freedom as license.

In the first season, for instance, the tempter is another serial killer wreaking havoc in Miami, who turns out to be his long-lost biological brother, Brian. After the trauma of witnessing his mother's murder, Dexter's mind had blocked out memories of Brian. His brother's carnage has been, Dexter learns, a carefully orchestrated ruse designed to pique Dexter's attention, teach him about his forgotten past, and finally invite him to take up a life of violence together. Unlike Dexter's killings, which end with him stealthily tossing his victims' bodies over the side of his boat in the dark of night, Brian's violent acts reflect excess and ego. After he kills Miami prostitutes, Brian drains them of their blood, cuts their remains into precisely equal segments, and freeze-dries them before leaving them on display in public areas.

The contrast between Brian and Dexter reveals who Dexter might have become had he not ended up in a traditional family. While Dexter was being raised in a family, we learn, Brian was dumped in a state hospital. "He was institutionalized for anti-social personality disorder. At 21, they said he was cured. They released him," Dexter's learns.[51] When brother and brother do finally discuss their past, Brian explains that he was raised by "doctors, therapists, group leaders," adding, sarcastically, "what a family they were."[52] In Brian's fate we can appreciate Dexter's good fortune: unconditional love, coupled with fatherly discipline, something the state could never have provided, civilized Dexter's violent instincts.

The state's inability to control crime, the show suggests, is a symptom of the declining importance of fathers and the inability of the state to act as a father. Indeed, the state's ineffectiveness comes from its forced reliance on psychological expertise rather than fatherly wisdom to handle social problems.[53] Harry did more than train Dexter to channel his pathological instincts. He worked hard, when Dexter was young, to keep mainstream state psychiatrists from discovering that his son was a psychopath. Various storylines in the show justified in hindsight Harry's distrust of the therapeutic. Multiple villains on the show, not only Brian, are the products of state mental hospitals, their psychotic violence linked to the government's disastrous efforts to treat them. However, the show also indicts more common and informal therapeutic forms of behavior management like counseling and self-help programs, suggesting that they create vulnerability, require copious amounts of self-disclosure, and revolve around a dangerously narcissistic search for an authentic self. In one season a gang of wealthy white torturer-rapists is inspired (and, as we find out, actively led) by a nationally known self-help guru who urges followers to "TAKE IT!"—a mantra that inspires them to seize what they want in life without self-doubt.[54] When professional or amateur psychologists are not callously detached from their patients or incompetent, they are encouraging a kind of unsafe loosening of the inhibitions that make civilization possible.

When he finally meets Brian, we see that Dexter is tempted to cast off those inhibitions and let loose an unrestrained, violent self in order to achieve total freedom. ("A killer. Without reason or regret. You're free," Dexter says enviously of Brian.)[55] In the end, however, an unexpected and authentic sense of obligation to Debra, his adopted sister, keeps Dexter from giving in to the temptation to abandon his rule-bound life for one of unchecked violence. In the finale of the show's first season, Dexter kills his brother to incapacitate the threat he poses to Debra. His father's influence, we see, has done more than channel his sadistic urges; it has transformed him morally—something that Dexter, his father, and the audience had previously thought impossible.

In the seasons that follow, the show develops the fantasy of Dexter as a one-man killing state grounded in family values by making him more domestic and heteronormative. When we first meet Dexter he is dating Rita, a sitcom-like mom type whom he uses as a cover. Like all social arrangements, to Dexter their relationship initially seems awkward. As the series progresses, however, he finds that in pretending to be normal, the domestic sphere of the nuclear family becomes a genuine source of empowerment: "I've come to appreciate the comfortable moments with Rita, the easy, quiet moments. This . . . might be better," he tells us at one point.[56] In the next season he remarks, summoning nostalgia for the postwar domestic ideal, "Right now, all I can think about is the smell of Rita's kitchen, the breathy cadence of her sleepy children, the warmth of her flesh."[57] He gradually becomes a father to Rita's preteen children, teaching them games, attending their school functions, disciplining them when they step out of line. The third season of the show ends with Dexter's marriage to Rita and her becoming pregnant with his child. As he takes his vow ("I promise to be the very best husband and father I can be"),[58] Dexter becomes, in his words, "a married man. . . . Drawn to the safety of belonging or being part of something bigger than me."[59] Harry's tutelage has not simply channeled Dexter's violence, it has transformed Dexter into a wise father. Leadership of a nuclear family becomes a task

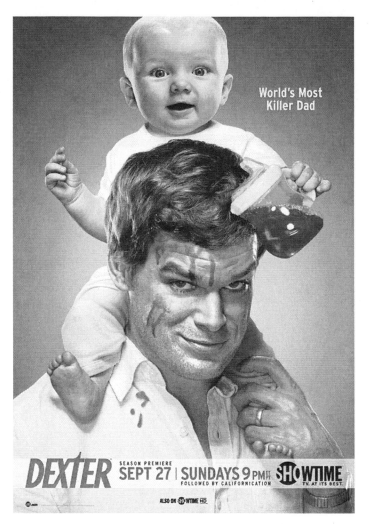

FIGURE 9. *Dexter* season four poster (2009). Visual double entendres like this one reflected the show's initial efforts to make lethal punishment compatible with the traditional family values that are at the heart of social conservatism.

that organically reinforces the artificial nature of the code Harry prescribed in order to regulate Dexter's violence. Now that he is able to experience intimacy in its most traditional forms, the show suggests he may no longer fit the profile of the psychopath. "Somewhere along the line the fake life we created as a cover for me to kill became real. It's not fake to me anymore," he says in an imagined conversation with his father.[60]

## Unraveling the Fantasy

Analyzing the ideology underlying pro–death penalty politics in the post-*Gregg* era and noting their expression in the television show *Dexter*, I have argued that family values libertarianism shaped the meaning of capital punishment in contemporary America. For many, capital punishment came to express the will of the aggrieved family on whose behalf the state was acting.

That image became increasingly difficult to sustain. *Dexter* premiered in a world where the death penalty had become stymied by appellate processes that stretched on for one and sometimes two decades and frequently resulted in reversals and retrials. Those few condemned inmates who did die at the hands of the state were put to permanent sleep on hospital gurneys rather than electrocuted or gassed. The show offered Americans a fantasy of the death penalty in which justice could be delivered with a speed, moral clarity, and zeal that legal execution lacked, all the while retaining the impartiality and orderliness that made law's violence distinctive.

That all changed in the show's concluding seasons, as Dexter tries to be both a father and a righteous killer. The hero's burgeoning humanity gets in the way of his ability to uphold the code he has inherited from his father. Dexter the father, the show suggests, cannot transcend his own parochial instincts the way Dexter the reined-in psychopath could. By the end of the series, Dexter's violence pollutes rather than purifies his city, his family, and his own self-image. The show ended by dismantling the fantasy it had initially stoked. Whereas the first three seasons cultivated a desire for a lethal punishment that was both fair and personalized, rule-bound and pathos-generating, the show's final three seasons were devoted to showing just how incompatible these values could be.

The unraveling begins with the arrival of Dexter's biological son, Harrison. The show offers comic relief as Dexter tries to maintain his commitment to his family while still satisfying his violent urges. "I'm killing for two now," he says wryly as he tries to work the occasional kill into a schedule dominated by work and family.[61] The show goes to great lengths, however, to show how psychologically, and not just logistically, difficult it is to be both a father and a killer. Dexter's emotional entanglements with his family members interfere with his ability to punish justly. He is overwhelmed with protective fatherly instincts that block his ability to evaluate situations clearly. Emotionally involved in the killing he is doing, he becomes error-prone. Dexter's "guilty without a doubt" record is broken when he kills a man later exonerated by DNA evidence.

Through a series of murderous interactions with foils—killers who have destroyed their own families in the pursuit of their dark desires—Dexter unsuccessfully attempts to reconcile his life as a killer with his life as a husband and father. That pattern culminates in the game of cat and mouse he plays over the course of a season with Arthur Mitchell, a serial killer known as "Trinity" (memorably played by John Lithgow). Mitchell initially seems like a model father: by day he is a teacher with a wife and well-behaved children. When he is not leading community service trips as a Christian deacon, though, he goes on killing jags. As Dexter investigates him, he learns that Mitchell's outward appearance of wholesomeness is a lie: he terrorizes his current family, beating his wife and son and chaining his daughter in her bedroom. Dexter wrestles with the possibility that he is as unfit for family life as Mitchell, but he quickly rejects the comparison: "He's destroyed everyone in that family. . . . I'm nothing like him! My family is nothing like that." Rita, he says, is "much more" than cover.[62] When Dexter ultimately kills Mitchell, he makes the punishment more about asserting his difference from his target than about doing justice on behalf of Mitchell's victims. "I have a family," he says before the kill. "I'm good for them."[63]

The season ends not on this moment of triumph, however, but in family disaster. Dexter comes home to find his wife Rita murdered in the bathtub and his infant son sitting in a pool of her blood. Mitchell, we learn, had made Rita his last victim earlier that day, just before Dexter apprehended him. The irony—and this is an irony that appears again in the seasons that follow—is that Rita would have lived had Dexter permitted the police department to apprehend Mitchell. The police were closing in on him, but Dexter pushed them off his trail so he could do the deed himself and exorcise his own demons. "I have to be the one to kill him," he has said earlier in a voice-over. "I have to know he's gone. For my family."[64] Little does he know how impaired his judgment has become by his self-image as a family man.

The show shifts, in the second half of the series, to charting Dexter's efforts to pick up the pieces following Rita's murder. While he continues to dispatch depraved criminals who have evaded justice, Dexter comes to see the trappings of his lethal work—the slides of blood, the antiseptic plastic wrap—as disturbing. His ritualistic executions of other killers become rare in the show's last few years. At one point in the show's last season, he throws away his trophy case of blood slides, renouncing his dark passenger. As his psychopathic violence wanes, a new, more human violence takes its place. Dexter begins killing those whose "crimes" are nonviolent or personally offensive, like a man who callously disparages Rita's memory or the long-lost father of his new girlfriend, who shows up in her life and starts to extort money from her. While this new kind of violence is initially celebrated as evidence of Dexter's burgeoning humanity, it is ultimately part of his unraveling, his gradual inability to channel his lethal instincts for the greater good.

Dexter's work starts to pollute his son, Harrison, and Debra—the very people he wants to protect. Harrison's own nature is a source of anxiety. As Dexter wrestles with his own capacity for evil, he imagines his influence on his son. Like Dexter, Harrison was exposed to his mother's violent death. As the father and son dress up as lions for the Noah's Ark pageant at Harrison's preschool, Dexter wonders whether there is room in the world for predators like himself and, potentially, his son—whether, as he puts it, "that boat has a place for all the animals, not just the sheep and the zebras, but the lions too."[65] However, when Harrison's stuffed animal—a lamb, no less—is smeared with blood, a casualty of one of Dexter's exploits, the show retreats from its functionalist fantasy of violence. Lions, like Dexter, soil innocence; they do not protect it. As Dexter throws away the stained stuffed animal and lies to his son about its disappearance, he realizes the lion cannot lie down with the lamb.

Vigilante violence similarly spoils Debra. At the beginning of the series, Debra is a by-the-book police officer. In the series' final years, though, that commitment erodes as she develops a romantic attraction to Dexter, an attraction drawn out of her by—who else?—a psychiatrist. Her desire to know her brother in a new way, a symptom of an illicit, unconscious attraction to his darkness, culminates in her decision to confess her love to him. That plan, however, is interrupted—or consummated, one might argue—when she walks in on him during one of his killings. Finding him psychologically naked, knife in hand, she recoils in disgust; but she nonetheless decides to protect him, putting family loyalty to her brother ahead of her professional loyalty to the law. That decision has psychic costs. In moving from unconscious attraction to Dexter to full-blown awareness of his dark passenger, Debra becomes a captive to it. In a perversion of family loyalty, she murders Maria LaGuerta, the Miami chief of police who discovers Dexter's secret—an

act that is psychologically devastating. "Whoever Deb was before killing LaGuerta—that person is dead," Dexter ruminates.[66] What takes her
place is, we see, a shell of her former self: she quits the police force, spi-
rals into drug and alcohol addiction, and, working as a private investiga-
tor, goes so far as to kill a man when he tries to obstruct her investigation.

Polluted by her knowledge of Dexter, Debra dies in the show's very
last episode. Like Rita, she ends up a victim of Dexter's failure to kill his
prey in time because of family obligations.[67] As a hurricane forms off the
Miami coast, Dexter wraps his sister in a white shroud and takes her out
into the ocean, where he inters her, as he has interred his other victims.
As the show visually suggests in the image of Dexter unloading his sister's body into the ocean, she has become his final victim, her death the
ultimate sign that Dexter's violence is degenerative and his desire to reconcile the roles of father and vigilante a lost cause. If the show first announced Dexter's journey to humanity in his decision to save his sister
at the climactic end of the first season, it signals his exile from it with her
burial at sea. "I used to think I was special . . . a special kind of killer,"
he tells viewers in a voice-over. Now, he has come to realize that he is
not. "I'm just a creep motherfucker."[68] In fact, the show's subplots in its
final season gradually push Dexter toward this conclusion. In one of the
final episodes, as he prepares to kill one of his last victims, a cannibal, he
identifies with the man. "You're disgusting. . . . There was a time when
I couldn't imagine anyone being what you are. . . . But now I realize I'm
just like you. I consume everyone I love," he says.[69] Whereas in earlier
seasons Dexter had killed serial killers in a moment of frenzied disiden-
tification, a moment of saying "I am not like you," this kill, viewers are
asked to consider, is an act of illusion-shattering self-hate.

Though Dexter dies spiritually, he survives physically. In the series finale, Dexter leaves his son with his girlfriend and stages his own death.
In the last scene in the series we see him as a lumberjack, living alone
in a run-down house in the Pacific Northwest. The cinematography of
the final scene contrasts remarkably with the show's normal surrealist
style. Gone are the bright hues and salsa music of Miami. In its place is
an overcast grayness shot through with the harsh, monotonous sound of
logs being loaded onto trucks. The spell of possibility once created by
the show's cinematography and soundtrack is gone, replaced by images
and sounds of a dismal, unforgiving reality. Gone too are Dexter's voice-
overs, which enabled our sympathetic understanding of his choices. In
the last shot of the series, the camera seems to want to break his silence.

It slowly zooms in on him as he sits alone at a barren table looking out the window of a dreary bachelor's apartment. He turns toward the camera and gazes at it, as if about to speak. Then his eyes, filled with vulnerability, close momentarily, only to reopen in a glare, defiantly shutting out his audience—and his humanity.

Having fantasized about transferring a monopoly on violence from the bureaucratic state to the traditional father, *Dexter* ultimately declares that experiment a failure. Civilization is not, as the show's first seasons suggested, regenerated through paternalistic vigilantism; instead, the vigilante's own narrow interests, born out of his position as a father, cloud his judgment, making his violence—and his calculations about how to deploy it—destructive.[70] The moral clarity that lethal punishment seeks to express fails to appear. The father's violence is in the end too messy, too parochial, too mired in private survival to be relevant to the public good. Dexter's exile ultimately amounts to an admission by the show's writers that punishment can generate sublime feelings of awe only when there is an emotional separation between the punisher and the beneficiaries of punishment (or, as one viewer put it on an online discussion board, the creators "messed up giving Dex a family so now they cleaned the slate")[71]

Writing in 1985, just as execution chambers across the nation were sputtering back to life, William Raspberry adopted this kind of perspective in a *Washington Post* column. He warned that the death penalty could not ultimately separate lawful and lawless violence:

> The people who act out our darker impulses seldom turn out, on closer examination, to be people to admire. There aren't any good-guy lynch mobs and vigilantes in real life. And what is true of armed vigilantes acting outside the law may also be true of societies who, in moments of fear, frustration, and outrage, turn to official vigilantism. It is, I suspect, why we keep vacillating, as individuals and as a society, on the question of capital punishment. We let savage behavior turn us into savages, but only for a time. After a while, we reflect on what we have become, and we are repulsed by the reflection. And finally we ask the legislatures and the courts to stop us before we kill again.[72]

We might read the show's ending as an articulation of the same thought. Dexter's recognition that there are not any "good-guy vigilantes" represents a broader indictment of lethal punishment's capacity to wed ideals to action.

Negative reaction to the show's ending was revealing. To many of his fans, Dexter's self-imposed isolation and the show's contention that vigilante violence pollutes were profoundly disillusioning. We might read some of the backlash against the show's ending as a refusal to let the illusion die. Journalists reported—unscientifically, of course—widespread disappointment with the ending. A few on the network's online bulletin board wanted Dexter to leave violence behind altogether. They were disappointed that he did not flee with his son and girlfriend to a new, violence-free life in another part of the world. But others noted with dismay that the creators of the show had, toward its end, "turned the series int[o] a cautionary tale. The politically correct Showtime elites had to make sure that the audience knew that it was wrong to kill people even if they were sadistic serial killers. . . . They just didn't have the guts to do something daring and bold because it might offend the sensibility of certain people."[73] The television critic for the Associated Press agreed, complaining that the show had "surrendered without cause." Noting Dexter's self-loathing in the series' final episode, he wrote, "Dexter you were better than that! And until its disappointing, desperate conclusion, so was the show."[74] Another viewer respected the show's final insistence on an absolute separation between humanity and lethal violence but noted mournfully, "I think we all kinda wanted Dexter to have a happy ending in which he gets to have his humanity and continue to be a vigilante."[75]

The stubborn persistence of that desire for a perfect death penalty merging public and private justice—lethal punishment that is stateless, yet statelike—might also be seen in the timing of changes to the laws on self-defense in many states. As the death penalty stalled in the early 2000s, plagued by delays and the ever-widening gap between sentencing and execution, states across the country began expanding the rights of citizens to kill one another legally. In 2005, the year before *Dexter* debuted, the Florida legislature passed a "stand your ground" law, broadening where and how its citizens could use force to confront threats against them. These laws allowed those who felt threatened to attack their aggressors in places other than their homes—in the shops they owned, for instance, or in their cars. By 2009, twenty-two states had joined Florida in passing expanded self-defense statutes.[76] As critics on the left and right questioned the government's ability to put people to death righteously or speedily, states began reinforcing legal homicide in other ways.

Dexter and the stand your ground legislation that came of age alongside him have shown that a desire for righteous, stateless violence persists even as the death penalty no longer seems to satisfy it. It persists, moreover, in a punitivism that is politically promiscuous. In July 2013, shortly after a jury in Florida acquitted George Zimmerman of the murder of seventeen-year-old Trayvon Martin under that state's Stand Your Ground statute, a doctored image began circulating on the Internet. Dexter Morgan, America's favorite serial killer, stands in front of a Miami cityscape holding open a tabloid newspaper. On the front page we see Zimmerman's smiling, relieved face under the headline "ZIMMERMAN NOT GUILTY!" Dexter's eyes are looking off to the right, his lips on the verge of a smile. He will do, the photo suggests, what the law could not and deliver justice for Trayvon (see fig. 10).

FIGURE 10. George Zimmerman's acquittal in 2013 of the murder of Trayvon Martin spawned an Internet meme that suggests how far Dexter's violence was whitewashed.

The image was deeply ironic. Through Dexter, the meme's creators fantasized a vigilante killing as a satisfying and appropriate punishment for an act of racist vigilante killing. Yet based on the discussion it provoked on Twitter, the image was not received as satire.[77] To express their frustration with Zimmerman's acquittal, some who saw Trayvon Martin's death as a reprehensible act of murder turned for solace to the very vigilantism they decried. At precisely the moment when it might have been criticized, the desire for lethal punishment was reinforced. The image suggests what *Dexter* had fantasized about for the past eight years: that lethal punishment could be cleansed from its racial past and present and deployed anew in ways that purify rather than pollute. *Dexter*'s writers may have relegated their antihero to the margins of civilization in the series' conclusion, but the punitive ideal he initially stood for still lingered troublingly close to home.

# Disabling Freedom

[O]ne of them passed the knife over K. to the other, who then passed it back over K. to the first. K. now knew it would be his duty to take the knife as it passed from hand to hand above him and thrust it into himself. But he did not do it, instead he twisted his neck, which was still free, and looked around. He was not able to show his full worth, was not able to take all the work from the official bodies, he lacked the rest of the strength he needed and this final shortcoming was the fault of whoever had denied it to him.[1] — Franz Kafka, *The Trial* (1925)

If I'd known that redemption was the goal, this case would've been a lot easier and I wouldn't have suffered as much  I thought we were trying to save a man's life.[2] — Millard Farmer, defense attorney for Patrick Sonnier, responding to the depiction of Sonnier in *Dead Man Walking* (1995)

Up "until very recently," Charles J. Ogletree and Austin Sarat wrote in 2009, "no one could have predicted that today we would be as far as we are on the road to abolition."[3] When they wrote those words, New Mexico, New York, and New Jersey had abolished the death penalty. Since then, Connecticut, Illinois, Maryland, and Nebraska have also abandoned capital punishment.[4] The number of annual executions and death sentences has continued to decline, and Americans' support for capital punishment, as measured by public opinion polls, has sunk to levels not seen since 1972. In October 2014, 63 percent of Americans indicated support for the death penalty in cases of first-degree murder, down from an all-time high of 80 percent in 1994.[5]

Experts have pointed to many factors to explain the death penalty's slow decline. After September 11, 2001, falling crime rates and rising fear of terrorism made external enemies a more pressing concern than domestic criminals.[6] The 2008 financial crisis highlighted the enormous cost of the death penalty as cash-strapped states began looking for ways to reduce their financial liabilities.[7] Life without parole provided juries with an alternative that feels just as safe and punitive; the 2005 adoption in Texas of a life without parole option for juries in capital cases contributed to the notable decline of death sentences in the state that accounts for nearly 40 percent of all American executions.[8] Drug supply problems have interfered with states' ability to carry out executions. Finally, and to some scholars most significantly, concerns about executing innocent people after years of spectacular and not-so-spectacular exonerations may have finally mobilized distrust of the state in a new direction: against the death penalty. And while the challenges these developments pose to the survival of the death penalty may be surmountable,[9] temporary,[10] geographically limited,[11] illusory,[12] or ideologically problematic,[13] by 2016 they have made abolition seem more possible than it has seemed in decades.

Despite all these recent developments, we can find the most potent source of the death penalty's recent decline by returning to its period of rebirth in the 1970s. Across the country, juries had sentenced over a thousand inmates to death since state legislatures revamped their sentencing statutes in the aftermath of the Supreme Court's *Furman* decision. In 1976, the Court's *Gregg* decision allowed states to resume where they had left off. When John Spenkelink became the first inmate to be executed involuntarily in 1979, some thought a dam had broken. "As many as 40 persons could be institutionally killed in 1979—which may well be remembered as the Year of the Execution," the *New York Times* informed its readers in a decidedly sober tone. By the 1980s, the paper predicted, the number of annual executions might come to "equal that reached in the heyday of capital punishment in the post-lynching era: 199 in 1935."[14]

None of this came to pass, however. There was only one other execution in the nation in 1979. Fully four years after the state of Florida executed Spenkelink, it had not succeeded in executing anyone else. "Florida's construction and application of the death penalty are a monumental bust," *New York Times Magazine* writer Robert Sherrill wrote in 1983. Governor Bob Graham had signed fifty-four death warrants in five years, yet only Spenkelink had been executed. On death row, the magazine reported, "veterans of six or seven years are commonplace." A dozen inmates had been there for nine years, it added. "It has left both sides embittered and infuriated. . . . Those who want to get on with the job of killing murderers feel cheated." No one was more frustrated than Florida attorney general Jim Smith, who, at that early date in the modern history of the American death penalty, was already declaring that the capital punishment seemed to exist "only on paper."[15]

This was but the first of many acknowledgments supporters of the death penalty would make of the gap between the anti–big government ethos that underlay support for the death penalty and the reality that it had become a big government program. For years, cultural constructions of executable subjects and the killing state have attempted to maintain the death penalty's sublime possibilities in spite of its increasingly prosaic form. From dying declarations on Texas's death row website, to prosecutorial rhetoric in Houston courtrooms, to the redemption narratives of films like *The Green Mile*, the cultural life of capital punishment has continuously worked to deinstitutionalize the act of sentencing people to death and executing them. In these practices, speeches, and stories, imposing a death sentence was a spiritually regenerating and morally meaningful act. Promulgated by film, embedded in sentencing protocols, maintained by anachronistic execution traditions, a vision of those punished as morally autonomous—and thus worthy of condemnation—has constantly tried to veil the absorption of the death penalty into a more machinelike, antihumanistic approach to governance.

Over time, however, retributive rhetoric has lost its ability to compensate for technocratic reality. Disillusion with the death penalty, the result of this failure, is perhaps the most crucial and irreversible part of this story of decline. Crime trends reverse themselves. Economics improve. States can change their execution methods, as they have for over a century, with the promise that innovations in killing technologies will make lethal punishment fail-safe.[16] The racial and class background of death row inmates limits the effect innocence has had on diminishing support for the death penalty.[17] But while conservatives have symbolically battered bureaucracy and constitutional law over the past forty years, those elements of modern governance are here to stay, and they will continue to shape the death penalty in ways that will undermine its retributive character. Ultimately, recognition that capital punishment cannot be made to live up to its retributive promise, not some moral awakening, will produce a majoritarian consensus against the death penalty. It will end not in fire but in ice, when those unmoved by exonerations or botched executions or evidence of race disparities give up on it.

Time, uncertainty, and technology have led us to this point. In the 1950s, before the organized effort to abolish the death penalty judicially got fully under way, the average time between sentencing and execution was two years. Rather than resolving the constitutionality of the death penalty, *Gregg* spawned a massive federal jurisprudence that, over time, lengthened appeals times across the nation, from six and a half years in 1984 to fifteen and a half years in 2016, the most recent year for which data are available.[18] The delays, however, have not always been as gratuitous as conservatives have claimed. High error rates in capital trials, often the result of states' unwillingness to provide adequate counsel for indigent capital defendants, are often to blame rather than the manipulation of loopholes and technicalities.[19] Whatever the source, delays project a kind of ambivalence about harsh punishment that the death penalty was supposed to cure, a problem only exacerbated because the vast majority of those sentenced to death since the 1970s have not been executed. The numbers are staggering. From 1973 to 2012, judges sentenced 8,374 people to death. During the appellate process, often years after judges originally imposed the death sentence, state and federal appellate courts overturned the conviction or sentence of 3,118 of those sentenced to death and commuted the sentences of 392. This meant new proceedings in front of new juries. When prosecutors succeeded in winning a new death sentence, the cycle would begin all over again. Testifying in front of the Senate Judiciary Committee in 1993, Miriam Shehane told Senators that

> the frustrations the families go through when they think justice will soon prevail, only to receive jolt after jolt as they learn the case is going back for trial due to technicalities, is enough to cause fatal health problems. In reality, this happens quite frequently. The strategy seems to be aimed at wearing you down by endless reversals. Unfortunately, this causes the victim's family to plead with the district attorney to accept a lesser sentence because they are mentally and physically unable to cope with opening fresh wounds all over again by the detailed facts of their loved one's heinous murder.[20]

Even Texas, the nation's capital punishment capital, cannot deliver on the promise of the death penalty. In the 2011 Republican presidential primary debates, Texas governor Rick Perry celebrated his state's reputation, proudly telling the cheering audience, "If you come into our state and you kill one of our children, you kill a police officer, you're involved with another crime and you kill one of our citizens, you will face the ultimate justice."[21] The reality, however, is that even an inmate sentenced to death in Texas has a good chance of never facing more than penultimate justice. At the end of 2011, over half of those sentenced to death in Texas since 1973 had not been executed; judges had overturned or commuted their sentences, they had died while awaiting execution, or they were still on death row, waiting.[22] A death sentence there, like anywhere else, launches a tortuous, decade-long series of appeals—the rule of law authorizing (and often deauthorizing, and then sometimes reauthorizing) death at a slow speed. Indeed, comparing the experiences of Minnesota homicide survivors in cases where the offenders had received sentences of life without parole to Texas survivors in cases where offenders had received death sentences, Marilyn Peterson Armour and Mark S. Umbreit found that Miriam Shehane's testimony did indeed represent a common experience for death penalty survivors. While proponents of the death penalty touted it as "the ultimate justice," grieving Minnesotans actually fared better than their Texan counterparts:

> In Minnesota, survivors had greater control, likely because the appeals process was successful, predictable, and completed within two years after conviction; whereas . . . the appeals process in Texas was drawn out, elusive, delayed, and unpredictable. It generated layers of injustice, powerlessness, and in some instances, despair. Although the grief and depth of sorrow remained high for Minnesotans, no longer having to deal with the murderer, his outcome, or the criminal justice system allowed survivors' control and energy to be put into the present to be used for personal healing.[23]

By deferring closure for well over a decade, the death penalty in Texas and elsewhere has worsened the well-being of the grieving.

Delay has also diminished the capacity for executions to be moments of moral reckoning. After the harsh words of condemnation at a sentencing hearing, the condemned in the modern period of the American death penalty have entered large, bureaucratically superintended warehouses.[24] Consigned to at least a decade on death row, they often are forgotten by all except those their crimes had directly affected. These changes may have had consequences for the public's will to punish. Noting that the decline of the death penalty has been part of a broader, across-the-board trend toward restraint in the use of punishment, Patricia Ewick has suggested that a diminution in our will to punish is not "merely or primarily because of [the punitive state's] cost, its demonstrable failure, or because we increasingly pity inmates. Instead, the cause . . . may be that the punishing state is so effective at mortifying prisoners that it has lost its capacity to degrade them."[25] Punishment is meaningful, Ewick explains, only when it can "paradoxically sustain the punished as sacred, as human, even while it seeks to degrade them. To fail in this regard, that is to profane that which is not sacred, is a semiotically futile gesture. The futility of the act transforms acts of alleged punishment into little more than the infliction of pain."[26]

For those unlucky few death row inmates who do make it to the execution chamber (and for the even fewer whose executions are covered by the media), "mortification," the institutional transformation of persons into docile objects, is not easily undone. Technology in the execution chamber has stripped the execution ritual of its punitive qualities, turning it, bizarrely, into something resembling a medical procedure. Journalistic coverage of executions in the era of lethal injection has had an undercurrent of desperation as writers struggle to find the tiniest details—a twitch, for instance—to make the infliction of death tangible to readers.

Changes in execution protocols, moreover, continue to diminish opportunities for the state to acknowledge the humanity of the condemned when it comes time to carry out the sentence. In 2011, after Lawrence Russell Brewer requested a feast and then did not touch the food that was brought to him, Texas ceased its practice of offering the condemned a meal of their choosing on the day of their deaths. In response to a letter from an outraged senator who threatened legislation that would abolish the specially prepared final meal, the Department of Criminal Justice announced that henceforth inmates would receive the standard fare served to all the other inmates on their execution day.[27] In ending the last meal tradition, the department took away a humanizing element of the ritual of punishment, one of the few remaining vestiges of the past that has worked to keep inmates from appearing "mortified" by execution protocols that treat them as if they were animals rather than humans. The end of last meal requests in Texas became the latest step in a two-century transformation of executable subjects from souls being punished to "bare life" being incapacitated.[28] Ten years earlier, reporters and members of the public had so frequently wanted to know the last meal requests of inmates that the department had taken to posting them on its website. Now the public desire for this bit of humanizing information would go unsatisfied.

Will an intractable appellate process and the technocratic transformation of executions into nonevents eventually be the death penalty's undoing? Lacking any dramatic changes on other fronts, will the passage of time gradually disillusion more and more supporters of capital punishment until it loses majority support? Some say yes. Bernard E. Harcourt argues that delays will eventually be fatal to the death penalty.[29] Opposition to the death penalty—or at least erosion of political support for it—will occur when Americans begin to realize that the control and clarity that executions promise are permanently located on an ever-receding horizon.[30]

Such optimism, however, may not be fully warranted. The conditions that make it increasingly difficult for the death penalty to generate retributive meaning have existed for years, and it is unclear whether they can, on their own, erode support for capital punishment. As "penal spectators," most Americans exist in a "shadow world of moral judgment and penal logics . . . beyond prison walls," a place where popular imaginings rather than harsh realities form the basis of knowledge about the death penalty.[31] To wear down political support for capital punishment, abolitionists must demonstrate to the occupants of that shadow world that, trapped permanently in an iron cage of rationality, the death penalty can only be an emotionally unsatisfying act of neutralization. It is not enough for material reality to persist at odds with cultural imaginings. Those cultural imaginings must change.

That work will not be easy. It is challenging to prove, let alone popularize, a negative—to demonstrate the absence of punitive meaning. Translating the dehumanizing toll that years of confinement on death row take on inmates requires documenting changes in them, capturing their gradual adaptation to indignities, charting their loss of agency. These are profoundly difficult, counterhegemonic tasks in a culture dominated by narratives of growth, evolution, and individual triumph over structure.[32] As we have seen, those seeking to argue that a punishment as a whole has become meaningless are up against decades of rhetoric, generated by opponents as well as supporters of the death penalty, who have suggested just the opposite. Even ostensibly neutral renderings of capital punishment deliver dominant meanings. Reporters covering executions inevitably vivify the condemned and their victims, including, as much as the event allows, details like the inmates' last words, the facial expressions of the witnesses watching the execution, or manifestations of grief or relief. All of these details allow reporters to impute a punitive essence to events that have become ever more sterile.

Abolitionists, moreover, have sought to humanize capital defendants. If juries and the public can see a capital defendant as someone's son instead of as a monster, this thinking goes, support for the death sentence will decline. The courtroom oratory of skillful defense attorneys can indeed have a powerful effect on those judges and juries who hold defendants' lives in their hands. But it likely does little to affect the opinions of those who do not hold the fate of capital defendants in their hands, casual supporters of the death penalty who continue to support the sanction despite years of widely publicized death row exonerations and botched executions. Humanizing portraits of death row inmates may even perversely work to preserve the retributive quality of executions that makes the death penalty appealing. From the displays of death row inmates' artwork by nonprofit abolitionist organizations to cinematic renderings of dynamic characters like Matthew Poncelet, to oversized books that tell the stories of the condemned through photographs, abolitionists' attempts to humanize the condemned may have unintended consequences. As Ewick suggests, "It is precisely [the] denial of the humanity of prisoners by the punishing state that may ultimately be the source of its demise. By destroying the very thing it requires—a sacred subject capable of being profaned—ceaseless, degrading and totalizing punishment inevitably becomes a casualty of its own success."[33] By humanizing the condemned, though, death penalty opponents present them as persons whose deaths will have retributive meaning.

A rhetoric that seeks to end the death penalty's romance with humanism creates an ethical quandary for abolitionists. Most opponents of the death penalty are motivated by a commitment to human dignity. To portray the condemned as lifeless beings whose deaths mean very little is to participate in the dehumanizing of the death house. Yet to confer dignity on them is to make their executions, when they occur, successful degradation ceremonies for many penal spectators, meaningful events that satisfy retributive demands.

Still, there are ways to change the message without sacrificing the ideals. First, without losing their moral commitments, opponents of the death penalty might shift their focus to the damage capital punishment is doing to the survivors of homicide victims. They might spend more time calling attention to the dissonance caused by an appeals process that makes closure depend on an execution that may never happen. While delays in the past inspired federal legislation designed to speed up the appellate process, they may now, nearly two decades after the Anti-terrorism and Effective Death Penalty Act was signed into law, be credibly portrayed as endemic to the system and unavoidable. In short, rather than appealing to arguments that murderers are better than their worst acts, they might portray the death penalty as another failed government program that harms those that many supporters of capital punishment *do* care about: the family members of victims.

Second, while it is ethically dubious and practically difficult to present the condemned as faceless automatons whose executions stand for very little, those who generate fictional and perhaps even nonfictional images of the condemned might find a middle ground by portraying executions as events that prevent moral closure for offenders. As we saw, *Dead Man Walking* exemplified the pitfalls of 1990s abolitionist narratives about the death penalty that presented executions as rehabilitating. Obsession with the achievements of the soul has long deflected attention from destruction of the body. To create subversive, disillusioning death penalty narratives, abolitionists need to resist the romance of closure and depict the consequence of an execution not as a soul redeemed or a debt paid or a tragedy nobly borne but as a life abruptly interrupted.

Lars von Trier's *Dancer in the Dark* (2000) is perhaps the only post-*Gregg* film that depicts executions in this manner. Icelandic singer-songwriter Björk played Selma Ježková, a Czech immigrant put to death in Washington State in the 1960s. A musical that mixes Broadway fantasy with Victorian melodrama, the film tells the story of Selma, a factory worker who is desperately saving money for an operation to save her son's eyesight while she herself is slowly going blind from the same eye disease. Her only respite from this dreary existence is an escape into the fantasy world of musicals. Selma's plight worsens when she is fired from the factory and her landlord steals the cash she's been squirreling away for her son's operation. She kills the landlord during a confrontation and reclaims the money, but she pays the ultimate price for trying to save her son's eyesight: she is convicted of murder and sentenced to death.

The film recalls melodramatic depictions—in plays and films of the 1920s and 1930s—of executions as acts of valiant self-sacrifice, yet it resists the prospect of closure endemic to that genre. At her hanging, Selma collapses in fear and, hyperventilating, is strapped to a board designed to hold her upright so that the execution can proceed. Her panic attack stalls the execution, though, and while the authorities decide how to proceed, her friend rushes up, places her son's eyeglasses in her hands, and tells her he has had the operation to save his eyesight. The film appears, for a moment, to be indulging the romance of successful self-sacrifice, showing its protagonist finding certitude in the news of her son's sight. With the noose around her neck, Selma begins singing, her voice growing louder and more confident with each note. Like her beloved musicals, the song is an escapist fantasy. "This isn't the last song / There is no violin / The choir is so quiet / And no-one takes a spin / This is the next-to-last song / And that's all, all," she sings, refusing the reality of her imminent demise.[34]

The song—and the existential triumph it signifies—is unceremoniously cut short. As Selma begins a new verse, the camera's frame tight around her face, the executioner springs the trap without warning, the shot abruptly yanked wide to show Selma's body falling as she's about to sing the highest note in a three-note progression. The breaking of her neck literally stops the music, replacing the romance of transcendence with the physical reality of death. The "next-to-last song" is actually the last song, an irony that becomes evident as the film silently displays, superimposed over Selma's dangling body, its last defiant, yet unsung, and patently false verse: "They say it's the last song / They don't know us, you see / It's only the last song / If we let it be." Earlier in the film, Selma told a friend that she used to leave movie musicals before the ending—after the next-to-last song—so that the show would "go on forever" in her head.[35] The film refuses to indulge that fantasy for Selma or for us. She dies not after the next-to-last song, but without warning in the midst of it. In the silence that follows, we are asked to recognize what she could not: that the condemned cannot transcend the structures that bind them. Like the music, both the film we are watching and the one in Selma's mind stop abruptly and forever, casualties of the killing state.

It is telling that cultural outsiders, a Danish director and an Icelandic performer, would portray capital punishment in the United States in a way that undermines our dominant cultural logic by calling attention, as one critic put it, to the "conflict between the liberating power of pure imagination and the intractable authority of the market and the state."[36] For too long that conflict has been nonexistent. In the cultural life of capital punishment, pure imagination has long masked, and thus sustained, the stark realities of state killing, balancing our most illiberal form of punishment with humanist invocations of negative freedom and spiritual redemption. As support for the death penalty weakens, abolition's greatest prospects may lie not in appeals to human dignity, or in arguments about whether we can avoid the execution of innocents or transcend our racist past, but in the failure of the punitive state to generate meaning. Abolition of the death penalty may depend, in the end, on our ability to free ourselves from our punitive fantasies of freedom.

# Notes

## Introduction

1. Kirk Makin, "Bundy Makes Final Bid to Beat Chair," *Globe and Mail* (Toronto), April 11, 1988.

2. One might argue that the Florida example is inapt, since it expresses anger with Tallahassee, not Washington. But the degree to which the federal courts got involved in supervising the states' use of the death penalty mirrors the way federal transportation funding has been used to exact reforms from otherwise reluctant state legislatures over the years. Both the death penalty and transportation infrastructure took on the veneer of "big, centralized government" that many associated with Washington, DC.

3. "Trust the Federal Government, 1958–2008," *American National Election Studies*, http://www.electionstudies.org/nesguide/toptable/tab5a_1.htm accessed June 8, 2015).

4. Roper Poll, cited in House Committee on the Judiciary, Abolition of Capital Punishment: Hearing before Subcommittee No. 2 of the Committee on the Judiciary. 86th Cong., 2nd Sess., May 25, 1960, 87. The temporally closest available Gallup data is from 1957, when 47 percent of Americans indicated their support of the death penalty for a person convicted of murder.

5. "Trust the Federal Government, 1958–2008." After the steep decline in the 1970s, the numbers have risen and fallen over the years, with the lowest number—21 percent—recorded in 1994 "Trust" is the sum of the percentages of respondents who said they trusted Washington to do what is right "most of the time" and "almost always."

6. "Trust the Federal Government, 1958–2008," and Gallup, Inc., "Gallup Historical Trends: The Death Penalty," *Gallup*, http://www.gallup.com/poll/1606/death-penalty.aspx (accessed June 8, 2015).

7. See Franklin E. Zimring, *The Contradictions of American Capital Punishment* (Oxford: Oxford University Press, 2003), and David Garland, *Peculiar*

*Institution: America's Death Penalty in an Age of Abolition* (Cambridge, MA: Harvard University Press, 2010).

8. See Lawrence M. Friedman, *Crime and Punishment in American History* (New York: Basic Books, 1993), and Theodore Hamm, *Rebel and a Cause: Caryl Chessman and the Politics of the Death Penalty in Postwar California, 1948–1974* (Berkeley: University of California Press, 2001). For instance, a folk knowledge about the prison and parole systems that developed in the 1970s and 1980s led many to believe that dangerous killers were regularly released after serving fractions of their original sentences. Benjamin D. Steiner, William J. Bowers, and Austin Sarat, "Folk Knowledge as Legal Action: Death Penalty Judgments and the Tenet of Early Release in a Culture of Mistrust and Punitiveness," *Law and Society Review* 33 (1999): 461–505.

9. Steven F. Messner, Eric P. Baumer, and Richard Rosenfeld, "Distrust of Government, the Vigilante Tradition, and Support for Capital Punishment," *Law and Society Review* 40 (2006): 559–90.

10. Samuel Adams, quoted in Thomas Thacher, *A Tribute of Respect to the Memory of Samuel Adams, L.L.D. A.A.S. Late Governor of the Common-wealth of Massachusetts* (Dedham, MA, 1803), quoted in William V. Wells, *The Life and Public Services of Samuel Adams*, vol. 3 (Boston: Little, Brown, 1866), 246, quoted in Louis P. Masur, *Rites of Execution: Capital Punishment and the Transformation of American Culture, 1776–1865* (New York: Oxford University Press, 1989), 30.

11. Gustave de Beaumont and Alexis de Tocqueville, *On the Penitentiary System in the United States and Its Application in France; with an Appendix on Penal Colonies and Also Statistical Notes*, trans. Francis Lieber (Philadelphia: Carey, Lea, and Blanchard, 1833), 47, https://archive.org/details/onpenitentiarysy00beauuoft.

12. Bertie [County], "The Penitentiary Question," *North Carolina Standard*, April 22, 1846, quoted in Edward L. Ayers, *Vengeance and Justice: Crime and Punishment in the 19th Century American South* (New York: Oxford University Press, 1984), 49.

13. Isaiah Berlin, "Two Concepts of Liberty," 1958, in Isaiah Berlin, *Four Essays on Liberty* (Oxford: Oxford University Press, 1969).

14. Eric Foner, *The Story of American Freedom* (New York: W. W. Norton, 1999).

15. Ibid.

16. Perry R. Duis, "No Time for Privacy: World War II and Chicago's Families," in *The War in American Culture: Society and Consciousness during World War II*, ed. Lewis A. Erenberg and Susan E. Hirsch (Chicago: University of Chicago Press, 1996), 17.

17. Some have called this ethos a liberal consensus forged between Demo-

crats and Republicans. Its tenets included a faith in Keynesian capitalism, belief that increased production would meet social needs, belief that interests could be harmonized among groups in a society, faith that social problems could be solved by social science, the expectation of a struggle against communism, and a sense that the United States ought to bring capitalism to the rest of the world. Godfrey Hodgson, *America in Our Time: From World War II to Nixon—What Happened and Why* (New York: Doubleday, 1976; repr., Princeton, NJ: Princeton University Press, 2005), 76. Citations refer to the Princeton edition. More recent work has identified the way a consensus vision of 1950s politics ignores important differences in attitudes and realities about race, class, and political strategy during the period. See, e.g., Gary Gerstle, "Race and the Myth of Liberal Consensus," *Journal of American History* 82 (1995): 579–86, and Kent M. Beck, "What Was Liberalism in the 1950s?" *Political Science Quarterly* 102 (1987): 233–58. Nonetheless, it does seem that a dominant vision of the country was promulgated by elites that demanded, if not always successfully, the perception that social problems and social conflicts were rare and, when they did exist, were being ameliorated by a competent, benignly paternalistic state.

18. On the rise of the liberal order and Americans' attachment to it, see Foner, *Story of American Freedom*; Alan Brinkley, *The Unfinished Nation. A Concise History of the American People* (New York: McGraw-Hill, 2009); Paul S. Boyer, *Promises to Keep: The United States since World War II*, 3rd ed. (Boston: Houghton Mifflin, 2004), Hodgson, *America in Our Time*; Terrence Ball, "The Politics of Social Science in Postwar America," in *Recasting America: Culture and Politics in the Age of Cold War*, ed. Lary May (Chicago: University of Chicago Press, 1988); and Gary Gerstle, *American Crucible: Race and Nation in the Twentieth Century* (Princeton, NJ: Princeton University Press, 2002). On strains to the liberal order and resistance it faced, see Alan Brinkley, "The New Deal and the Idea of the State," in *The Rise and Fall of the New Deal Order, 1930–1980*, ed. Steve Fraser and Gary Gerstle (Princeton, NJ: Princeton University Press, 1990); Gerstle, "Race and the Myth of Liberal Consensus," 579–86; and Kent Beck, "What Was Liberalism in the 1950s?" *Political Science Quarterly* 52 (1987): 233–58. For examples of the way the imagined beneficiaries of midcentury liberal reforms were white, see Alice Kessler-Harris, *In Pursuit of Equity: Women, Men, and the Quest for Economic Citizenship in 20th Century America* (Oxford: Oxford University Press, 2003); Jonathan Simon, *Governing through Crime: How the War on Crime Transformed American Democracy and Created a Culture of Fear* (Oxford: Oxford University Press, 2007); and Volker Janssen, "From the Inside Out: Therapeutic Penology and Postwar Liberalism in Postwar California," *Osiris* 22 (2007): 116–34.

19. See Michael Willrich, *City of Courts: Socializing Justice in Progressive Era Chicago* (Cambridge: Cambridge University Press, 2003), and Terrence

Ball, "The Politics of Social Science in Postwar America," in *Recasting America: Culture and Politics in the Age of Cold War*, ed. Lary May (Chicago: University of Chicago Press, 1988).

20. Terrence Ball has shown that the state funded a postwar boom in the social sciences to advance a cold "war of ideas and ideologies. . . . In the in-house literature and public pronouncements of the postwar period, social scientists are likened repeatedly to technicians, to engineers, even to physicians concerned with the 'health' of American society." "Politics of Social Science," 82.

21. Retributivists often see the pain of punishment as a compensatory response to the undeserved, elevated status a criminal assumes by breaking the law. It restores a balance of the benefits and burdens of life lived under the rule of law that the criminal's crime disrupted. Philosophers have debated the soundness of its logic. Andrew von Hirsch offered it as a partial defense in his 1976 book *Doing Justice* but later came to question the idea that the "unfair advantage" an offender gains in the act of lawbreaking "can somehow (in other than a purely metaphorical sense) be eliminated or cancelled by punishing him. In what sense does his being deprived of rights now offset the extra freedom he has arrogated to himself then by offending? And why is preserving the balance of supposed advantages a reason for invoking the coercive powers of the state?" Andrew von Hirsch, "Censure and Proportionality," in *A Reader on Punishment*, ed. Anthony Duff and David Garland (New York: Oxford University Press, 1994), 117. I am interested less in how retribution might be justified and more in what its enactment entails.

22. Williams v. People of State of New York 337 U.S. 241 (1949) at 248.

23. David Garland, *The Culture of Control: Crime and Social Order in Contemporary Society* (Chicago: University of Chicago Press, 2001). Prisoner lawsuits in the wartime and postwar period, from a lawsuit against Georgia in 1943 to one against Arkansas in 1970, document the persistence of brutality in prisons, but federal courts' receptiveness to claims of abuse and the sometimes voluntary changes states made after revelations of abuse were made public reflect how much the penological terrain had changed. See Lawrence Friedman, *Crime and Punishment in American History* (New York: Basic Books, 1994), 309–16.

24. Byron E. Eshelman with Frank Riley, *Death Row Chaplain* (Englewood Cliffs, NJ: Prentice-Hall, 1962), 62.

25. Stuart Banner, *The Death Penalty: An American History* (Cambridge, MA: Harvard University Press, 2003).

26. Rudolph v. Alabama 375 U.S. 889 (1963).

27. Furman v. Georgia, 408 U.S. 238 (1972). For analyses of the road to *Furman*, see Marie Gottschalk, "The Long Shadow of the Death Penalty: Mass Incarceration, Capital Punishment, and Penal Policy in the United States," in *Is the Death Penalty Dying? European and American Perspectives*, ed. Austin Sarat and Jurgen Martschukat (Cambridge: Cambridge University Press, 2011),

and Evan J. Mandery, *A Wild Justice: The Death and Resurrection of Capital Punishment in America* (New York: W. W. Norton, 2014).

28. Grace Elizabeth Hale, *A Nation of Outsiders: How the White Middle Class Fell in Love with Rebellion in Postwar America* (New York: Oxford University Press, 2011).

29. William H. Whyte, *The Organization Man* (New York: Simon and Schuster, 1956), and David Riesman, Nathan Glazer, and Reuel Denney, *The Lonely Crowd: A Study of the Changing American Character* (New Haven, CT: Yale University Press, 1950).

30. Erika Dross, "The Art of Cultural Politics: From Regionalism to Abstract Expressionism," in *Recasting American Liberty: Culture and Politics in the Age of Cold War*, ed. Lary May (Chicago: University of Chicago Press, 1989).

31. David Harvey, *A Brief History of Neoliberalism* (Oxford: Oxford University Press, 2007).

32. See, e.g., Erving Goffman, *Asylums: Essays on the Social Situation of Mental Patients and Other Inmates* (Garden City, NY: Anchor, 1961), and Stanley Milgram, *Obedience to Authority: An Experimental View* (New York: Harper and Row, 1974).

33. On momism and gay baiting see, respectively, K. A. Cuordileone, "'Politics in an Age of Anxiety': Cold War Political Culture and the Crisis in American Masculinity, 1949–1960," *Journal of American History* 87 (2000): 515–45, and David K. Johnson, *The Lavender Scare: The Cold War Persecution of Gays and Lesbians in the Federal Government* (Chicago: University of Chicago Press, 2004)

34. On suburbanization, see Kenneth Jackson, *Crabgrass Frontier: The Suburbanization of the United States* (Oxford: Oxford University Press, 1987); Thomas J. Sugrue, *The Origins of the Urban Crisis: Race and Inequality in Postwar Detroit* (Princeton, NJ: Princeton University Press, 1996); Robert Self, *American Babylon: Race and the Struggle for Postwar Oakland* (Princeton, NJ: Princeton University Press, 2005); and Kevin Kruse, *White Flight: Atlanta and the Making of Modern Conservatism* (Princeton, NJ: Princeton University Press, 2007).

35. Michael Flamm, *Law and Order: Street Crime, Civil Unrest, and the Crisis of Liberalism in the 1960s* (New York: Columbia University Press, 2005).

36. For a race-based critique of the historiographic idea of a liberal consensus during this period, see Gerstle, "Race and the Myth of Liberal Consensus," 579–86.

37. Simon, *Governing through Crime*, 3.

38. Ibid.

39. On the antipsychiatry movement in the United States, see Michael E. Staub, *Madness Is Civilization: When the Diagnosis Was Social, 1948–1980* (Chicago: University of Chicago Press, 2011).

40. See, e.g., Angela Davis, "The Soledad Brothers," *Black Scholar* 2 (April–May 1971): 2–7, and Jessica Mitford, *Kind and Unusual Punishment: The Prison Business* (New York: Knopf, 1973).

41. Naomi Murakawa, *The First Civil Right: How Liberals Built Prison America* (New York: Oxford University Press, 2014), 43.

42. John Maynard Keynes, *The General Theory of Employment, Interest, and Money* (1936; repr. New York: Harcourt and Brace, 1965).

43. On the macroeconomic level, a neoliberal faith in free markets, espoused most famously by Margaret Thatcher and Ronald Reagan, justified the deregulation of industries, the movement of industrial production to countries with cheaper labor costs, and the migration overseas of well-paid unskilled industrial jobs. On the rise of the neoliberal political order, see Harvey, *Brief History of Neoliberalism*.

44. As James Ferguson notes, scholars use the term neoliberalism to denote not only macroeconomic policies but "specific mechanisms of government and recognizable modes of creating subjects. . . . [N]ew constructions of 'active' and 'responsible' citizens and communities are deployed to produce governmental results that do not depend on direct state intervention. The 'responsibilized' citizen comes to operate as a miniature firm, responding to incentives, rationally assessing risks, and prudently choosing from among different courses of action." James Ferguson, "The Uses of Neoliberalism," *Antipode* 41 (2010): 166–84, 171, 172. From self-help books to reality television to daytime talk shows, popular culture has played a key role in promulgating the disciplinary strategies used to "responsibilize" citizens. See, e.g., Barbara Cruikshank, *The Will to Empower: Democratic Citizens and Other Subjects* (Ithaca, NY: Cornell University Press, 1999); Laurie Ouellette and James Hay, *Better Living through Reality TV: Television and Post-Welfare Citizenship* (Malden, MA: Wiley-Blackwell, 2008); and Janice Peck, *The Age of Oprah: Cultural Icon for the Neoliberal Era* (Boulder, CO: Paradigm, 2008).

45. See Roger N. Lancaster, *Sex Panic and the Punitive State* (Berkeley: University of California Press, 2011), chap. 8 ("The Victimology Trap: Capitalism, Liberalism, and Grievance").

46. Ruth Wilson Gilmore, *Golden Gulag: Prisons, Surplus, Crisis, and Opposition in Globalizing California* (Berkeley: University of California Press, 2007).

47. These ideologies all invoked negative freedom in selective and contradictory ways to achieve different goals: the centering of family in public life (moral traditionalism), the limiting of the state's police powers (civil libertarianism), the limiting of the state's regulation of markets (neoliberalism). As Patricia Ewick and Susan S. Silbey have shown, contradictions in ideologies are normal. Following them, I understand ideology not as a "grand set of ideas that in its seamless coherence precludes all other ideas" but as a unique pattern, assembled out

of a culture's concepts, binary oppositions, "logics, hierarchies of value, and conventions" that people use to make sense of the world. Ideologies are continually made, remade, and sometimes transformed in consciousness, in our ongoing efforts to apprehend, respond to, and reflect on our lived experiences. It is in that process of making meaning that an ideology "embeds power," reinforcing the structures and practices that distribute resources within a society (or, when oppositional, justifying resistance to those structures and practices). Patricia Ewick and Susan S. Silbey, *The Common Place of the Law: Stories from Everyday Life* (Chicago: University of Chicago Press, 1998), 225, 40, 225.

48. This was the only reason, Michel Foucault argued, that the state would use the death penalty in an age of biopower. Michel Foucault, *The History of Sexuality: An Introduction*, trans. Richard Hurley (New York: Random House, 1990), 138.

49. On spectacle lynchings and their connection to executions in the late nineteenth- and early twentieth-century South, see Amy Louise Wood, *Lynching and Spectacle: Witnessing Racial Violence in America, 1890–1940* (Chapel Hill: University of North Carolina Press, 2009). On the connections between the contemporary death penalty and lynching, see Garland, *Peculiar Institution*.

50. M. Watt Espy and John Ortiz Smykla, *Executions in the United States, 1608–2002: The Espy File* [computer file]. 4th ICPSR ed. Compiled by M. Watt Espy and John Ortiz Smykla (Ann Arbor, MI: Inter-university Consortium for Political and Social Research, 2004). I have included all executions they have coded as having been carried out for "rape," "attempted rape," "burglary-attempted rape," and "rape-robbery." The case of the Martinsville Seven was particularly illustrative: in the name of preserving "stability," a code word for white male supremacy, seven black men were executed for the rape of one white woman in Virginia in 1951. Eric W. Rise, "Race, Rape, and Radicalism: The Case of the Martinsville Seven, 1949–1951," *Journal of Southern History* 58 (1992): 461–90.

51. Garland, *Peculiar Institution*.

52. Austin Sarat, ed., *The Killing State: Capital Punishment in Law, Politics, and Culture* (Oxford: Oxford University Press, 1998); Kerry Dunn and Paul J. Kaplan, "The Ironics of Helping: Social Interventions and Executable Subjects," *Law and Society Review* 43 (2009): 337–68.

53. For an example of this type of scholarship, see Lary May, *The Big Tomorrow: Hollywood and the Politics of the American Way* (Chicago: University of Chicago Press, 2002).

54. For an example of this type of scholarship, see Tom Engelhardt, "The Victors and the Vanquished," in *History Wars: The Enola Gay and Other Battles for the American Past*, ed. Edward T. Linethal and Tom Engelhardt (New York: Henry Holt, 1996), and George Lipsitz, *Time Passages: Collective Memory and American Popular Culture* (Minneapolis: University of Minnesota Press, 1990).

55. Even though nearly 40 percent of all executions since 1977 have happened in Texas, some Texas counties have not sent a capital murderer to the state's execution chamber in decades. Other factors beyond the scope of this book make a significant difference in determining whether state actors ever reinstituted the death penalty after *Furman*, asked a judge or jury to sentence an offender to death, or carried out an execution. Anyone wanting to understand, in a nuanced way, why a particular state has the death penalty, or why a particular county uses it, must pay attention to these variables. See, e.g., James S. Liebman and Peter Clarke, "Minority Practice, Majority's Burden: The Death Penalty Today," *Ohio State Journal of Criminal Law* 9 (2011): 255–352. For a critique of approaches to the death penalty rooted in American exceptionalism, see David Garland, "Capital Punishment and American Culture," *Punishment and Society* 7 (2005): 347–76. Garland notes that the United States is home to Michigan, which abolished the death penalty in 1846 and has never had an execution since, as well as to Texas. Joachim Savelsberg has demonstrated the importance that the structure of political institutions plays in channeling punitive sentiment or insulating it from political policymaking. Joachim Savelsberg, "Knowledge, Domination, and Criminal Punishment," *American Journal of Sociology* 99 (1994): 911–43. Vanessa Barker has used Savelsberg's findings to explain the different outcomes gained by the victims' rights movement in different US states. Vanessa Barker, "The Politics of Pain: A Political Institutionalist Analysis of Crime Victims' Moral Protests," *Law and Society Review* 41 (2007): 619–63.

56. Jenifer Warren, One in 100: Behind Bars in America, 2008 (Washington, DC: Pew Charitable Trust, 2008). Available at http://www.pewtrusts.org/en/research-and-analysis/reports/2008/02/28/one-in-100-behind-bars-in-america-2008 (accessed July 28, 2015).

57. See, e.g., Teri Figueroa and Mark Walker, "John Gardner Sentencing Filled with Emotion," *San Diego Union Tribune*, May 15, 2010. On shaming sanctions, see James Q. Whitman, "What Is Wrong with Inflicting Shame Sanctions?" *Yale Law Journal* 107 (1998): 1055–92. On the role of victim impact testimony in capital trials, see Austin Sarat, "Speaking of Death: Narratives of Violence in Capital Trials," *Law and Society Review* 27 (1993): 19–58. On humiliation on reality television, see Steven A. Kohm, "Naming, Shaming and Criminal Justice: Mass-Mediated Humiliation as Entertainment and Punishment," *Crime, Media, Culture* 5 (2009): 188–205.

58. Readers' comments on Gillian Mahoney, "Georgia Death Row Inmate's Last Meal Includes 2 Cheeseburgers, Cornbread and Popcorn," *ABCNews.com*, February 19, 2015. Available at http://abcnews.go.com/US/death-row-inmates-meal-includes-cheeseburgers-cornbread-popcorn/story?id=29074364#disqus_thread (accessed July 28, 2015).

59. James Whitman, *Harsh Justice: Criminal Punishment and the Widen-*

*ing Divide between America and Europe* (Oxford: Oxford University Press, 2005), 196.

60. Ibid., 198.

61. Immanuel Kant, *The Metaphysical Elements of Justice*, trans. John Ladd (1797; repr. Indianapolis: Bobbs-Merrill, 1965).

62. Jeannine Marie DeLombard, *In the Shadow of the Gallows: Race, Crime, and American Civic Identity* (Philadelphia: University of Pennsylvania Press, 2012), 30.

63. Antonin Scalia, "God's Justice and Ours," *First Things* 123 (May 2002): 17–21, 19.

64. Philip Smith, *Punishment and Culture* (Chicago: University of Chicago Press, 2008), 172.

## Chapter One

1. Byron E. Eshelman with Frank Riley, *Death Row Chaplain* (Englewood Cliffs, NJ: Prentice-Hall, 1962), 219.

2. Truman Capote, *In Cold Blood* (New York: Vintage, 1965), 124.

3. Seventeen months after the book's release, in May 1967, it had sold—in hardcover—310,337 copies in the United States, in addition to 347,479 sold by the Book of the Month Club and 158,844 by the Literary Guild. "Breakdown of Hardcover Sales," May 1967. Richard Brooks Papers, box 31a, folder 39 ("Legal"), Margaret Herrick Library, Academy of Motion Picture Arts and Sciences, Los Angeles.

4. George Plimpton, "The Story behind a Nonfiction Novel," *New York Times*, January 16, 1966.

5. For an account of the temporary judicial abolition of the death penalty, see Evan Mandery, *A Wild Justice: The Death and Resurrection of Capital Punishment in America* (New York: W. W. Norton, 2013).

6. Gallup, Inc., "Gallup Historical Trends: The Death Penalty," *Gallup*, http://www.gallup.com/poll/1606/death-penalty.aspx (accessed June 8, 2015).

7. Postwar America was, as Elaine Tyler May has termed it, the "age of the expert," and a confidence in technocrats' capacity to solve social problems had partly undergirded a period of dramatic growth for the nation's public universities. Elaine Tyler May, *Homeward Bound: America Families in the Cold War Era* (1999; repr. New York: Basic Books, 1988), 21. Private insurance, once seen as a form of gambling, was now touted, as Caley Horan has shown, as a statistically driven method for guaranteeing personal and social stability. Caley Dawn Horan, "Actuarial Age: Insurance and the Emergence of Neoliberalism in the Postwar United States" (PhD diss., University of Minnesota, 2011).

8. Faith in this sociological and psychological approach to punishment, "penal welfarism," as David Garland has termed it, seemed to be spreading to the point of becoming orthodoxy. The term punishment fell out of use in penological discourse, and retributive rationales for punishment were seen as distasteful hangovers of a premodern past that was being transcended. David Garland, *The Culture of Control: Crime and Social Order in Contemporary Society* (Chicago: University of Chicago Press, 2001). Prisoners' lawsuits in wartime and in the postwar period, from a lawsuit against Georgia in 1943 to one against Arkansas in 1970, document the persistence of brutality in prisons, but the receptiveness of federal courts to claims of abuse and the sometimes voluntary changes states made after revelations of abuse were made public reflect how much the penological terrain had changed. See Lawrence Friedman, *Crime and Punishment in American History* (New York: Basic Books, 1993), 309–16.

9. On Chessman's assuming the persona of amateur criminologist, see Theodore Hamm, *Rebel and a Cause: Caryl Chessman and the Politics of the Death Penalty in Postwar California, 1948–1974* (Berkeley: University of California Press, 2001).

10. Caryl Chessman, *Trial by Ordeal* (Englewood Cliffs, NJ: Prentice-Hall, 1955), 280.

11. To do this, they had to dismantle harmful myths about the death penalty that they found in classic stage and screen productions. Melodramas of the nineteenth century and Hollywood's classic era had often depicted the lead-up to an execution as a test of a man's mental mettle that he then passed with flying colors. In the popular imagination, the death penalty gave men the occasion to assert their negative psychological freedom—the state might have condemned them to death, but they retained possession of their minds until the very end. The death row inmates in John Wexley's 1929 Broadway play *The Last Mile*, for instance, discussed the way movies depicted French nobles going to the guillotine with dignity—"dancing and singing what they called the minuet" before dying. "That's nerve," one of them says admiringly. John Wexley, *The Last Mile* (New York: Samuel French, 1930), 70–71.

12. Of the 1,528 persons put to death between 1945 and the film's release in 1958, just 11 had been women. M. Watt Espy and John Ortiz Smykla, "Executions in the United States, 1608–2002: The Espy File" [Computer file]. 4th ICPSR ed. Compiled by M. Watt Espy and John Ortiz Smykla (Ann Arbor, MI: Inter-university Consortium for Political and Social Research, 2004).

13. Nelson Gidding and Don Mankiewicz, *I Want To Live!* directed by Robert Wise (1958; Culver City, CA: MGM, 2002), DVD.

14. Walter Wanger to Robert Wise, March 11, 1958, Walter Wanger Papers, box 80, folder 17 ("Correspondence—General, 1957–1960"), University of Wisconsin, Madison, Library.

15. Joseph Landon and Don Murray, *The Hoodlum Priest*, directed by Irvin Kershner (1961; Culver City, CA: MGM, 2002), DVD.

16. "God in a Gas Chamber," *Time*, March 3, 1961, 74.

17. Psychiatrists, Menninger told the public, had a much more nuanced understanding of the human mind that allowed them to reform convicts' behavior through therapy or, in those cases where there was little hope of reform, to provide for their long-term care in a confined setting. "Having arrived at some diagnostic grasp of the offender's personality, those in charge can decide whether there is a chance that he can be redirected into a mutually satisfactory adaptation to the world. If so, the most suitable techniques of education, industrial training, group administration, and psychotherapy should be selectively applied. . . . If, in due time, perceptible change occurs, the process should be expedited by finding a suitable spot in society and industry for him, and getting him out of prison control and into civil status (with parole control) as quickly as possible." Karl Menninger, "Verdict Guilty—Now What?" *Harper's Magazine*, August 1959, 62.

18. Transcript of interviews conducted between Richard Brooks and doctors of the Menninger Clinic, tapes 1–2, January 16, 1967, Richard Brooks papers, box 31c, folder 65 ("Menninger Clinic"), Margaret Herrick Library, Academy of Motion Picture Arts and Sciences, Los Angeles, 35.

19. Richard Brooks, *In Cold Blood*, directed by Richard Brooks, (1967; Hollywood, CA: Columbia Pictures, 2003), DVD.

20. Donald E. J. MacNamara to Marcel Frym, telegram, December 30, 1958, Walter Wanger Papers, box 80, folder 23 ("Screenings, September 1958–February 1959), University of Wisconsin, Madison, Library.

21. William O. Douglas to Walter Wanger, December 11, 1958, Walter Wanger Papers, box 80, folder 23 ("Screenings, September 1958–February 1959), University of Wisconsin, Madison, Library. Indeed, one wonders whether Barbara Graham's retort to the guard who told her to breathe the gas deeply to avoid pain—"How would you know?"—was on Douglas's mind during the oral arguments for *Aikens v. California*, which was another capital case heard the same day as *Furman v. Georgia*. Douglas challenged the contention made by Ronald George, the attorney for California, that "there is no cruel and unusual punishment, certainly not under our humane method. . . . In fact, the death that comes to such a prisoner is, perhaps, less cruel than the death by natural causes that comes to us all eventually." "Except nobody knows," Douglas pointedly responded. Quoted in Mandery, *Wild Justice*, 153.

22. Charles Champlin, "Brooks Turns Down TV 'Cold Blood' Bid," *Los Angeles Times*, July 24, 1969.

23. Gallup, "Gallup Historical Trends: The Death Penalty."

24. See, e.g., Mary D. Edsall and Thomas Byrne Edsall, *Chain Reaction: The*

*Impact of Race, Rights, and Taxes on American Politics* (New York: W. W. Norton, 1991), and Katherine Beckett, *Making Crime Pay: Law and Order in Contemporary American Politics* (New York: Oxford University Press, 1997).

25. After World War II, the South's annual execution numbers followed the national pattern of decline, but they remained consistently higher than, and occasionally doubled, the number of executions posted in all other census regions *combined*. Espy and Smykla, *Executions in the United States*.

26. The term psychopath had long been used to denote a person "whose every moral faculty appears to be of the normal equilibrium. He thinks logically, he distinguishes good and evil, and he acts according to reason. But of all moral notions he is entirely devoid." "Mmle. Semenova's Acquittal," *New York Times*, February 14, 1885. The term appeared in the nineteenth century to describe those who were once described as suffering from "moral insanity." Nicole Rafter, *The Criminal Brain: Understanding Biological Theories of Crime* (New York: New York University Press, 2008). By the middle of the twentieth century, however, the term would become attached to sex offenders. See Estelle B. Freedman, ""Uncontrolled Desires': The Response to the Sexual Psychopath, 1920–1960," *Journal of American History* 74 (1987): 83–106. The term returned to its original nineteenth-century sense toward the end of the twentieth century.

27. Truman Capote, *In Cold Blood* (New York: Vintage, 1965), 295.

28. Joseph Satten, Karl Menninger, Irwin Rosen, and Martin Mayman, "Murder without Apparent Motive: A Study in Personality Disorganization," *American Journal of Psychiatry* 117 (1960): 48–53, quoted in Capote, *In Cold Blood*, 300–301.

29. Schmid and Speck avoided execution by living long enough to see the Supreme Court's abolition of capital punishment in 1972. The other three were executed. For an in-depth analysis of how the Starkweather case called into question the tenets of Cold War liberalism, see Daniel LaChance, "Executing Charles Starkweather: Lethal Punishment in an Age of Rehabilitation," *Punishment and Society* 11 (2009): 337–58.

30. Grant Duwe has shown that while mass murder is often seen as originating in the mid-1960s, an earlier twentieth-century wave of mass murders occurred in the 1920s and 1930s but attracted comparatively less attention at the time because the killings were predominantly intrafamilial. Mass murder did increase sharply in the 1960s, but its salience and the sense that it was unprecedented were a result of media distortion. Grant Duwe, "The Patterns and Prevalence of Mass Murder in Twentieth-Century America," *Justice Quarterly* 21 (2004): 721–69.

31. "College Student Slays Both Parents, Sister," *Los Angeles Times*, November 30, 1958.

32. "Slayer of 3 'Not Sorry, Not Glad,'" *Washington Post and Times Herald*, November 30, 1958.

33. "2 Admit Killing 7, Joke about Getting Chair," *Newsday*, June 12, 1961.

34. "Pair Admit 7 Slayings," *Baltimore Sun*, June 13, 1961.

35. For work tracing this theme in nineteenth-century political philosophy, see Robert B. Pippin, *Hollywood Westerns and American Myth: The Importance of Howard Hawks and John Ford for Political Philosophy* (New Haven, CT: Yale University Press, 2010).

36. Solomon E. Asch, "Opinions and Social Pressure," *Scientific American* 193 (November 1955): 31–35.

37. Stanley Milgram, "Behavioral Study of Obedience," *Journal of Abnormal and Social Psychology* 67 (1963): 371–78, esp. 375. The experiment was in part inspired by Hannah Arendt's coverage of Adolf Eichmann's trial in Jerusalem in 1961. Eichmann had overseen the logistics of the Nazi genocide, and Arendt's portrait of him in *Eichmann in Jerusalem* was of a man under conditions in which evil had become easy to rationalize and thus "banal." Milgram specifically mentioned, in his article on the experiments, that the "facts of recent history" made his inquiry a pressing one. Milgram, "Behavioral Study of Obedience," 371. Hannah Arendt's *The Origins of Totalitarianism* (1951) had chronicled the modern human experience of rootlessness in the West. The rise of bureaucratic forms of statecraft and communication technologies that had made a totalitarian grip easier to establish and more difficult to resist in Europe was, of course, also present in America. As George Will wrote at her death, Arendt had taught Americans that the modern totalitarian state sought "to reduce masses to a malleable material. It is total war by the political sphere against the private sphere of life . . . the triumph of political force over 'the disturbing miracle contained in the fact that each of us is made as he is—single, unique, unchangeable.'" George F. Will, "Eichmann as Everyman," *Washington Post*, December 12, 1975.

38. Don Moser, "The Pied Piper of Tucson," *Life*, March 4, 1966.

39. Ed Meagher, "Jury Rules Death for Schmid," *Los Angeles Times*, March 2, 1966.

40. "Execution Set 5 Times Before Penalty Is Paid," *Omaha World Herald*, June 25, 1959.

41. Flannery O'Connor, "A Good Man Is Hard to Find," in *A Good Man Is Hard to Find and Other Stories* (New York: Harcourt, 1955), 9–29, 12.

42. Ibid., 28.

43. Ibid., 23–29.

44. Ibid., 28.

45. Ibid., 29.

46. Flannery O'Connor to A., August 28, 1955. In Flannery O'Connor, *Collected Works* (New York: Penguin, 1988), 949.

47. Joyce Carol Oates, "Where Are You Going, Where Have You Been?" *Epoch* (Fall 1966), http://www.usfca.edu/jco/whereareyougoing (accessed October 17, 2013).

48. Ibid.

49. Ibid.

50. Ibid.

51. She had, Capote notes, improved greatly when she went to Wichita under doctor's orders and got a position working as a clerk, but the guilt of neglecting her domestic duties had drawn her back to Holcomb and brought her depression back.

52. He dismissed men he employed who used alcohol, we learn, and he immediately slapped a lawsuit on the owner of a propeller plane that crashed on his property. Capote, *In Cold Blood*, 10–13.

53. Ibid., 69.

54. Rebecca West, "A Grave and Reverend Book," *Harper's Magazine*, February 1966, 114.

55. Malcolm Muggeridge, "Books," *Esquire*, April 1966.

56. Peter Bart, "Mann among Men," *New York Times*, July 24, 1966.

57. Indeed, the prototypical executable subject in the aftermath of *Gregg*, one scholar has suggested, is the criminal psychopath whose inability to feel empathy for others is part of a larger understanding of the self as a sovereign presiding over subjects who live and die at his whim. Robert Weisberg, "The Unlucky Psychopath as Death Penalty Prototype," in *Who Deserves to Die: Constructing the Executable Subject*, ed. Austin Sarat and Karl Shoemaker (Amherst: University of Massachusetts Press, 2011).

58. Walter Berns, *For Capital Punishment: Crime and the Morality of the Death Penalty* (New York: Basic Books, 1979), 176.

59. Ibid.

60. Ibid., 173.

61. Ibid., 176.

62. Richard O'Mara, "Rehabilitation versus Retribution," *Baltimore Sun*, March 28, 1976.

63. Robert Martinson, "What Works: Questions and Answers about Prison Reform," *Public Interest* 35 (Spring 1974): 22–54.

64. Jerome Miller, "Is Rehabilitation a Waste of Time?" *Washington Post*, April 23, 1989. As Eric Cummins has noted, the rhetoric of the rehabilitative ideal was at its apogee in 1965, but the material infrastructure needed to implement it was sorely deficient. A report issued by the National Commission on the Causes and Prevention of Violence observed that only 20 percent of the nation's 121,000 correctional positions were directed at rehabilitating prisoners. The ratios of mental health workers to prisoners reveal just how pie in the sky the rehabilitative ideal actually was: one psychiatrist for every 1,140 prisoners, one psychologist for every 803 prisoners, one social worker for every 295 prisoners, and one classroom teacher for every 104 prisoners. The liberal state's eyes were bigger than its belly. David P. Stang, "The Inability of Corrections to Correct," in

*Law and Order Reconsidered: A Staff Report to the National Commission on the Causes and Prevention of Violence,* ed. James S. Campbell, Joseph R. Sahid, and David P. Stang (Washington, DC: US Government Printing Office, n.d.), 25–40, quoted in Eric Cummins, *The Rise and Fall of California's Radical Prison Movement* (Stanford, CA: Stanford University Press, 1994), 91.

65. Gray Cavender, "Media and Crime Policy: A Reconsideration of David Garland's *The Culture of Control,*" *Punishment and Society* 6 (2004): 335–48, 341.

66. Quoted in ibid., 341.

67. Garry Wills, *Nixon Agonistes: The Crisis of the Self-Made Man* (Boston: Houghton Mifflin, 1970), 588, quoted in Michael McCann and David T. Johnson, "Rocked but Still Rolling: The Enduring Institution of Capital Punishment in Historical and Comparative Perspective," in *The Road to Abolition? The Future of Capital Punishment in the United States,* ed. Charles J. Ogletree Jr. and Austin Sarat (New York: New York University Press, 2009), 150.

68. Mike Hammer was the protagonist of a series of novels by Mickey Spillane; he was first introduced in *I, the Jury* (New York: Signet, 1947).

69. James Warner Bellah and Willis Goldbeck, *The Man Who Shot Liberty Valance,* directed by John Ford (1962; Burbank, CA: Paramount Pictures, 2001), DVD.

70. David W. Livingstone, "Spiritedness, Reason, and the Founding of Law and Order: John Ford's *The Man Who Shot Liberty Valance,*" *Perspectives on Political Science* 38 (2009): 217–27; Sidney A. Pearson Jr., "It's Tough to Be the Second Toughest Guy in Town: Ask the Man Who Shot Liberty Valence," *Perspectives on Political Science* 36 (2007): 23–28; Mike Yawn and Bob Beatty, "John Ford's Vision of the Closing of the West: From Optimism to Cynicism," *Film and History* 26 (1996): 6–19.

71. Harry Julian Fink, Rita M. Fink, and Dean Riesner, *Dirty Harry,* directed by Don Siegel (1971; Burbank, CA: Warner Home Video, 2001), DVD; Wendell Mayes, *Death Wish,* directed by Michael Winner (1974; Burbank, CA: Paramount Pictures, 2006), DVD.

72. Corey Robin, *The Reactionary Mind: Conservatism from Edmund Burke to Sarah Palin* (Oxford: Oxford University Press, 2011), 219.

73. Gene Siskel, "'Tis the Season to Be Dirty, Tough, Etc.," *Chicago Tribune,* March 16, 1973.

74. Mary Anne Rhyne, "Cop Killer Dies in Florida Electric Chair," Associated Press, January 30, 1985.

75. Terence Hunt, "Bush Outlines Anti-crime Program," *News-Journal* (Daytona Beach, FL), October 7, 1988.

76. Colman McCarthy, "America the Executioner," *Washington Post,* June 7, 1979.

77. This understanding of punishment, of course, is at the heart of Émile

Durkheim's sociology. Punishment, for Durkheim, reassures members of a community that their collective morality is still intact and that the crime was an aberration; the act of punishment maintains "inviolate the cohesion of society by sustaining the common consciousness in all its vigour." In the end, the suffering of the offender exacted by the punishment "is not a gratuitous act of cruelty. It is a sign indicating that the sentiments of the collectivity are still unchanged, that the communion of minds sharing the same beliefs remains absolute, and in this way the injury that the crime has inflicted upon society is made good. . . . Without this necessary act of satisfaction what is called the moral consciousness could not be preserved." Émile Durkheim, *The Division of Labor in Society*, trans. W. D. Halls (New York: Free Press, 1984), 63. As we will see in chapter 4, executions' ritualistic, regenerating qualities were an integral part of the era of public executions in the United States, which lasted in some places until the 1930s.

78. "Growing Up in Tucson," *Time Magazine*, March 11, 1966, 40.

## Chapter Two

1. Norman Mailer, *The Executioner's Song* (New York: Little, Brown, 1979; repr. New York: Vintage, 1998), 833. Citations refer to the Vintage edition.

2. B. F. Skinner, *Beyond Freedom and Dignity* (New York: Knopf, 1971), 81.

3. Ibid., 66.

4. Walter Berns, *For Capital Punishment: Crime and the Morality of the Death Penalty* (New York: Basic Books, 1979), 176.

5. A sense of freedom waxes as "visible control wanes," Skinner argued. Behavioral incentives and disincentives, rewards and punishments, were everywhere, but Americans were willfully blind to their presence in all but those clearly demarcated areas where discipline was appropriate (the barracks, the classroom, and the playground) or consciously sought (the gymnasium or the music lesson). By clearly demarcating those spaces and persons subjected to surveillance and psychological manipulation, Americans could pretend that such control was nonexistent everywhere else and that they, not their environment, were sovereign over themselves. Skinner, *Beyond Freedom and Dignity*, 70.

6. "Skinner's Utopia: Panacea, or Path to Hell?" *Time*, September 20, 1971.

7. Milos Forman, *One Flew over the Cuckoo's Nest*, directed by Milos Forman (1975; Burbank, CA: Warner Home Video, 2011), DVD.

8. Frederic Wertham, "Psychoauthoritarianism and the Law," *University of Chicago Law Review* 22 (Winter 1955): 336–38.

9. See, e.g., Angela Davis, "The Soledad Brothers," *Black Scholar* 2 (April–May 1971): 2–7; Willard Gaylin, "No Exit," *Harper's Magazine*, November 1971, 86–94; and Alan Dershowitz, "Let the Punishment Fit the Crime," *New York Times*, December 28, 1975. For a scholarly analysis of the movement against the

indeterminate sentence written during the decade, see Marvin Zalman, "The Rise and Fall of the Indeterminate Sentence," *Wayne Law Review* 24 (November 1977): 45–94.

10. Writing in the *Wayne Law Review* in 1977, Marvin Zalman astutely observed that the left, too, seemed drawn to the antimodern qualities of retribution: "The present desire for simple justice seems to reflect a broader uneasiness over the ability of the general-welfare state to solve the problems of the postindustrial era. Thus, the surprising consensus of liberals and conservatives in favor of sentencing uniformity may be a bit of nostalgic fundamentalism—a mythical recreation of a sure and stable past that never was." Zalman, "Rise and Fall of the Indeterminate Sentence," 93–94.

11. Their arguments framed retribution in a way similar to that of the Enlightenment philosopher Immanuel Kant. Kant had argued that punishment ought to be a retributive act that recognized the criminal's status as a responsible human being whose actions were being given their due. "If legal justice perishes," Kant had written—if the criminal was treated as a means to an end rather than an end in himself—"then it is no longer worth while for men to remain alive on this earth." Immanuel Kant, *The Metaphysical Elements of Justice*, trans. John Ladd (Indianapolis: Bobbs-Merrill, 1965), 100.

12. Michael E. Staub, *Madness Is Civilization: When the Diagnosis Was Social, 1948–1980* (Chicago: University of Chicago Press, 2011).

13. "Big Brother," the state, in Orwellian parlance, was as irrational as it was effective, Orwell showed. It insisted on converting the rebels it detected before it killed them. Winston, the protagonist, initially thinks that "to die hating them—that was freedom" when, trying to foment a rebellion, he is initially apprehended by the state. But it is only after a period of brainwashing, when he genuinely learns to love the state again, that he is executed—his physical death a mere symbol of his mental death. George Orwell, *1984* (1949; repr. London: Penguin, 1973), 226.

14. Staub. *Madness Is Civilization*, 72.

15. Ibid., 75.

16. Erving Goffman, *Asylums: Essays on the Social Situation of Mental Patients and Other Inmates* (Garden City, NY: Anchor, 1961).

17. Ibid., 16.

18. For an analysis of the romance of the middle-class white outsider and the seminal role that *The Catcher in the Rye* played in launching it, see Grace Elizabeth Hale, *A Nation of Outsiders: How the White Middle Class Fell in Love with Rebellion in Postwar America* (New York: Oxford University Press, 2011).

19. These films fit into a larger category of film that Nicole Rafter calls "crime films." As she notes, a key source of crime films' enduring attraction is that they provide "a cultural space for the expression of resistance to authority. . . . Simultaneously radical and conservative, crime films can appeal to nearly everyone."

Nicole Rafter, *Shots in the Mirror: Crime Films and Society* (Oxford: Oxford University Press, 2006), 13.

20. Thomas E. Gaddis and Guy Trosper, *Birdman of Alcatraz*, directed by John Frankenheimer (1962; Hollywood, CA: MGM, 2001), DVD.

21. Ibid.

22. Michael Tonry, *Sentencing Matters* (New York: Oxford University Press, 1996), 164. Quoted in Cassia C. Spohn, "Thirty Years of Sentencing Reform: The Quest for a Racially Neutral Sentencing Process," *Criminal Justice* 3 (2000): 427–501.

23. Angela Davis, for instance, argued that George Jackson, Fleeta Drumgo, and John Clutchette, who were accused of murdering a guard at Soledad State Prison in 1970, had been the victims of indeterminate sentences: "Only after having conceded the state's unqualified right to dictate the principles governing their lives, would the prison officials and the Adult authority consider them sufficiently 'rehabilitated' to warrant their release. Like so many of our brothers and sisters today they would not acquiesce in their victimization and continued to challenge the assumptions underlying this distorted concept of rehabilitation." Davis, "Soledad Brothers," 2. For an overview of the radical prison movement in California, see Eric Cummins, *The Rise and Fall of California's Radical Prison Movement* (Palo Alto, CA: Stanford University Press, 1994).

24. Naomi Murakawa, *The First Civil Right: How Liberals Built Prison America* (New York: Oxford University Press, 2014), 96–97.

25. Jessica Mitford, *Kind and Unusual Punishment: The Prison Business* (New York: Knopf, 1973), 48, 52. Indeed, in California, enhanced vulnerability to capital punishment was a by-product of the indeterminate sentence. Anyone serving an indeterminate life sentence was statutorily eligible for the death penalty if found guilty of a premeditated assault on a fellow prisoner or guard while incarcerated. Such was the case of Robert Wells, sentenced to death for throwing a cuspidor at a guard, and such was the possibility for George Jackson when he was charged, along with Fleeta Drumgo and John Clutchette, in the murder of a white guard at Soledad State Prison in California. See Cummins, *Rise and Fall of California's Radical Prison Movement*.

26. Anthony Burgess, *A Clockwork Orange* (1962; repr. New York: W. W. Norton, 1995).

27. Anthony Burgess, "The Clockwork Condition" (1973), *New Yorker*, June 4, 2012, 69–76, 76.

28. Arthur L. Mattocks and Charles Jew, "Assessment of an Aversive Treatment Program with Extreme Acting-Out Patients in a Psychiatric Facility for Criminal Offenders" (unpublished paper, California Department of Corrections, n.d.), quoted in Michael H. Shapiro, "Legislating the Control of Behavior Control: Autonomy and the Coercive Use of Organic Therapies," *Southern California Law Review* 47 (February 1974): 237–356, 246, 246n13.

29. Senate Committee on the Judiciary, *Report on Individual Rights and the Federal Role in Behavior Modification, 93rd Congress*, S. Rep. No. 88–744 (1974). Some accounts of the program held that prisoners began their experience in sensory deprivation naked; their first "reward" was underwear. Alan Eladio Gómez, "Resisting Living Death at Marion Federal Penitentiary, 1972," *Radical History Review* 96 (2006): 58–86. On the philosophical implications of the START program, see Lisa Guenther, *Solitary Confinement: Social Death and Its Afterlives* (Minneapolis: University of Minnesota Press, 2013), chap. 4 ("From Thought Reform to Behavior Modification").

30. Senate Committee on the Judiciary, *Report on Individual Rights and the Federal Role in Behavior Modification, 93rd Congress*, S. Rep. No. 88–744 (1974).

31. Jessica Mitford covered the experiment in "Clockwork Orange," a chapter of her muckraking book about prisons, *Kind and Unusual Punishment*. Syndicated columnist Nick von Hoffman wrote a column titled "California 'Clockwork,'" noting that the local medical ethics board failed to intervene. Why? Atascadero, he sarcastically explained, was "in modern, sunny, up-to-date California where they've just outlawed capital punishment, which, of course, you don't need if you're going to reinstitute torture." Nick von Hoffman, "California 'Clockwork,'" *Boston Globe*, April 9, 1972.

32. Phil Stanford, "A Model, Clockwork-Orange Prison," *New York Times*, September 17, 1972.

33. McNeil v. Director, Patuxent Institution 407 U.S. 245 (1972).

34. Stanford, "Model, Clockwork-Orange Prison."

35. The results of the investigation were released in a 1974 report. Senate Committee on the Judiciary, *Report on Individual Rights and the Federal Role in Behavior Modification, 93rd Congress*, S. Rep. No. 88–744 (1974).

36. Knecht v. Gillman, 488 F. 2d. 1136.

37. California Penal Code 2670.5 §1.

38. See Keramet Reiter, "Experimentation on Prisoners: Persistent Dilemmas in Rights and Regulations," *California Law Review* 97 (2009): 501–66.

39. William Claiborne, "New Prison Stirs Experiment Fears," *Washington Post*, December 17, 1973.

40. George Blue, "Prison Revolution or Inmate Solidarity: Two Views," *Chicago Defender*, June 29, 1974.

41. "Black Leaders to Meet in March against Racism," *New York Amsterdam News*, June 29, 1974.

42. The facility opened with an announced commitment to the "Morris Model," an approach to punishment developed by University of Chicago penologist Norval Morris that adopted a minimalist approach to punishment calling for determinate sentences, maximum prisoner autonomy within the context of confinement, and inmates who feel secure in their persons and property. The year it

was dedicated, Norman Carlson, director of the Bureau of Prisons, had written in his introduction to the federal system handbook, "Within the Federal Prison System we are trying to strike a new balance which recognizes that retribution and deterrence are also valid reasons for incarceration. Medical terms such as 'treatment' have been dropped since they imply that offenders are sick, that we know the causes of their crimes and we know how to effect cures, none of which is true." Quoted in Warren Uzzle, "Experimental Prison Is Troubled by Same Old Problems," *New York Times,* June 13, 1977.

43. Litigation over prison conditions also reflected this pattern. Keramet Reiter, "The Most Restrictive Alternative: A Litigation History of Solitary Confinement in U.S. Prisons, 1960–2006," *Studies in Law, Politics and Society* 57 (2012): 71–124.

44. Edward M. Opton Jr., "Psychiatric Violence against Prisoners: When Therapy Is Punishment," *Mississippi Law Journal* 45 (1974): 605–44, 607, 622.

45. On the limits of Eighth Amendment jurisprudence, see Reiter, "Most Restrictive Alternative," and Sharon Dolovich, "Cruelty, Prison Conditions, and the Eighth Amendment," *New York University Law Review* 84 (2009): 881–979.

46. Murakawa, *First Civil Right.*

47. Neal B. Kauder and Brian J. Ostrom, "State Sentencing Guidelines: Profiles and Continuum," National Center for State Courts (Williamsburg, VA), 2008. Available at http://tinyurl.com/qyy39z7 (accessed August 12, 2015).

48. As Murakawa explains, Marvin Frankel, whom Edward M. Kennedy called the "father of sentencing reform" and author of the treatise *Criminal Sentencing: Law without Order,* "wanted sentencing commissions to teach 'the public to accept a more civilized (generally less harsh) sentencing regime.'" Murakawa, *First Civil Right,* 108 (citation omitted).

49. Benjamin D. Fleury-Steiner, "Solitary Confinement and the Official Denial of Human Rights Abuses in U.S. Prisons" (paper presented at the annual meeting of the Law and Society Association, Minneapolis, May 2014)

50. For an overview of this literature, see Peter Scharff Smith, "The Effects of Solitary Confinement on Prison Inmates: A Brief History and Review of the Literature," *Crime and Justice* 34 (2006): 441–528.

51. Indeed, the lack of a positive right to mental integrity is evident in the de facto toll that solitary confinement exacts on mental health. See Keramet Reiter, "The Supermax Prison: A Blunt Means of Control, or a Subtle Form of Violence?" *Radical Philosophy Review* 17 (2014): 457–75.

52. Murakawa, *First Civil Right.*

53. One of the architects of the California legislation banning the administration of involuntary behavior modification therapies on inmates recognized that its focus on "intrusive therapies"—which he described as irreversible, aimed at changing rather than restoring a person's thought processes, rapidly effective, permanent, and irresistible—still left inmates vulnerable to psychological degra-

dation and suffering, particularly those in solitary confinement. "Although confinement alone may produce profound changes in mentation, it generally does so gradually, and we normally would not consider such confinement a direct intrusion on mentation," he wrote. In the occasional tension between individuals' right to freedom from unwanted government intrusion into thoughts and their interest in having the kinds of ordered thinking we commonly recognize as necessary to making meaningful and logical choices, the state might sometimes have to sacrifice the latter to preserve the former. Shapiro, "Legislating the Control of Behavior Control," 266.

54. People v. Robert Page Anderson, 6 Cal. 3d 628 (1972).

55. Ibid. at 646.

56. Roy G. Spece Jr. and J. Anthony Kouba, "A Convict's Brain: Is It Really His Own?" *Los Angeles Times*, April 2, 1972.

57. Shapiro, "Legislating the Control of Behavior Control," 337, 338n.

58. Herbert Morris, "Persons and Punishment," *Monist* 52 (1968): 475–501, 487.

59. Walter Berns, *For Capital Punishment: Crime and the Morality of the Death Penalty* (New York: Basic Books, 1979), 154.

60. Furman v. Georgia, 408 U.S. 238 (1972).

61. Stuart Banner, *The Death Penalty: An American History* (Cambridge, MA: Harvard University Press, 2002).

62. Furman v. Georgia, 408 U.S. 238 (1972) at 245 (Douglas, Concurring).

63. Ibid. at 293, 295 (Brennan, Concurring).

64. Ibid. at 309 (Stewart, Concurring).

65. Ibid. at 253 (Douglas, Concurring).

66. Indeed, in a speech urging the passage of federal determinate sentencing laws, Edward M. Kennedy, the bill's sponsor, praised the protections procedural due process offered to an offender's freedom. The current system left defendants without a "way of knowing or reliably predicting whether he or she will walk out of the courtroom on probation or be locked up for a term of years that may consume the rest of his or her life, or somewhere in between." *Congressional Record*, February 2, 1984, 1644, quoted in Murakawa, *First Civil Right*, 106.

67. National Advisory Commission on Criminal Justice Standards and Goals, *Report on the Criminal Justice System* (Washington, DC: Government Printing Office, 1973), 181, quoted in Murakawa, *First Civil Right*, 133.

68. Of course, this would not completely guarantee fairness; the classification of a crime is in many cases subjective, and prosecutors would still retain the discretion to charge defendants with capital murder or a noncapital form of murder, thereby maintaining the opportunity for similarly situated defendants to incur different punishments.

69. Gregg v. Georgia 428 U.S. 153 (1976) at 222 (White, Concurring).

70. Woodson et al. v. North Carolina 428 U.S. 280 (1976) at 304.

71. Ibid.

72. Yet "guided" as it might have been, the discretion the Court preserved in *Gregg* undermined the fairness it had demanded four years earlier. Justice Brennan had warned in *Furman* that "crimes and criminals simply do not admit of a distinction that can be drawn so finely as to explain, [on a rational basis], the execution of such a tiny sample of those eligible." Furman v. Georgia at 294. And even if they did, none of the statutes states created had standards so clear that two differently constituted juries would inevitably arrive at the same sentence. All of them included words and standards that required jurors to respond in ways that were subjective. The result was, predictably enough, the observable influence of constitutionally impermissible variables on sentencing decisions. By the mid-1980s, the Court was presented with statistical evidence that the leeway built into the standards of "guided discretion" sentencing statutes was enabling unlawful discrimination. Presented in *McClesky v. Kemp* with evidence that, all other relevant factors being equal, juries in Georgia were more likely to sentence defendants convicted of capital murder to death when their victims were white, the Court nonetheless refused to overturn the death sentence of an African American man who had murdered a white person. Statistical patterns were not enough to prove discriminatory intent. "We decline to assume that what is unexplained is invidious" the Court wrote, backing away from the commitment it had made in *Furman* to ensuring fair outcomes in capital cases. McClesky vs. Kemp 481 U.S. 279 (1987) at 312–13.

73. Callins v. Collins, 510 U.S. 1141 (1994) at 1145 (Blackmun, Dissenting).

74. David Garland, *Peculiar Institution: America's Death Penalty in an Age of Abolition* (Cambridge, MA: Harvard University Press, 2010).

75. Michael McCann and David T. Johnson have argued that the fear of totalitarianism that underlay the abolition of the death penalty in Europe after World War II was absent in the United States. In the United States, they write, "domestic political elites could justifiably distance themselves from the murderous fascism and imperial militarism of totalitarian European states defeated in World War II. Even more than in Britain and France, leaders in the United States found little reason to increase legal limits on state power or to refrain from exercising violence against persons who wantonly broke the law." Michael McCann and David T. Johnson, "Rocked but Still Rolling: The Enduring Institution of Capital Punishment in Historical and Comparative Perspective," in *The Road to Abolition? The Future of Capital Punishment in the United States*, ed. Charles J. Ogletree Jr. and Austin Sarat (New York: New York University Press, 2009), 147. And yet, as I suggest here, the Court did seem sensitive to the contribution American eugenics had made to the development of Nazi ideology, and a fear of American susceptibility to totalitarian power was at the heart of Cold War domestic culture and the suspicious attitude many Americans eventually adopted toward technocratic, welfare-oriented forms of social engineer-

ing. From the individualizing sentencing law mandated by the Court in *Woodson* to the self-presentation of prominent death-seeking district attorneys as lawmen in the Old West, the death penalty in the United States has been just as deliberately distanced from the totalitarianism of the fascist European state as from the anarchy of racist vigilantism.

76. Furman v. Georgia, 408 U.S. 238 (1972) at 357 (Marshall, Concurring).

77. Murakawa, *First Civil Right.*

78. Mona Lynch, "The Disposal of Inmate #85271: Notes on a Routine Execution," *Studies in Law, Politics, and Society* 20 (2000): 3–34, 6.

79. Thomas Szasz, "The Right to Die," *New Republic*, December 11, 1976, 8–9.

## Chapter Three

1. Robert Johnson, *Death Work: A Study of the Modern Execution Process*, 2nd ed. (Belmont, CA: Wadsworth, 1998), 43.

2. "Offender Information: Earl Behringer," *Texas Department of Criminal Justice (TDCJ)*, https://www.tdcj.state.tx.us/death_row/dr_info/behringcrearllast .html (accessed July 18, 2015).

3. Truman Capote, *In Cold Blood* (New York: Vintage, 1965), 341.

4. Norman Mailer, *The Executioner's Song* (1979; repr. New York: Vintage, 1998), 934.

5. Ibid., 984.

6. Ibid., 979.

7. While Gilmore's dogged pursuit of his death sentence made volunteering for execution an opportunity to thumb his nose at the state, the drama he created by seeking his own death was atypical, the result of his status as the first prisoner executed since the *Furman* moratorium was imposed. While volunteering can easily be read as suicide, and thus as subverting the state's power to punish, Meredith Martin Rountree has shown that defendants seeking to drop their appeals often hesitate to frame their cases in that way: "Consciously or not, the prisoners may have recognized that in seeking the sovereign's permission, they were better off acceding to its power than insisting that the Court recognize that they have rights and claims requiring respect and accommodation." As a result, the procedures followed when a defendant wishes to stop appeals legitimate capital punishment. Meredith Martin Rountree, "'I'll Make Them Shoot Me': Accounts of Death Row Prisoners Advocating for Execution," *Law and Society Review* 46 (2012): 589–622, 604.

8. Wayne King, "Florida Executes Killer as Plea Fails," *New York Times*, May 26, 1979.

9. Appearance, it is important to note, does not always reflect reality. In a

recent survey, Austin Sarat found that lethal injection was botched more often than executions by other methods used in the twentieth century. While 3 percent of executions have gone awry in some way since 1900, over 7 percent of lethal injections have not gone according to plan. Austin Sarat, *Gruesome Spectacles: Botched Executions and America's Death Penalty* (Palo Alto, CA: Stanford University Press, 2014).

10. Indeed, in the 1950s the British Royal Commission rejected lethal injection as a mode of execution because it was too emasculating. Timothy V. Kaufman-Osborn, "The Death of Dignity," in *Is the Death Penalty Dying? European and American Perspectives*, ed. Austin Sarat and Jürgen Martschukat (Cambridge: Cambridge University Press, 2011).

11. "Number of Executions by State and Year," *Death Penalty Information Center*, http://www.deathpenaltyinfo.org/number-executions-state-and-region -1976 (last updated July 15, 2015).

12. "Executed Offenders," *Texas Department of Criminal Justice (TDCJ)*, https://www.tdcj.state.tx.us/death_row/dr_executed_offenders.html (accessed July 18, 2015).

13. Jason Clark, e-mail message to author, March 4, 2014. According to Clark, the public information director of the Texas Department of Criminal Justice, the purpose of the website was efficiency; since last statements were the most requested pieces of information about an execution, "TDCJ places the last statements on the website because it eliminates the need to respond to individual requests." For reasons I discuss later, publishing the last meal requests, also justified by efficiency, was eliminated in 2003 and existing information about the meals was deleted.

14. On executions during the seventeenth, eighteenth, and early nineteenth centuries, see Louis Masur, *Rites of Execution: Capital Punishment and the Transformation of American Culture, 1776–1865* (New York: Oxford University Press, 1989); Stuart Banner, *The Death Penalty: An American History* (Cambridge, MA: Harvard University Press, 2002); Michel Foucault, *Discipline and Punish: The Birth of the Prison*, trans. Alan Sheridan (1975; New York: Vintage Books, 1995). Citations refer to the Vintage edition. See also Karen Halttunen, *Murder Most Foul: The Killer and the American Gothic Imagination* (Cambridge, MA: Harvard University Press, 2000).

15. "Executed Offenders," *TDCJ*.

16. "Offender Information: Jonathan Marcus Green," *Texas Department of Criminal Justice (TDCJ)*, https://www.tdcj.state.tx.us/death_row/dr_info/green jonathon.html (accessed July 18, 2015).

17. Ibid.

18. Ibid.

19. Émile Durkheim, *The Division of Labor in Society*, 1893, trans. W. D. Halls (New York: Free Press, 1984), 58, 63.

20. Sensational forms of punishment declined, Foucault argues, as disciplinary forms of power became dominant in the eighteenth and early nineteenth centuries. In contrast to spectacles of sovereign might, power was life-affirming rather than life-denying, present in the quotidian rather than in the occasional spectacle, continuous rather than "on again, off again." Its object was no longer to maintain sovereign power but to maximize and expand capital or other forms of utility by systematically using knowledge about the mind and the body to train and reshape them. And yet, as Foucault himself acknowledges, harsh bodily punishments like the death penalty persisted well beyond the developments he documents. Foucault accounts for the persistence of the death penalty in modern societies by claiming they are framed differently: "As soon as power gave itself the function of administering life, its reason for being and the logic of its existence—and not the awakening of humanitarian feelings—made it more and more difficult to apply the death penalty. How could power exercise its highest prerogatives by putting people to death, when its main role was to ensure, sustain, and multiply life, to put this life in order? For such a power, execution was at the same time a limit, a scandal, and a contradiction. Hence capital punishment could not be maintained except by invoking less the enormity of the crime itself than the monstrosity of the criminal, his incorrigibility, and the safeguard of society. One had the right to kill those who represented a kind of biological danger to others." Michel Foucault, *The History of Sexuality: An Introduction*, trans. Richard Hurley (New York: Random House, 1990), 138.

21. Penry v. Lynaugh 492 U.S. 302 (1989) at 310.

22. Ibid. at 328.

23. The language used by courts in Texas varies slightly from case to case. This wording was taken from a 2008 case. Charge to the Jury, State of Texas v. Juan Leonardo Quintero, Harris County District Court (Houston, TX), Case No. 1085704, 2008, available at "Jury Charges in Sentences in Capital Cases," Texas Judicial Branch, http://www.txcourts.gov/All_Archived_Documents/JudicialInformation/oca/pdf/jchgs/Harris052008JChgSnt.pdf (accessed July 18, 2015). The current sentencing scheme outlined here was instituted in 1991.

24. Final Argument on Punishment, State of Texas v. Herman Addison, Punishment Phase Trial Record, Argument Volume, Harris County District Clerk's Office (Houston, TX), Case No. 723380, 1997, 68. Addison received a life sentence from his jury after it deadlocked eight to four in favor of death. Stefanie Asin, "Brain-Damaged Man Escapes Death Penalty," *Houston Chronicle*, July 17, 1997.

25. Ibid., 68–69.

26. Ibid., 69.

27. Ibid., 70.

28. Prosecutors articulate choice as a fundamental part of what Paul Kaplan

calls the "American Creed." Paul Kaplan, *Murder Stories: Ideological Narratives in Capital Punishment* (Lanham, MD: Lexington Books, 2012).

29. Final Argument on Punishment, State of Texas v. Herman Addison, 69.

30. Ibid., 72–73.

31. Final Argument on Punishment, State of Texas v. Danny Dean Thomas, Punishment Phase Trial Record, Argument Volume, Texas Court of Criminal Appeals (Austin, TX), Case No. AP-73,351, 1998, 41.

32. Final Argument on Punishment, State of Texas v. Derrick Jackson, Punishment Phase Trial Record, Argument Volume, Texas Court of Criminal Appeals (Austin, TX), Case No. AP-73,081, 1998, 69.

33. Final Argument on Punishment, State of Texas v. Jeffrey Williams, Punishment Phase Trial Record, Argument Volume, Texas Court of Criminal Appeals (Austin, TX), Case No. AP-73,796, 2000, 49.

34. Final Argument on Punishment, State of Texas v. Eric Cathey, Punishment Phase Trial Record, Argument Volume, Texas Court of Criminal Appeals (Austin, TX), Case No. AP-72,772, 1997, 101.

35. Ibid., 100.

36. "Death Sentences in the United States from 1977 by State and by Year," *Death Penalty Information Center*, http://www.deathpenaltyinfo.org/death-sentences-united-states-1977–2008 (last updated July 15, 2015). These data do not indicate how many life sentences juries handed out, thus limiting our ability to know whether other variables, such as a higher number of cases in which death was sought, may be masking a negative effect *Penry* had on death sentences. Nonetheless, we can say that death row grew faster after *Penry* than before it.

37. David Garland, *Peculiar Institution: America's Death Penalty in an Age of Abolition* (Cambridge, MA: Harvard University Press, 2010), 268.

38. Roper v. Simmons 543 U.S. 551 (2005).

39. Atkins v. Virginia 536 U.S. 304 (2002).

40. Ford v. Wainwright 477 U.S. 399 (1986) and Panetti v. Quarterman 551 U.S. 930 (2007).

41. Studying the closing arguments of defense attorneys in California, Paul Kaplan has found that attorneys must walk a "narrow tightrope" when arguing about mitigating evidence: when telling their client's life stories to juries, he explains, they avoid directly challenging an American "creed" that posits individuals as the uncaused cause of their acts. To question the concept of personal responsibility was to risk alienating the jury. Kaplan, *Murder Stories*, 110.

42. Woodson et al. v. North Carolina 428 U.S. 280 (1976) at 304.

43. The emergence of modern technologies of power and processes of rationalization in the eighteenth century, Foucault has shown, gradually led Western nation-states to abandon public executions as an unreliable strategy for social control. Instead, disciplinary, institutionalized approaches to punishment

allowed the state to extract data from each subject that could then be used, in congruence with a rapidly expanding body of social scientific knowledge, to govern the person. Because it was so targeted, this method was thought to be much more efficient at controlling the population than the spectacle of a public execution, whose impact could be distorted by any number of variables or "third part[ies]." Foucault, *Discipline and Punish*, 129.

44. Annulla Linders, "The Execution Spectacle and State Legitimacy: The Changing Nature of the American Execution Audience, 1833–1937," *Law and Society Review* 36 (2002): 607–56.

45. Timothy V. Kaufman-Osborn, "The Metaphysics of the Hangman," *Studies in Law, Politics, and Society* 20 (2000): 35–70, 48.

46. See, e.g., Johnson, *Death Work*; Mona Lynch, "The Disposal of Inmate #85271: Notes on a Routine Execution," *Studies in Law, Politics, and Society* 20 (2000): 3–34; and Stephen Trombley, *The Execution Protocol: Inside America's Capital Punishment Industry* (New York: Doubleday, 1993).

47. Johnson, *Death Work*, 50.

48. For scholarly analyses, see, e.g., Johnson, *Death Work*; Kaufman-Osborn, "Metaphysics of the Hangman"; Lynch, "Disposal of Inmate #85271"; and Trombley, *Execution Protocol*. For commentary in major newspapers, see Joseph L. Zentner, "Lethal Injection Is Still Killing," *Chicago Tribune*, May 7, 1985; Mike Jendrzejczyk, "'Sanitized' Execution Is Still Dirty," *Los Angeles Times*, January 10, 1982; David C. Anderson, "Who Wears the Blindfolds at Executions?" *New York Times*, February 26, 1995; Kurt Andersen, Sam Allis, and David Beckwith, "A 'More Palatable' Way of Killing," *Time*, December 20, 1982.

49. Trombley, *Execution Protocol*, and Johnson, *Death Work*.

50. Johnson, *Death Work*, and Linda Ross Meyer, "The Meaning of Death: Last Words, Last Meals," in *Who Deserves to Die: Constructing the Executable Subject*, ed. Austin Sarat and Karl Shoemaker (Amherst: University of Massachusetts Press, 2011).

51. Meyer, "Meaning of Death."

52. Tracy L. Snell, *Capital Punishment, 2011—Statistical Tables* (Washington, DC: Bureau of Justice Statistics, 2014). Available online at http://www.bjs .gov/content/pub/pdf/cp11st.pdf (accessed August 7, 2015).

53. Ibid.

54. Johnson, *Death Work*, 93.

55. This kind of risk management model was widely adopted by prison managers over the course of the 1980s. Malcolm M. Feeley and Jonathan Simon, "The New Penology: Notes on the Emerging Strategy of Corrections and Its Implications," *Criminology* 30 (1992): 449–74.

56. David Garland, *The Culture of Control: Crime and Social Order in Contemporary Society* (Chicago: University of Chicago Press, 2001), 184.

57. Lynch, "Disposal of Inmate #85271."

58. On the contrary, offenders' last words, last meal requests, and their subsequent broadcast to the public may enable or even encourage sympathetic identification with offenders while diluting portrayals of them as irredeemable figures unworthy of sympathy or rehabilitation. Eating and coming to terms with death are two tasks—one mundane, the other existential—that observers will inevitably share with those executed.

59. Austin Sarat has also identified this oxymoronic conception of executable subjects. Austin Sarat, *When the State Kills: Capital Punishment and the American Condition* (Princeton, NJ: Princeton University Press, 2001).

60. States do not always make this work easy. These practices are not always mandated by or mentioned in execution manuals. Some states do not invite inmates to speak in the execution chamber, instead asking them to write a statement that is released to the media after the execution. Others do not provide a microphone in the chamber, making it impossible for witnesses, sitting in a separate room behind a glass partition, to hear what an offender is saying. Even in these states, however, journalists go out of their way to report what they see. When Stanley "Tookie" Williams was executed in California in 2005, witnesses could see, but not hear, the execution. The *Los Angeles Times* reported that Williams's supporters "mouthed 'God bless you' and 'We love you' and blew kisses to Williams. Williams also seemed to mouth statements." The reporters also noted that, when the execution was delayed because personnel were having difficulty finding a vein suitable for the injection, "Williams repeatedly lifted his head off the gurney, winced visibly, and at one point appeared to say: 'Still can't find it?'" Even when final words were not a scripted part of the execution, journalists were determined to accurately report the last words spoken by the condemned. Jenifer Warren and Maura Dolan, "Tookie Williams Is Executed," *Los Angeles Times*, December 13, 2005.

61. Kevin Francis O'Neill, "Muzzling Death Row Inmates: Applying the First Amendment to Regulations That Restrict a Condemned Prisoner's Last Words," *Arizona State Law Journal* 33 (2001): 1159–1218.

62. Ibid.

63. The state's commitment to its tradition of last meals has been more uneven. Until 2003, the Texas Department of Criminal Justice reproduced condemned inmates' final meal requests word for word on its website. In response to complaints that independently broadcasting inmates' final meal requests was in poor taste, the department took them off the website, but they continued to release the information to the media. Its long-standing commitment to publishing and releasing to the media offenders' last words and last meal requests has, like the Supreme Court's retention of juries' sentencing discretion, maintained an image of a state that recognized the distinctiveness of each offender's life. When the department removed the information from its website, an independent website, the Memory Hole, archived the last iteration of the web page on

which the state reported the final meal requests. The Memory Hole eventually went offline, but its reproduction of the state's last meals web page has itself been archived by the Stanford University Social Sciences Research Group using Archive-It. The state's last meals website is thus available at http://wayback .archive-it.org/924/20100423172233/http://www.thememoryhole.org/deaths/ texas-final-meals.htm.

64. For the sake of efficiency, the individual URL of each statement quoted is not given. These statements may be accessed by clicking the link labeled last statement next to a particular inmate's name on the state's "Executed Offenders" web page. "Executed Offenders," *TDCJ* (William Davis).

65. Ibid.

66. In front of crowds that had come to watch them die, the righteous tried to evoke sympathy, potentially making the sovereign's punishment seem cruel rather than just. The deviant, on the other hand, questioned the seriousness of the sanction, potentially making the state look impotent. Philip Smith, "Executing Executions: Aesthetics, Identity, and the Problematic Narratives of Capital Punishment Ritual," *Theory and Society* 25 (1996): 235–61, 241.

67. "Executed Offenders," *TDCJ* (Robert Atworth and Brian Roberson).

68. Ibid. For claims of innocence, see the last statements of Gary Graham, Leonel Herrera, Cameron Willingham, Gregory Wright, Orien Joiner, Martin Vega, Henry Dunn, Preston Hughes, Keith Thurmond, Roy Pippin, Jonathan Green, Thomas Mason, Paul Nuncio, Richard Duncan, Cary Kerr, Clifford Phillips, Odell Barnes, Reginald Blanton, Kenneth Ransom, Billy Hughes, Richard Jones, Willie Pondexter, Robert Drew, Johnny Anderson, Mack Hill, and Carl Johnson. For examples of inmates who criticized the criminal justice system in their final statements, see the last statements of Roy Pippin, Milton Mathis, and Lee Taylor.

69. Ibid.

70. Ibid.

71. See, e.g., Ethan Blue, "The Culture of the Condemned: Pastoral Execution and Life on Death Row in the 1930s," *Law, Culture, and the Humanities* 9 (2013): 114–32, and Meyer, "Meaning of Death."

72. "Executed Offenders," *TDCJ* (Jonathan Green).

73. Frank R. Baumgartner, Suzanna L. De Boef, and Amber E. Boydstun, *The Decline of the Death Penalty and the Discovery of Innocence* (Cambridge: Cambridge University Press, 2008).

74. On the meaning of punishment to distant observers of it, see Michelle Brown, *The Culture of Punishment: Prison, Society, and Spectacle* (New York: New York University Press, 2009).

75. Erving Goffman, *Asylums: Essays on the Social Situation of Mental Patients and Other Inmates* (Garden City, NY: Anchor, 1961), 4.

76. "Executed Offenders," *TDCJ* (Jamie McCoskey).

77. Bruce Jackson and Diane Christian, *In This Timeless Time: Living and Dying on Death Row in America* (Chapel Hill: University of North Carolina Press, 2012).

78. Meyer, "Meaning of Death," 191.

79. These are excerpts from the final statements of Vincent Cooks, Michael Richard, Dennis Dowthitt, Jerry Martin, Richard Jones, Robert Morrow, Robert Carter, John Lamb, Timothy Gribble, G. W. Green, and Rex Mays, respectively. "Executed Offenders," *TDCJ.*

80. Sara Rimer, "In the Busiest Death Chamber, Duty Carries Its Own Burdens," *New York Times,* December 17, 2000.

81. "Deleted List of Texas Inmates' Last Meals," *Archive-It,* http://wayback .archive-it.org/924/20100423172233/http://www.thememoryhole.org/deaths/ texas-final-meals.htm (accessed July 22, 2015).

82. Ibid.

83. Karen Hillebrand, "Sanderson's Life Comes to End," *Lexington (NC) Dispatch,* January 30, 1998. North Carolina's death row website appears to no longer catalog its condemned inmates' final words.

84. Brian Price, "The Last Supper," *Legal Affairs,* March/April 2004, 31.

85. "Deleted List of Texas Inmates' Last Meals," *Archive-It.*

86. "We're not trying to entertain anyone by putting this information out," Lyons told a reporter in 2003. "We're putting it out because it's what the public wants to know." Carlos Campos, "Prisoners' Last Meals Satisfy Appetite for Curious Facts," *Atlanta Journal-Constitution,* December 1, 2003.

87. These practices and their broadcast to the public undoubtedly served multiple purposes in addition to the one I am emphasizing here. Morbid curiosity is one compelling explanation. Wendy Lesser argues that details like these titillate observers; they offer a voyeuristic glimpse into a world most of us will never know, an opportunity to safely imagine what we would say or eat if we were mere minutes from the noose or the needle. They allow us to enter for a fleeting moment the mind of someone close to death. Wendy Lesser, *Pictures at an Execution: An Inquiry into the Subject of Murder* (Cambridge, MA: Harvard University Press, 1993). Indeed, the *Houston Chronicle* reported that the details of offenders' final meals (perhaps a more voyeuristic object than final statements) were the most popular feature of the Department of Criminal Justice's website when they were posted. Allan Turner, "Last Meals Considered Tasteless," *Houston Chronicle,* December 15, 2003. An entire genre of privately published books developed around the final meal requests of prisoners in Texas and elsewhere, with titles like *Dead Man Eating* (2006), *Last Suppers: Famous Final Meals from Death Row* (2001), and *Meals to Die For* (2005). These details of executions have become commodities, privileged information that can sell newspapers and books. Other interpretations abound. The traditions of last meals and last words may keep offenders and the public from responding to the violence of execu-

tions. They pacify prisoners by giving them personally meaningful or satisfying tasks in their final moments, tasks that require their cooperation with authorities. For the public, the practice of allowing the offender to speak immediately before execution signifies to the public the state's commitment to due process; procedural rights to speak and object serve as a distraction from violations of the offender's substantive rights. In that sense, the last speech further distinguishes the state's lawful killing from the lawless killing it is punishing and, in so doing, enhances the public's perception of the state as just. Noting how Christ's Last Supper shapes the meaning of last meals in their contemporary context, Meyer argues that the practice signifies forgiveness. Meyer, "Meaning of Death." Others interpret it as generating exactly the opposite sentiment. Applying René Girard's mimetic theory of culture to executions, Donald L. Beschle sees the last meal as a ritual designed to incite animosity toward the condemned person. Through this practice, the condemned gets to engage temporarily in role reversal, commanding that the state serve him his favorite meal. Such a role reversal amplifies and focuses the community's collective anger. Donald L. Beschle, "What's Guilt (or Deterrence) Got to Do with It? The Death Penalty, Ritual, and Mimetic Violence," *William and Mary Law Review* 38 (1997): 487–538. One might make the same case for offenders' last words. The opportunity to have the last word is another kind of role reversal, wherein the condemned gains undue attention in his final moments. This interpretation of the final meal and final statement is confirmed by letters to the editor that sometimes surface, indignantly comparing the offender's easy, luxury-filled death with the victim's cruel, unadorned one. A letter to the *Nevada Appeal*, for example, said about offenders' deaths, "They have a nice last meal and in six minutes are put to sleep on a nice, clean cot, no blood, no gore—with protesters out front praying for them. That is definitely not 'an eye for an eye.'" Patrice Heeran, letter, *Nevada Appeal*, May 27, 2006. It is also reflected in Antonin Scalia's 1994 concurrence in *Callins v. Collins*, which held that capital punishment did not violate the Eighth Amendment. He described the case as "the murder of a man ripped by a bullet suddenly and unexpectedly, with no opportunity to prepare himself and his affairs, and left to bleed to death on the floor of a tavern." He continued, "How enviable a quiet death by lethal injection compared with that!" The offender's final meal and final statement, opportunities to "prepare himself and his affairs," thus became in this telling the basis of a perverse kind of envy. Scalia's words called attention to this imbalance in a way that invites hostility toward offenders. *Callins v. Collins*, 510 U.S. 1141 (1994) at 1142–43 (Scalia, Concurring).

88. "Executed Offenders," *TDCJ* (Troy Kunkle).

89. Walter Berns, *For Capital Punishment: Crime and the Morality of the Death Penalty* (New York: Basic Books, 1979).

90. Campos, "Prisoners' Last Meals," quoted in Meyer, "Meaning of Death," 182.

91. Patricia Ewick, "The Return of Restraint: Limits to the Punishing State," *Quinnipiac Law Review* 31 (2013): 577–97, 591.

## Chapter Four

1. Arthur Miller, *The Crucible: A Play in Four Acts* (New York: Penguin, 2003), 134.

2. Karen Halttunen, *Murder Most Foul: The Killer and the American Gothic Imagination* (Cambridge, MA: Harvard University Press, 2000), and Stuart Banner, *The Death Penalty: An American History* (Cambridge, MA: Harvard University Press, 2002).

3. Halttunen, *Murder Most Foul*.

4. The salvation of the condemned person's soul was often at the heart of premodern execution rituals. In colonial New England, Puritans executed those they condemned to death after shrift periods in which the offender worshipped alongside them in church. Then, on execution day, clergy would urge the crowd to identify with the reformed sinner, to pray that God's grace would save them all from hell. Halttunen, *Murder Most Foul*, and Banner, *Death Penalty*.

5. The notion that a date with the gallows could catalyze the redemption of sinners persisted even after the arrival of the Enlightenment in North America pushed the state and civil society in secular directions. When abolitionist progressives like Benjamin Rush sought to replace the gallows with penitentiaries, conservative religious leaders balked. As Louis P. Masur explains, a number of them claimed the executed were more likely to be saved than the imprisoned. "Eternal reformation, the ascent from the gallows to glory, was far more important than far-fetched schemes for temporal reform," they insisted. Louis P. Masur, *Rites of Execution: Capital Punishment and the Transformation of American Culture, 1776–1865* (New York: Oxford University Press, 1989), 70.

6. Furman v. Georgia, 408 U.S. 238 (1972) at 382 (Burger, Dissenting).

7. Ibid. at 289–90 (Brennan, Concurring).

8. Ibid. at 346 (Marshall, Concurring).

9. Stuart Banner, "Traces of Slavery: Race and the Death Penalty in Historical Perspective," in *From Lynch Mobs to the Killing State: Race and the Death Penalty in America*, ed. Charles J. Ogletree Jr. and Austin Sarat (New York: New York University Press, 2006).

10. David Garland, *Peculiar Institution: America's Death Penalty in an Age of Abolition* (Cambridge, MA: Harvard University Press, 2010).

11. Andrea Shapiro, "Unequal before the Law: Men, Women and the Death Penalty," *American University Journal of Gender, Social Policy, and the Law* 8 (2000): 427–70.

12. For women it deepened. Twice as many women were killed from 1930 to 1967 (thirty-one) as were executed from 1977 to 2014 (fifteen), despite enormous population growth over that time. Data on women executed from 1930 to 1967 come from M. Watt Espy and John Ortiz Smykla, *Executions in the United States, 1608–2002: The Espy File* [computer file], 4th ICPSR ed., compiled by M. Watt Espy and John Ortiz Smykla (Ann Arbor, MI: Inter-university Consortium for Political and Social Research, 2004). Data on women executed from 1977 to 2014 come from the Searchable Execution Database of the Death Penalty Information Center, available at http://www.deathpenaltyinfo.org/views-executions (accessed August 5, 2015). The finding of racial bias comes from Steven E. Barkan and Steven F. Cohn, "Racial Prejudice and Support for the Death Penalty by Whites," *Journal of Research in Crime and Delinquency* 31 (1994): 202–9.

13. On the rise of crime control as a strategy for manipulating anxiety about race, see Katherine Beckett, *Making Crime Pay: Law and Order in Contemporary American Politics* (New York: Oxford University Press, 1997).

14. Michelle Alexander, *The New Jim Crow: Mass Incarceration in an Age of Colorblindness* (New York: New Press, 2010). On the role race has played in the incarceration boom, see also Michael Tonry, *Malign Neglect: Race, Crime, and Punishment in America* (Oxford: Oxford University Press, 1996) also Ruth Wilson Gilmore, *Golden Gulag: Prisons, Surplus, Crisis, and Opposition in Globalizing California* (Berkeley: University of California Press, 2007).

15. See John Blume, Theodore Eisenberg, and Martin T. Wells, "Explaining Death Row's Population and Racial Composition," *Journal of Empirical Legal Studies* 1 (2004): 165–207; Lowell Dodge, Laurie E. Eckland, et al., "Death Penalty Sentencing," in *The Death Penalty in America*, ed. Hugo A. Bedau (New York: Oxford University Press, 1990); Raymond Paternoster, *Capital Punishment in America* (New York: Lexington Books, 1991).

16. David Jacobs and Jason T. Carmichael, "The Political Sociology of the Death Penalty: A Pooled Time-Series Analysis," *American Sociological Review* 67 (2002): 109–31.

17. Steven E. Barkan and Steven F. Cohn, "Racial Prejudice and Support for the Death Penalty by Whites," *Journal of Research in Crime and Delinquency* 31 (1994): 202–9, and Joe Soss, Laura Langbein, and Alan R. Metelko, "Why Do White Americans Support the Death Penalty?" *Journal of Politics* 65 (2003): 397–421.

18. Benjamin Fleury-Steiner, *Jurors' Stories of Death: How America's Death Penalty Invests in Inequality* (Ann Arbor: University of Michigan Press, 2004), 8.

19. David C. Baldus, Charles Pulaski, and George Woodworth, "Comparative Review of Death Sentences: An Empirical Study of the Georgia Experience," *Journal of Criminal Law and Criminology* 74 (1983): 661–753.

20. McCleskey vs. Kemp 481 U.S. 279 (1987) at 313.

21. While popular culture has sometimes mapped images of a comforting and familiar past onto newer social practices in order to soothe anxiety about change, in the case of the death penalty it operated on a landscape in which inertia—the nation's failure to overcome its racist past—rather than change, was the source of anxiety. On the way consumer capitalism was reconciled with nostalgia for traditional values, see George Lipsitz, *Time Passages: Collective Memory and American Popular Culture* (Minneapolis: University of Minnesota Press, 1990).

22. Only four films made more than passing reference to the execution of a black prisoner; the rest depicted or focused on the execution of a white inmate. Of the four films in which a black man's execution earned more attention, only two depicted the actual execution. Of the two movies that did not depict the execution, in one the African American inmate was saved at the last minute by a white reporter, and in the other the execution occurred offscreen. These films were *The Green Mile* (1999), *True Crime* (1999), *A Lesson Before Dying* (2001), and *Monster's Ball* (2001). On-screen executions of black men occur only in *The Green Mile* and *Monster's Ball*. Only *A Lesson Before Dying* depicts the executed black man as a multilayered, complex character who changes over the course of the film. See Frank Darabont, *The Green Mile*, directed by Frank Darabont (1999; Hollywood, CA: Warner Home Video, 2007), DVD; Larry Gross, Stephen Schiff, and Paul Brickman, *True Crime*, directed by Clint Eastwood (1996; Hollywood, CA: Warner Home Video, 1999), DVD; Ann Peacock, *A Lesson Before Dying*, directed by Joseph Sargent (1999; Hollywood, CA: HBO Home Video, 2000), DVD; Milo Addica and Will Rokos, *Monster's Ball*, directed by Marc Forster (2001; Hollywood, CA: Warner Home Video, 2002), DVD.

23. David W. Rintels, Gerald I. Isenberg, Hans Proppe, Julian Marks, and Michael B. Seligman, *The Execution of Raymond Graham*, directed by Daniel Petrie (1985; Sunrise, FL: Alliance Entertainment, 2000), DVD.

24. Robert Eisele, Mary McLaglen, and Charles Weinstock, *Last Light*, directed by Kiefer Sutherland (1993; Santa Monica, CA: Lionsgate, 2007), DVD.

25. William Goldman and Chris Reese, *The Chamber*, directed by James Foley (1996; Hollywood, CA: Universal Studios, 1998), DVD.

26. Randy C. Baer and Marlane X. Meyer, *Better Off Dead*, directed by M. Neema Barnette (1993; Burbank, CA: Warner Home Video, 1995), VHS.

27. *Raymond Graham* was read by critics as a "protest against capital punishment," and ABC pressured its producers to voice more pro–capital punishment sentiment in telling the story. Tom Shales, "The Deathwatch: 'Execution'; ABC's Gripping Live Drama," *Washington Post*, November 18, 1985; Stephen Farber, "They Watch What We Watch: A Controversy Heats Up Over Whether TV's Censors Do Too Much or Too Little," *New York Times*, May 7, 1989. John Grisham's opposition to the death penalty is widely known. Critics perceived

his abolitionist viewpoint when *The Chamber* was first released as a novel. See, e.g., Walter Goodman, "Getting to Know Grandpa under Penalty of Death," *New York Times*, July 29, 1994. Grisham's subsequent 2006 nonfictional study of a wrongful conviction in *An Innocent Man* and his fictional treatment of that theme in *The Confession* in 2010 have continued to reveal the depths of his abolitionist commitment. Gloria Steinem was driven by similar motivations. As she explained to the Associated Press in an interview about the movie, "What too few people understand is that capital punishment has no impact on cutting down crime, and that there's considerable evidence that it does the reverse: encourages crime. Worse, it is administered in such a way that the system waits until the person is rehabilitated. Then the sentence is finally carried out." "Gloria Steinem Produces 'Better Off Dead,'" *Lodi (CA) News-Sentinel*, January 14, 1993.

28. Stephen Farber, "Minority Villains Are Touchy Network Topic," *New York Times*, March 1, 1986. Bruce J. Sallan, ABC's vice president of motion pictures for television, was wrong about this statistic. African Americans were disproportionately represented on death row, but they were not a strict numerical majority. In 1984, 585 of 1,405 persons under the sentence of death were black. Lawrence A. Greenfeld and David G. Hinners, "Capital Punishment 1984," *Bureau of Justice Statistics Bulletin* (Washington, DC: US Department of Justice, 1985). Available at http://www.bjs.gov/index.cfm?ty=pbdetail&iid=3511 (accessed July 27, 2015).

29. Farber, "Minority Villains." This too was misleading because it did not consider minority representations on news programming. A sampling of news coverage in Chicago taken in 1989 found that African Americans most often appeared in news stories about violent crime when they were the perpetrators. Robert M. Entman, "Modern Racism and the Images of Blacks in Local Television News," *Critical Studies in Mass Communication* 7 (1990): 332–45. This claim was also challenged by a report that studied a sampling of television in 1987 and found that minorities on fictional television programming were more than twice as likely to be criminals or delinquents as their white counterparts. Marsha E. Williams and John C. Condry, "Living Color: Minority Portrayals and Cross-Racial Interactions on Television" (presentation, Biennial Meeting of the Society for Research in Child Development, Kansas City, MO, April 1989). Available at http://files.eric.ed.gov/fulltext/ED307025.pdf (accessed July 27, 2015).

30. Her method of operation is to extort money from johns by threatening to accuse them of rape. Her white crime partner, also her boyfriend, bursts into the motel room and is shot by the cop. Kit shoots the officer while he's down, then spits out the epithet Nigger! as she stands over his body.

31. Steven Haft and Rob Koslow, *Last Dance*, directed by Bruce Beresford (1996; Hollywood, CA: Walt Disney Video, 2003), DVD.

32. Darabont, *Green Mile.*

33. Susan Gonzalez, "Director Spike Lee Slams 'Same Old' Black Stereotypes in Today's Films," *Yale Bulletin and Calendar,* March 2, 2001. Available at http://www.yale.edu/opa/arc-ybc/v29.n21/story3.html (accessed July 27, 2015).

34. Darabont, *Green Mile.*

35. In depicting sympathetic white men as the victims of a culture that unfairly holds them responsible for the historical oppression of women and minorities, the film was symptomatic of a broader trend in depictions of white masculinity in middlebrow culture of the 1970s, 1980s, and 1990s. Sally Robinson, *Marked Men: White Masculinity in Crisis* (New York: Columbia University Press, 2000). David Savran has also studied masochistic expressions of white masculinity in this period. See David Savran, *Taking It Like a Man: White Masculinity, Masochism, and Contemporary American Culture* (Princeton, NJ: Princeton University Press, 1998).

36. Peacock, *Lesson Before Dying.*

37. Goldman and Reese, *Chamber.*

38. Haft and Koslow, *Last Dance.*

39. Eisele, *Last Light.*

40. As Roger Lancaster puts it, "A complex set of cultural values related to forbearance, forgiveness, rehabilitation, and second chances has progressively ceded ground to an equally complicated set of values that revolve around vigilance, accusation, detection, the assertion of guilt, and spectacles of punishment." Roger Lancaster, *Sex Panic and the Punitive State* (Berkeley: University of California Press, 2011), 189.

41. On neoliberalism, see David Harvey, *A Brief History of Neoliberalism* (Oxford: Oxford University Press, 2007), and James Ferguson, "The Uses of Neoliberalism," *Antipode* 41 (2010): 166–84.

42. George Lipsitz has argued that reactionary rhetoric worked to channel the frustration working-class white men felt as a result of neoliberal policies of dispossession. The source of their angst, socially conservative ideologies told them, was not economic policy change, but the cultural change wrought by the countercultural, feminist, gay, and civil rights movements. George Lipsitz, *The Possessive Investment in Whiteness: How White People Profit from Identity Politics,* rev. and exp. ed. (Philadelphia: Temple University Press, 2006).

43. Tim Robbins, *Dead Man Walking,* directed by Tim Robbins (1995; Hollywood, CA: MGM, 2000), DVD.

44. Ibid.

45. Ibid.

46. Ibid.

47. Ibid.

48. Daniel Patrick Moynihan, "The Negro Family: The Case for National Action," *Office of Policy Planning and Research* (Washington, DC: US Depart-

ment of Labor, 1965). Available at http://tinyurl.com/oqkt3xr (accessed July 27, 2015).

49. I have previously explored this theme in representations of white men in prison films in the 1990s. See Daniel LaChance, "Rehabilitating Violence: White Masculinity and Harsh Punishment in 1990s Popular Culture," in *Punishment in Popular Culture*, ed. Charles Ogletree Jr. and Austin Sarat (New York: New York University Press, 2015), 161–96.

50. Recognition of the pain of working-class white dispossession (let alone that of racial minorities) was not, in the neoliberal political culture of the 1980s and 1990s, readily available from the state or the culture. Indeed, some have argued that the readiness of Americans to identify with crime victims and support them financially and symbolically was in part a way of safely expressing a desire to be protected and taken care of that was no longer culturally acceptable in the realm of economic policy. See, e.g., Lancaster, *Sex Panic*. Here a bizarre inversion of that theme plays out: the condemned gains recognition as a penitent criminal rather than an aggrieved victim.

51. Austin Sarat, *When the State Kills: Capital Punishment and the American Condition* (Princeton, NJ: Princeton University Press, 2001), 225.

52. Caryl Chessman, *Trial by Ordeal* (Englewood Cliffs, NJ: Prentice Hall, 1955), 92, quoted in Theodore Hamm, *Rebel and a Cause: Caryl Chessman and the Politics of the Death Penalty in Postwar California, 1948–1974* (Berkeley: University of California Press, 2001), 68.

53. Goldman and Reese, *Chamber*.

54. Rather than calling attention to the foundational nature of racism in America, the film consigns it to the hearts of elite white supremacists who will, the audience learns, be vanquished by the law.

55. Goldman and Reese, *Chamber*.

56. Ibid.

57. Goodman, "Getting to Know Grandpa under Penalty of Death."

58. Before *Furman*, in the years 1961–70, Hugo Adam Bedau found a death sentence to clemency ratio of 6.3:1. After *Gregg*, from 1979 to 1988, he found that ratio had increased dramatically, to 40.2:1. The data, Bedau notes, do not account for potential, unknown differences between the numbers of applications for clemency during these two periods. Hugo Adam Bedau, "The Decline of Executive Clemency in Capital Cases," *New York University Review of Law and Social Change* 18 (1990 91): 255 72.

59. Harold G. Grasmick, Elizabeth Davenport, Mitchell B. Chamlin, and Robert J. Bursik Jr., "Protestant Fundamentalism and the Retributive Doctrine of Punishment," *Criminology* 30 (1992): 21–46.

60. "This is not the same person who committed those heinous crimes. Why? Because Carla Fay Tucker has given her heart and life to the Lord Jesus Christ and He is the only person who can change and turn people's lives around," a sup-

porter wrote. Bruce Alexander to Ann Richards, n.d., General Counsel's Execution Files, Texas Governor George W. Bush, Archives and Information Services Division, Texas State Library and Archives Commission (Austin, TX), box 2002/151–97. In Texas the governor does not have the authority to grant clemency without the recommendation of a clemency board. The Texas Board of Pardons had not recommended clemency for Tucker when these letters were written (and they did not do so when she was eventually put to death in 1998).

61. Teresa Malcolm, "Tucker's Death Affected Robertson Views," *National Catholic Reporter*, April 23, 1999. His comments were echoed in an editorial published that year in *Christianity Today* in which the magazine's editorial staff guardedly came out in opposition to the death penalty, noting that it was applied unequally to minorities and that it did not seem to be making the country safer. Unsigned editorial, "The Lesson of Karla Faye Tucker: Evangelical Instincts against Her Execution Were Right, but Not Because She Was a Christian," *Christianity Today*, April 6, 1998.

62. Kimberly Sevcik, "Has Stanley Williams Left the Gang?" *New York Times Magazine*, August 10, 2003.

63. Arnold Schwarzenegger, "Statement of Decision: Request for Clemency by Stanley Williams," December 12, 2005. Available at http://graphics8.nytimes .com/packages/pdf/national/Williams_Clemency_Decision.pdf (accessed July 27, 2015).

64. On the efforts to save Tucker's life, Gregory Curtis wrote, "No matter how the laws read, executing a woman is an act that offends some deep value we have held in Texas from 1863 until now. Our reluctance must be the most visible vestige of the belief that it is, after all, worse to hurt a woman than to hurt a man, that somehow the whole point of civilization is to protect women. . . . Yet, this view—unstated, uncodified in law, but persistent and powerful—is directly counter to current thinking. In all the debate over the death penalty, no one argues publicly that if there is a death penalty, it should apply only to men and not to women. The whole tenor of the times is to treat women and men the same. But does that belief extend even to the execution chamber?" Gregory Curtis, "Seven Women," *Texas Monthly*, October 1997.

65. Robyn E. Blumer, "Equality, Even in Death," *St. Petersburg (FL) Times*, January 11, 1998.

66. Sam Howe Verhovek, "As Woman's Execution Nears, Texas Squirms," *New York Times*, January 1, 1998.

67. Darabont, *Green Mile*.

68. Linda Ross Meyer, "The Meaning of Death: Last Words, Last Meals," in *Who Deserves to Die: Constructing the Executable Subject*, ed. Austin Sarat and Karl Shoemaker (Amherst: University of Massachusetts Press, 2011), 178.

69. Panetti v. Quarterman 551 U.S. 930 (2007) at 958.

## Chapter Five

1. Bill R. Boyd, "Macy Shows Old West Values," Editorial, *Oklahoman*, June 24, 1997.

2. Frederick Jackson Turner, "The Significance of the Frontier in American History" (presentation, American Historical Association, Chicago, IL, July 12, 1893). Available at http://nationalhumanitiescenter.org/pds/gilded/empire/text1/turner.pdf (accessed July 30, 2015).

3. For a review of these critiques and of the stubborn staying power of Turner's paradigm in spite of them, see William Cronon, "Revisiting the Vanishing Frontier: The Legacy of Frederick Jackson Turner," *Western Historical Quarterly* 18 (1987): 157–76.

4. Robert B. Pippin, *Hollywood Westerns and American Myth: The Importance of Howard Hawks and John Ford for Political Philosophy* (New Haven, CT: Yale University Press, 2010), 69.

5. Ibid., 98.

6. Richard Slotkin, *The Fatal Environment: The Myth of the Frontier in the Age of Industrialization, 1800–1890* (New York: Atheneum, 1985), and Slotkin, *Gunfighter Nation: The Myth of the Frontier in Twentieth-Century America* (New York: Atheneum, 1992). Slotkin argues that the myth collapses in the wake of the Vietnam War. My work argues that it has retained its power and popularity.

7. See, e.g., Jonathan Simon, *Governing through Crime: How the War on Crime Transformed American Democracy and Created a Culture of Fear* (Oxford: Oxford University Press, 2007), esp. chap. 3 ("We the Victims"); Austin Sarat, "Vengeance, Victims, and the Identities of Law," *Social and Legal Studies* 6 (1997): 163–89, and Roger N. Lancaster, *Sex Panic and the Punitive State* (Berkeley: University of California Press, 2011), esp. chap. 7 ("Constructing Victimization: How Americans Learned to Love Trauma").

8. Frank Baumgartner, Spreadsheet of Executions by County, available at http://www.unc.edu/~fbaum/Innocence/NC/execs-by-county-since-1976.xlsx (accessed July 30, 2015).

9. In 1980 Governor George Nigh appointed Macy to take the spot vacated by then-district attorney Andy Coats. Macy went on to win reelection as Oklahoma County district attorney five times, running unopposed for his last election in 1998. Nolan Clay and Bryan Dean, "Former Oklahoma County DA Bob Macy Dies," *Oklahoman*, November 19, 2011. He won each of his contested elections by a landslide: 60 percent in 1982, 80.2 percent in 1986, 73.1 percent in 1990, 70.7 percent in 1994. See "The Final State Tallies Are In," *Oklahoman*, November 7, 1982; "Election '86," *Oklahoman*, November 9, 1986; Dave Seldon, "7 DAs Get Heave-Ho from Voters," *Oklahoman*, November 8, 1990; and "District Attorneys," *Oklahoman*, November 10, 1994. When Carol Vance left the

office of Harris County district attorney in 1980, Holmes won election to replace him. Holmes won the office four more times before announcing his retirement in 1999. He won 60 percent of the votes in the 1988 election, then 60 percent in 1992, and ran unopposed in 1996. Pete Slover, "Big Wins Mark Races in County," *Houston Chronicle*, November 10, 1988; "Harris County at-a-Glance," *Houston Chronicle*, November 5, 1992; "Election at a Glance/District Attorney," *Houston Chronicle*, November 8, 1996.

10. Clay and Dean, "Former Oklahoma County DA Macy Dies."

11. Allan Turner, "Former DA Ran Powerful Death Penalty Machine: Mr. Law and Order," *Houston Chronicle*, July 25, 2007.

12. Clay and Dean, "Former Oklahoma County DA Macy Dies."

13. Armando Villafranca, "A Man of Conviction," *Houston Chronicle*, November 29, 1998.

14. *An Examination of the Death Penalty in the United States: Hearing before the Subcommittee on the Constitution, Civil Rights and Property Rights of the Committee on the Judiciary, United States Senate, February 1, 2006*, 109th Cong. 6 (2006) (Statement of Mrs. Ann Scott, Tulsa, Oklahoma).

15. Ibid., 7.

16. Ibid., 6.

17. Ibid., 12.

18. David E. Rosenbaum, "Bush Talks Tough on Crime, Criticizing Criminal Furlough Program," *New York Times*, June 23, 1988.

19. John J. Larivee, "Dukakis and Prisoner Reform," *Wall Street Journal*, May 25, 1988, quoted in Tom Wicker, "In the Nation: Bush League Charges," *New York Times*, June 24, 1988.

20. Robin Toner, "Prison Furloughs in Massachusetts Threaten Dukakis Record on Crime," *New York Times*, July 5, 1988.

21. Ibid.

22. Ibid.

23. This position reflects one side of an important inconsistency in contemporary crime discourse: on the one hand, there is an expectation that citizens ought to be able to live their lives with zero risk of crime; on the other hand, there is an assumption that life involves risks and that we must all bear the burden of them. Simon, *Governing through Crime*.

24. Rector was so mentally impaired that he did not eat the dessert served with his last meal because he planned to eat it after his execution. Sharon LaFraniere, "Governor's Camp Feels His Record on Crime Can Stand the Heat," *Washington Post*, October 5, 1992.

25. Steven A. Kohm, "The People's Law vs. Judge Judy Justice: Two Models of Law in American Reality-Based TV," *Law and Society Review* 40 (2006): 693–728, 698.

26. Ibid., 708.

27. *Antiterrorism and Effective Death Penalty Act, 1996*, Pub. L. No. 104–132, 104th Cong., 2nd Sess. (March 14, 1996), ProQuest Congressional.

28. Senator Orrin Hatch, speaking on S. 735, 104th Cong., 1st Sess., *Congressional Record* 141 (June 7, 1995): S 15062.

29. Ibid.

30. On the rise of a legal-rational form of political domination in the West, see Max Weber, *Economy and Society* (Berkeley: University of California Press, 1978). On the rationalizing of capital punishment in modern political orders, see Timothy V. Kaufman-Osborn, *From Noose to Needle: Capital Punishment and the Late Liberal State* (Ann Arbor: University of Michigan Press, 2002). On the rise of disciplinary forms of power aimed at normalization, see Michel Foucault, *Discipline and Punish: The Birth of the Prison*, trans. Alan Sheridan (1975; New York: Vintage Books, 1995). Citations refer to the Vintage edition. On the rise of disciplinary forms of power aimed at neutralizing risk through incapacitation, see Malcolm M. Feeley and Jonathan Simon, "The New Penology: Notes on the Emerging Strategy of Corrections and Its Implications," *Criminology* 30 (1992): 449–74.

31. In modern states, legal theorists like Robert Cover have taught us that the violence that underlies law is carefully organized and deployed by many actors: "In order to do that violence safely and effectively, responsibility for that violence must be shared; law must operate as a system of cues and signals to many actors who would otherwise be unwilling, incapable or irresponsible in their violent acts. . . . [N]o single mind and no single will can generate the violent outcomes that follow from [legal decisions]." Robert M. Cover, "Violence and the Word," *Yale Law Journal* 95 (1986): 1601–29, 1628. When bringing capital charges against a defendant, prosecutors have a monopoly on being able to request the state's violence; juries and judges have a monopoly on deciding whether that violence will indeed be deployed against a defendant; prison personnel have a monopoly on being able to physically inflict authorized violence.

32. Jan Krocker, "Holmes Spoke the Truth, Never Feared the Bad Guy," *Houston Chronicle*, December 31, 2000.

33. Ibid.

34. Clay and Dean, "Former Oklahoma County DA Macy Dies."

35. Diana Baldwin, "Macy Returns to Court for Killer's Sentencing," *Oklahoman*, March 7, 2003.

36. Ibid.

37. Steve Brewer, "Holmes Won't Seek Re-election," *Houston Chronicle*, October 13, 1999.

38. Turner, "Mr. Law and Order."

39. Villafranca, "Man of Conviction."

40. Ibid.

41. Ibid.

42. Brian Rogers, "Passing Down a Biblical Tradition: An Inscribed Holy Book Has Provided Words of Wisdom to DAs over the Years," *Houston Chronicle*, December 22, 2008.

43. Turner, "Mr. Law and Order."

44. Villafranca, "Man of Conviction."

45. Ibid.

46. Stephen Johnson, "Voter Guide: District Attorney," *Houston Chronicle*, October 25, 1992.

47. Bruce Tomaso, "Death Row from Different Perspectives: The District Attorney," *Dallas Morning News*, October 1, 1995.

48. Thom Marshall, "Realistic Rules and Regulations," *Houston Chronicle*, June 30, 2000.

49. Duckett v. Mullin, 306 F.3d 982 (2002) at 992. The opinion was reported in Robert E. Boczkiewicz, "Macy Criticized as Sentence Upheld," *Oklahoman*, September 10, 2002.

50. Duckett v. Mullin at 994.

51. Nolan Clay, "Nichols State Trial Opposed," *Oklahoman*, January 23, 2000.

52. Nolan Clay, "Macy Off Bombing Case," *Oklahoman*, October 17, 2000.

53. Ibid.

54. Ibid.

55. Nolan Clay, "Bombing Victims Angry over Removal of Macy," *Oklahoman*, October 18, 2000.

56. "Macy to the Sidelines: In Nichols Case, Should DA Step Aside?" *Oklahoman*, October 18, 2000.

57. Ibid.

58. At times Macy responded legalistically to accusations of overzealousness. In defending his decision to seek a state trial for Terry Nichols against poll results showing that up to 68 percent of Oklahomans opposed such a trial, Macy, following Johnny Holmes's response to questions about his own punitive inclinations, disclaimed his prosecutorial charging discretion, incorrectly telling the newspaper, "It's my job. I don't have any choice in the matter. . . . These crimes were committed in Oklahoma County, and it's my job to prosecute him." Clay, "Nichols State Trial Opposed." In response to coverage of appellate courts' chastisement of his misconduct in numerous cases, Macy dutifully acknowledged his obligation to respond to their directives: "I never deliberately violated the Canons of Ethics," Macy said in an article published at the time of his retirement. "Anytime they criticized me, I'd try to make sure that I didn't repeat the conduct in the criticism. Sometimes, I did repeat the conduct because the first defendant's ruling had not come down when I tried the next case. They would get

after me because it looked like I'd deliberately ignored their ruling of the court. When in fact, that ruling had not come down at the time I had done the subsequent trial." Diana Baldwin, "Macy Leaving Behind Renowned DA Career," *Oklahoman*, July 1, 2001.

59. Charolette Aiken, "Macy Called 'True Patriot' at Fund-Raiser," *Oklahoman*, September 29, 1993.

60. Boczkiewicz, "Macy Criticized as Sentence Upheld."

61. Malcolm Feeley has observed elsewhere how self-denying pronouncements by legal authorities can ironically enhance their majesty and power. In writing about Felix Frankfurter's jurisprudence, Feeley observes, "At times his appeal for restraint is almost theological: Lawyers and judges in their infinite wisdom probably can devise good solutions to solve social problems, but (for God) to intervene might undermine the free will of humankind. So it is the task of the high priest, in the name of the awesome power, to urge self-restraint. Humankind is allowed to engage in folly if it wishes; that is the price that must be paid for political maturity. Thus even the most powerful counsel to embrace judicial restraint is framed in such a way as to assume awesome powers of the Court." Malcolm Feeley, "Hollow Hopes, Flypaper, and Metaphors," *Law and Social Inquiry* 17 (1992): 745–60, 759.

62. Lisa Teachey, "D.A. Reached for a Shotgun, Not a Law Book," *Houston Chronicle*, November 13, 1996.

63. Nolan Clay, "Bob Macy," *Oklahoman*, October 5, 2008.

64. Pat McGuigan, Chris Querry, and Dryon J. Will, *Bob Macy: The Man Behind the String Tie (as Told by Bob Macy)* (Mustang, OK: Tate, 2011), 152.

65. Ibid., 85.

66. Ibid., 84.

67. Ibid., 85.

68. Teachey, "D.A. Reached for a Shotgun."

69. Readers' identification with Holmes and Macy was always meant to be vicarious. While Holmes and Macy trusted themselves to bring criminals to justice in vigilante fashion, they were more guarded in endorsing others' vigilante inclinations. When a man Macy prosecuted was acquitted of killing a jilted lover under the state's "make my day" statute, which authorized citizens to use lethal violence against any intruder they suspected would harm their home's occupants, Macy was furious: "When this law was first proposed, district attorneys across the state opposed it for criminal cases. We were concerned there would be instances [when] the 'Make My Day' law would be used as a mechanism for people to eliminate their enemies," Macy said. Charlotte Aiken, "Judge Sentences Man to 80 Years," *Oklahoman*, February 4, 1994. Likewise, Holmes cautioned those who read about his apprehending a thief by gunpoint that the "average Joe" should not do what he had done. Teachey, "D.A. Reached for a Shotgun."

70. Gail Bederman, *Manliness and Civilization: A Cultural History of Gen-*

*der and Race in the United States, 1880–1917* (Chicago: University of Chicago Press, 1995).

71. Amy Louise Wood, *Lynching and Spectacle: Witnessing Racial Violence in America, 1890–1940* (Chapel Hill: University of North Carolina Press, 2009).

72. Smoking gun evidence of racial bias was not produced by Macy's critics during or after his tenure as Oklahoma City district attorney. He was, however, indirectly accused of racism by Oklahoma City activist Clara Luper, who told the *Tulsa World* in 1991 that the culture of Oklahoma County had become one in which "when you really want to lynch a person, you lynch them not with a rope, but with a legalized process." The paper, for its part, noted that the county was sending a "very high" number of blacks to death row: "Since Macy took over the prosecutor's office, 41.5 percent of the condemned criminals have been black. In the other 76 counties, the rate of blacks being sent to death row is markedly lower. Of 82 non-Oklahoma County prisoners on Death Row, only 14 are black, or 17.1 percent." Data in the article suggest a 1991 black death row incarceration rate of 20.4 per 100,000 African Americans in Oklahoma County, compared with 9.6 per 100,000 in the rest of the state. The nonblack death row incarceration rate was 5.3 per 100,000 residents in Oklahoma County, compared with 2.3 per 100,000 residents in the rest of the state. (The article did not take up other variables, like the demographics of homicide convictions.) Wayne Greene, "Death Sentence Prompts Cries of Racism in Oklahoma County," *Tulsa World*, November 21, 1991. Evidence of racial bias in Harris County is less circumstantial. One study showed that Holmes had, in practice if not in principle, set the bar lower for seeking death sentences against black defendants than against white ones. Scott Phillips, "Racial Disparities in the Capital of Capital Punishment," *Houston Law Review* 45 (2008): 807–40. In 2000, moreover, prosecutors across Texas were criticized for introducing to juries, during the penalty phase of capital trials of African American and Hispanic defendants, statistical evidence claiming that members of these demographic groups were statistically more prone to violence than their counterparts in other races. James Kimberly, "Death Penalties of 6 in Jeopardy: Attorney General Gives Result of Probe into Race Testimony," *Houston Chronicle*, June 10, 2000. Two of those cases happened in Harris County on Holmes's watch. In addition, antiquated racist imagery found its way into prosecutorial rhetoric on at least one occasion. Urging a death sentence for a twenty-two-year-old African American defendant, one of Holmes's assistant district attorneys asked the jury to see its task as akin to that of a wildlife official protecting tourists from African beasts: "Do you know what we do in the parks to the wild bears who attack humans and to the tigers in Africa that attack the people that are touring over there? What do we do to those people [*sic*] that smell the hunt and kill the human?" he asked jurors. "That's right, we kill them. Because forevermore they will understand the concept of killing. They will never lose the notion or the smell of how to kill. He is a future

danger. There is no doubt about it." Final Argument on Punishment, State of Texas v. Calvin McGee, Punishment Phase Trial Record, Argument Volume, Texas Court of Criminal Appeals, Case No. AP-73,391, 1999, 42.

73. See, e.g., Kent Scheidegger, "Rebutting Myths about Race and the Death Penalty," Ohio State Journal of Criminal Law 10 (2012): 147–66.

74. On the rise of civic nationalism, see Gary Gerstle, *American Crucible: Race and Nation in the Twentieth Century* (Princeton, NJ: Princeton University Press, 2001).

75. Villafranca, "Man of Conviction."

76. McGuigan, Querry, and Will, *Bob Macy*, 51–52. Describing Macy's relationship with the black community in St. Petersburg, Florida, where he briefly worked, the biographers wrote, "Macy was tireless in his outreach to black citizens" and quoted a local news item that had a photograph of Macy standing among "eleven black women," one of whom praised his "knowledge and expertise in the area of crime prevention." Similarly, the biographers tell us that Macy held a high opinion of some women in legal careers. They quote him describing Fern Smith as "the equal of any man in any courtroom in Oklahoma. She tried more capital cases than anyone in my office. She was a lady and a professional." The defensive tone of these anecdotes suggests a figure concerned about his reputation on issues of race and gender and anxious to shore up a reputation as someone blind to both. Ibid., 106, 135. Indeed, in expressing his disdain for Rodney King, as he did elsewhere in the biography, Macy aligned himself with law enforcement in a case where the roadside beating of an African American man by police—and a jury's refusal to punish it—had produced outrage among African Americans about racism in the criminal justice system.

77. On militarism and white masculinity, see George Lipsitz, *The Possessive Investment in Whiteness: How White People Profit from Identity Politics*, rev. and exp. ed. (Philadelphia: Temple University Press, 1998), esp. chap. 4 ("Whiteness and War").

78. Liebman and Clarke, "Minority Practice, Majority's Burden."


## Chapter Six

1. *Dexter*, episode 4x01 ("Living the Dream"), first broadcast September 27, 2009, by Showtime. Directed by Marcos Siega and written by Clyde Phillips.

2. *State of Texas v. Robert Eugene Will III*, Trial Record, Voir Dire Volume 10, Texas Court of Criminal Appeals (Austin, TX), Case No. AP-74,306, 2001, 9–10.

3. This premise is at the heart of social contract theory. Writing in 1689, John Locke noted, "Those who are united into one body, and have a common established law and judicature to appeal to, with authority to decide controver-

sies between them, and punish offenders, are in *civil society* one with another: but those who have no such common appeal . . . are still in the state of nature, each being, where there is no other, judge for himself, and executioner; which is, as I have before shewed it, the perfect *state of nature*." John Locke, *Second Treatise of Government* (1690; repr. Indianapolis: Hackett, 1980), chap. 7, §87. Available at https://www.gutenberg.org/files/7370/7370-h/7370-h.htm (accessed August 4, 2015). A more modern iteration of this principle is Supreme Court Justice George Sutherland's majority opinion in *Berger v. United States.* Sutherland wrote, "The United States Attorney is the representative not of an ordinary party to a controversy, but of a sovereignty whose obligation to govern impartially is as compelling as its obligation to govern at all; and whose interest, therefore, in a criminal prosecution is not that it shall win a case, but that justice shall be done." Berger v. United States, 295 U.S. 78 (1935) at 88.

4. In 1968, the top ten network shows included three comedies set in the countryside, two westerns, and a number of shows centered on aging stars like Lucille Ball. Four years later that same list was almost unrecognizable, including *All in the Family*, about a white bigot in Queens forever fighting with his leftist son-in-law, *The Mary Tyler Moore Show*, about a thirty-something single woman starting over, and *Sanford and Son*, about a black family. Josh Ozersky, *Archie Bunker's America: TV in an Era of Change, 1968–1978* (Carbondale: Southern Illinois University Press, 2003).

5. On the rise of social conservatism of the 1970s out of right-wing anticommunism, see Donald T. Critchlow, *Phyllis Schlafly and Grassroots Conservatism: A Woman's Crusade* (Princeton, NJ: Princeton University Press, 2006); Lisa McGirr, *Suburban Warriors: The Origins of the New American Right* (Princeton, NJ: Princeton University Press, 2001); and Robert Self, *All in the Family: The Realignment of American Democracy since the 1960s* (New York: Hill and Wang, 2012).

6. Kirk Makin, "Bundy-Haters Cheer as Mass Killer Executed," *Globe and Mail* (Toronto), January 25, 1989.

7. See, e.g., a speech given in 1989 by William Bennett, drug czar for the Bush administration, at the Kennedy School of Government: "I'm reminded of what John Jacob, president of the Urban League, said recently: drugs are destroying more black families than poverty ever did. And I'm thankful that many of these poor families have the courage to fight drugs now, rather than declaring themselves passive victims of root causes," Bennett said. William Bennett, "Drug Policy and the Intellectuals," *Police Chief* 57 (May 1990): 30–33, 36.

8. Patrick Buchanan, "Death Penalty Only Justice," *Chicago Tribune*, July 8, 1976.

9. *Capital Punishment: Hearing before Subcommittee No. 3 of the Committee on the Judiciary, United States House of Representatives*, March 9, 15–17, May 10, 1972, 92nd Cong. 227 (1972) (Testimony of Frank G. Carrington, exec-

utive director, Americans for Effective Law Enforcement, Inc.), quoted in Raphael Ginsberg, "Mighty Crime Victims: Victims' Rights and Neoliberalism in the American Conjuncture," *Cultural Studies* 28 (2014): 911–46, 919.

10. Ginsberg, "Mighty Crime Victims."

11. As Franklin E. Zimring has noted, closure became a "central objective of the death penalty system" in the modern period. Franklin E. Zimring, *The Contradictions of American Capital Punishment* (Oxford: Oxford University Press, 2003), 61.

12. Ginsberg, "Mighty Crime Victims," 920.

13. Ibid.

14. My sample included thirty-one transcripts of hearings reviewed through a search of the Proquest Congressional Database for all hearings with the words capital punishment or death penalty in the title.

15. *Innocence and the Death Penalty: Hearing before the Committee on the Judiciary, United States Senate*, April 1, 1993, 103rd Cong. 69 (1994) (Statement of Miriam Shehane).

16. Ibid., 70.

17. *An Examination of the Death Penalty in the United States: Hearing before the Subcommittee on the Constitution, Civil Rights and Property Rights of the Committee on the Judiciary, United States Senate*, February 1, 2006, 109th Cong. 8 (2006) (Statement of Mrs. Ann Scott, Tulsa, Oklahoma).

18. The views of a victim's family had, of course, a long and sometimes racially charged influence over the historical practice of lethal punishment. In the nineteenth and early twentieth centuries, lynchings—a form of lethal punishment that had clear ties to capital punishment—often involved such public authentication. Amy Louise Wood writes that "in cases of alleged sexual assault, the female victim frequently played a prominent role in the lynching. Her presence was crucial to legitimize the violence and make manifest that the lynching was a direct act of vengeance." Amy Louise Wood, *Lynching and Spectacle. Witnessing Racial Violence in America, 1890–1940* (Chapel Hill: University of North Carolina Press, 2009), 100.

19. Between World War I and World War II, at least 133 films including capital punishment were produced, with plots that were set in the contemporary United States. Attention to the plight of victims' survivors was rare, in part because most death penalty films in the period—"83 out of 133—depicted sympathetic white men who were unjustly sent to death row and saved at the last minute by a revelation of their innocence or mitigating facts surrounding their crime, usually engineered by a female family member or romantic interest." Daniel LaChance, "Executing Humanity: Popular Representations of Capital Punishment in the United States, 1915–1940," unpublished manuscript, last modified October 14, 2014. Microsoft Word File. To create a list of films in which the death penalty appeared, I compiled the names of all films in the American

Film Institute (AFI) catalog that had capital punishment or executions listed as a keyword. I then excluded from the list films set on the frontier (most often, but not always, westerns), films set in the distant past (films about the Civil War), and films set outside the United States. The AFI catalog is not a perfect source for finding films that depict capital punishment; for instance, Michael Curtiz's *Angels with Dirty Faces* (1938), which ends with an execution, and D. W. Griffith's *Intolerance* (1916), which ends with a pardon, were not accompanied by any death penalty–related keywords. I have thus supplemented the list I created using the AFI catalog with information found on the Internet Movie Database (www.imdb.com) and a death penalty filmography from the now defunct website of the Prison Film Project, formerly at www.theprisonfilmproject.com. LaChance, "Executing Humanity."

20. Out of 408 executions that received media coverage by the major daily newspaper(s) in New York, California, Maryland, Massachusetts, and Georgia between 1915 and 1940, we found that 56 (13 percent) mentioned the family members of the murder victim, while 184 (45 percent) mentioned the family members of the condemned. Some caution is warranted here. The kinds of papers examined, large urban ones, may have covered news differently than their local and rural counterparts. The articles examined were coverage of the execution itself; omitted from consideration was broader coverage of each case. Data between World War II and 1967 have not yet been collected. Daniel LaChance, unpublished data, last modified July 27, 2015. Excel File.

21. "Teen-ager Seized in the Slaying of Ten," *New York Times*, January 30, 1958.

22. "Slayer of Eleven Dies," *New York Times*, June 25, 1959.

23. Jon Nordheimer, "Bundy Is Put to Death in Florida after Admitting Trail of Killings," *New York Times*, January 25, 1989.

24. Dirk Johnson, "For Families, Killer's Death Eases Doubts but Not Pain," *New York Times*, February 13, 1989.

25. See, e.g., Rick Santorum, *It Takes a Family: Conservatism and the Common Good* (Wilmington, DE: ISI Books, 2005).

26. *The Family: Preserving America's Future, Report to the President from the White House Working Group on the Family* (Washington, DC: Domestic Policy Council, 1986), 8, quoted in Robert O. Self, *All in the Family: The Realignment of American Democracy since the 1960s* (New York: Hill and Wang, 2012), 383.

27. Ibid., 400.

28. Ibid., 401.

29. Ibid., 400–401.

30. "Text of Robert Dole's Speech to the Republican National Convention August 15, 1996," *CNN: All Politics*, http://www.cnn.com/ALLPOLITICS/1996/

conventions/san.diego/transcripts/0815/dole.fdch.shtml (accessed August 5, 2015).

31. Santorum, *It Takes a Family*, 27, 45.

32. Ibid., 16.

33. On the decline of civic participation, see Robert D. Putnam, *Bowling Alone: The Collapse and Revival of American Community* (New York: Simon and Schuster, 2001).

34. Payne v. Tennessee, 501 U.S. 808 (1991). *Payne* overturned Booth v. Maryland, 482 U.S. 496 (1987), and South Carolina v. Gathers, 490 U.S. 805 (1989).

35. Quoted in Payne v. Tennessee, 501 U.S. 808 (1991) at 814–15.

36. Linda Greenhouse, "Court Hears Thornburgh on the Death Penalty," *New York Times*, April 25, 1991.

37. Payne v. Tennessee, 501 U.S. 808 (1991) at 832 (O'Connor, Concurring).

38. Payne v. Tennessee, 501 U.S. 808 (1991) at 838 (Souter, Concurring).

39. Ibid.

40. While a single television show cannot, on its own, serve as evidence that the meanings it generates are widely received, let alone adopted, it can do several things for the student of popular culture. Most modestly, it can confirm the existence of the relation between ideologies and particular practices that is evident in other texts, like Supreme Court opinions, bolstering the case for the relation's significance. Here, *Dexter* affirmed that family values libertarianism can be compatible with the practice of lethal punishment—a case I have made using *Payne v. Tennessee*, among other texts. But it can do more, making it worthy of a close reading. First, a cultural text can reveal the unexpected way an ideology can operate to shore up a particular practice. To make lethal punishment appealing to those who would otherwise find it repulsive, *Dexter* covered its family values libertarianism with a cosmopolitan veneer. Multiculturalist elements of the show offered distractions from its conservative foundations. Second, a cultural text can reveal the internal tensions an ideology must reconcile in order to confer positive meaning on a particular practice. To make lethal punishment sublime, *Dexter* offered a fantastical reconciliation of the public and private that lay at the heart of family values libertarianism. Third, and conversely, a cultural text can reveal how a practice can lose its meaning—and often its appeal—when the text stops managing those ideological tensions. Here the show's refusal to keep reconciling the public and private tensions turned Dexter's lethal punishment from a sublime practice to a vulgar one. Finally, the backlash a text incurs when its ideological tensions are not reconciled suggests the power of the fantasy over the minds of those who rebel against its dissolution. The harsh criticism the show's finale incurred reveals how far support for lethal punishment rests on its capacity to be both a public act of justice and a private act of vengeance. In the rise and fall of Dexter Morgan, I suggest, we might find valuable

insights into how capital punishment has reflected and reinforced family values libertarianism.

41. Gerard Gilbert, "Serial Thriller," *Independent Extra* (London), December 31, 2008.

42. The show's ratings rose each year. In its final two seasons it averaged between 2.1 and 2.2 million viewers per week, a large audience by premium cable television standards. Mike Hale, "Bad Guy as Hero: Happy Ending?" *New York Times*, September 20, 2013. Its series finale in September 2013 drew 2.8 million viewers, its highest ratings ever. Across all platforms, in its final year the show averaged 6.4 million weekly viewers. Rick Kissell, "Showtime's 'Dexter' Goes Out with Series-High Ratings," *Variety*.com, September 23, 2013, http://variety.com/2013/tv/ratings/showtimes-dexter-goes-out-with-series-high-ratings-1200662066.

43. *Dexter*, episode 1x03 ("Popping Cherry"), first broadcast October 15, 2006, by Showtime. Directed by Michael Cuesta and written by Daniel Cerone.

44. Michael Idato, "Dexter's Eighth Deadly Sin," *Age* (Melbourne, Australia), May 2, 2013.

45. Austin Sarat, "Vengeance, Victims and the Identities of Law," *Social and Legal Studies* 6 (1997): 163–89, 181.

46. *Dexter*, episode 1x03 ("Popping Cherry").

47. *Dexter*, episode 1x10 ("Seeing Red"), first broadcast December 3, 2006, by Showtime. Directed by Michael Cuesta and written by Kevin R. Maynard.

48. *Dexter*, episode 1x02 ("Crocodile"), first broadcast October 8, 2006, by Showtime. Directed by Michael Cuesta and written by Clyde Phillips. This last point of the code perhaps registered the way stories of DNA exonerations of wrongly convicted prisoners had brought new scrutiny to the death penalty. The show premiered the year that John Grisham published *The Innocent Man*, a best-selling account of how egregious prosecutorial misconduct landed an Oklahoma man on that state's death row for eleven years. John Grisham, *The Innocent Man: Murder and Injustice in a Small Town* (New York: Doubleday, 2006).

49. Jonathan Simon, *Governing through Crime: How the War on Crime Transformed American Democracy and Created a Culture of Fear* (Oxford: Oxford University Press, 2007), 154.

50. Victoria L. Smith, "Our Serial Killers, Our Superheroes, and Ourselves: Showtime's *Dexter*," *Quarterly Review of Film and Video* 28 (2011): 390–400.

51. *Dexter*, episode 1x11 ("Truth Be Told"), first broadcast December 10, 2006, by Showtime. Directed by Keith Gordon and written by Drew Z. Greenberg and Tim Schattmann.

52. Ibid.

53. In reality, as I have discussed earlier, the opposite is true: since the 1970s, criminal justice policy and mainstream criminological thought in the United States have been distinguished by a marked turn away from rehabilitation and

toward incapacitation and retribution. Loïc Wacquant, "The New 'Peculiar Institution': On the Prison as Surrogate Ghetto," *Theoretical Criminology* 4 (2000): 377–89; Michael Tonry, *Malign Neglect: Race, Crime, and Punishment in America* (Oxford: Oxford University Press, 1996); David Garland, *The Culture of Control: Crime and Social Order in Contemporary Society* (Chicago: University of Chicago Press, 2001); Joachim J. Savelsberg, Lara L. Cleveland, and Ryan D. King, "Institutional Environments and Scholarly Work: American Criminology, 1951–1993," *Social Forces* 82 (2004): 1275–1302.

54. *Dexter*, episode 5x08 ("Take It!"), first broadcast November 14, 2010, by Showtime. Directed by Romeo Tirone and written by Manny Coto and Wendy West.

55. *Dexter*, episode 1x12 ("Born Free"), first broadcast December 17, 2006, by Showtime. Directed by Michael Cuesta and written by Daniel Cerone and Melissa Rosenberg.

56. *Dexter*, episode 1x04 ("Let's Give the Boy a Hand"), first broadcast October 22, 2006, by Showtime. Directed by Robert Lieberman and written by Drew Z. Greenberg.

57. *Dexter*, episode 2x01 ("It's Alive"), first broadcast September 30, 2007, by Showtime. Directed by Tony Goldwyn and written by Daniel Cerone.

58. *Dexter*, episode, 3x12 ("Do You Take Dexter Morgan?"), first broadcast December 14, 2008, by Showtime. Directed by Keith Gordon and written by Scott Buck.

59. Ibid.

60. *Dexter*, episode 7x08 ("Argentina"), first broadcast November 18, 2012, by Showtime. Directed by Romeo Tirone and written by Arika Lisanne Mittman.

61. *Dexter*, episode 4x01 ("Living the Dream"), first broadcast September 27, 2009, by Showtime. Directed by Marcos Siega and written by Clyde Phillips.

62. *Dexter*, episode 4x09 ("Hungry Man"), first broadcast November 22, 2009, by Showtime. Directed by John Dahl and written by Wendy West.

63. *Dexter*, episode 4x12 ("The Getaway"), first broadcast December 13, 2009, by Showtime. Directed by Steve Shill and written by Wendy West and Melissa Rosenberg based on a story by Scott Reynolds and Melissa Rosenberg.

64. Ibid.

65. *Dexter*, episode 6x12 ("This Is the Way the World Ends"), first broadcast December 18, 2011, by Showtime. Directed by John Dahl and written by Scott Buck and Wendy West.

66. *Dexter*, episode 8x02 ("Every Silver Lining . . ."), first broadcast July 7, 2013, by Showtime. Directed by Michael C. Hall and written by Manny Coto.

67. Dexter has been tracking yet another serial killer while making plans to flee the country and live in Argentina with his new romantic partner and his son. When he has the serial killer incapacitated, he decides not to exact vigilante justice and instead calls the police and leaves the killer for the state to execute. In

the interim, however, the killer frees himself, and when Debra shows up to arrest him, he mortally shoots her.

68. *Dexter*, episode 7x12 ("Surprise, Motherfucker!"), first broadcast December 16, 2012, by Showtime. Directed by Steve Shill and written by Scott Buck and Tim Schlattmann.

69. *Dexter*, episode 8x03 ("What's Eating Dexter Morgan"), first broadcast July 14, 2013, by Showtime. Directed by Ernest Dickerson and written by Lauren Gussis.

70. Reflecting on the show's development, its star and executive producer Michael C. Hall said, "I think the tragedy of this character is that it's not his darkness that gets anyone in trouble, it's his appetite for life or connection or humanity. It's his desire to have his cake and kill it too." *The Writer's Room*, episode 1x03 ("Dexter"), first broadcast August 12, 2013, by SundanceTV. Hosted by Jim Rash.

71. "Kobe2k12," Comment on "Worse [*sic*] Ending in the History of TV," Showtime Online Message Boards, comment posted September 24, 2013, http://www.sho.com/site/message/thread.do?topicid=283357&boardid=5781&pagenum=2&groupid=1609 (accessed December 17, 2013).

72. William Raspberry, "Before We Kill Again," *Washington Post*, December 23, 1985.

73. "nycchris," Comment on "Worse [*sic*] Ending in the History of TV," Showtime Online Message Boards, comment posted September 23, 2013, http://www.sho.com/site/message/thread.do?topicid=283357&boardid=5781&pagenum=2&groupid=1609 (accessed December 17, 2013).

74. Frazier Moore, "'Dexter' Cuts Its Own Throat in Sappy Series End," Associated Press, September 23, 2013.

75. "funwithdexter," Comment on "Dexter Would Not Leave His Son," Showtime Online Message Boards, comment posted September 26, 2013, http://www.sho.com/site/message/thread.do?topicid=283468&boardid=5781&groupid=1609 (accessed December 17, 2013).

76. Denise Paquette Boots, Jayshree Bihari, and Euel Elliott, "The State of the Castle: An Overview of Recent Trends in State Castle Doctrine Legislation and Public Policy," *Criminal Justice Review* 34 (2009): 515–35.

77. Miles Klee, "'Dexter' Fans Want Their Hero to Kill George Zimmerman," *Daily Dot*, July 15, 2013, http://www.dailydot.com/entertainment/dexter-kill-george-zimmerman (accessed November 21, 2015).

**Epilogue**

1. Franz Kafka, *The Trial*, trans. David Wyllie (1925; Mineola, NY: Dover, 2012), 164.

2. Quoted in Carole Shapiro, "Do or Die: Does *Dead Man Walking* Run?" *University of San Francisco Law Review* 30 (1996): 1143–66, 1155.

3. Charles J. Ogletree Jr. and Austin Sarat, "Introduction: Toward and Beyond the Abolition of Capital Punishment," in *The Road to Abolition? The Future of Capital Punishment in the United States*, ed. Charles J. Ogletree Jr. and Austin Sarat (New York: New York University Press, 2009), 15.

4. For state-by-state accounts of these states' abolition process, see Larry W. Koch, Colin Wark, and John F. Galliher, *The Death of the American Death Penalty: States Still Leading the Way* (Boston: Northeastern University Press, 2012).

5. Jeffrey M. Jones, "Americans' Support for Death Penalty Stable," *Gallup News Service*, October 23, 2014, http://www.gallup.com/poll/178790/americans -support-death-penalty-stable.aspx.

6. The logics used to prosecute the war on terror have been strikingly similar to those used to justify the death penalty, perhaps indicating that punitive sentiments have been channeled away from the domestic criminal. Robin Wagner-Pacifici, "Torture, War, and Capital Punishment: Linkages and Missed Connections," in *The Road to Abolition? The Future of Capital Punishment in the United States*, ed. Charles J. Ogletree Jr. and Austin Sarat (New York: New York University Press, 2009).

7. Hadar Aviram, *Cheap on Crime: Recession Era Politics and the Transformation of American Punishment* (Berkeley: University of California Press, 2015). In 2012 abolitionists placed cost at the center of a campaign in California to abolish the death penalty by voter referendum that failed by a slim margin: 53 percent voted to retain the death penalty, while 47 percent voted in support of abolition. Howard Mintz, "Defeat of Proposition 34: California's Death Penalty Battle Will Continue," *San Jose Mercury News*, November 7, 2012.

8. "Number of Executions by State and Year since 1976," *Death Penalty Information Center*, http://www.deathpenaltyinfo.org/number-executions-state -and-region-1976 (last updated July 15, 2015).

9. States have already responded to legal challenges to lethal injection protocols and suppliers' refusal to manufacture and sell to the state the drugs used in lethal injections by using different drugs that are more easily obtainable and by passing laws keeping the names of drug providers from the public to insulate them from public pressure. Other states have raised the possibility of returning to the electric chair and the gas chamber. Manny Fernandez, "Executions Stall as States Seek Different Drugs," *New York Times*, November 9, 2013. The slowdown of executions in recent years may ultimately be a hiccup if these solutions remedy the problem.

10. DNA-based exonerations from wrongful convictions in the period predating the use of DNA fingerprinting will wane with time, and the use of DNA evidence to secure death sentences may create a sense that wrongful convictions are becoming less frequent; as Simon A. Cole and Jay Aronson put it, "The

use of DNA-based innocence as an abolitionist argument strengthens the perceived epistemic authority of DNA evidence in ways that may ultimately hasten the execution of death-row inmates whose convictions rested on DNA evidence." Simon A. Cole and Jay D. Aronson, "Blinded by Science on the Road to Abolition?" in *The Road to Abolition? The Future of Capital Punishment in the United States*, ed. Charles J. Ogletree Jr. and Austin Sarat (New York: New York University Press, 2009), 55.

11. The six states that have abolished the death penalty since 2000 accounted for less than 2 percent of executions that have happened nationally since 1976—and two of them had not executed anyone. "Number of Executions by State and Year since 1976," *Death Penalty Information Center*, http://www.deathpenaltyinfo.org/number-executions-state-and-region-1976 (last updated July 15, 2015). Abolition's prospects may be limited to states where commitment to the death penalty, in the post-*Gregg* era, had already been weak. It may be contingent, moreover, on conditions that are subject to change. Violent crime could once again rise, affect public opinion, and reverse the downward trend in support for the death penalty. State budgets may recover, easing the momentum that concerns about economic cost have given to abolitionism in places like California, which has the nation's largest death row population. Furthermore, while there are indicators of decline for support of the death penalty in high-executing states, there are also examples of aggressive efforts to keep execution chambers active. Elite maneuvers in Florida and Texas suggest that legislative abolition will be exceedingly difficult in death penalty strongholds. In 2013, Florida governor Rick Scott signed into law the "Timely Justice Act." The legislation, a kind of state-level version of the federal Antiterrorism and Effective Death Penalty Act of 1996, requires the governor to sign a death warrant thirty days after a condemned inmate has exhausted all appeals and requires the state to execute the defendant within six months of the warrant's signing. Sponsored by the legislature's ardent defender of the state's stand your ground laws, the act was designed to reduce the time between sentencing and execution in a state that leads the nation in exonerations of death row inmates since 1973. Mary Ellen Klas, "Gov. Rick Scott Signs Bill to Speed Up Executions in Florida," *Tampa Bay Times*, June 14, 2013. In Texas, meanwhile, popularly elected justices on the state's court of criminal appeals sidestepped the Supreme Court's putative ban on the execution of the mentally retarded by rejecting the use of an IQ cutoff and instead defining the standard for mental retardation as Lenny from John Steinbeck's *Of Mice and Men*, a character that Patricia Ewick notes is "a childlike innocent." *Ex parte* Briseno, 135 S.W. 3d 1, 6 and n.19 (Tex. Crim. App. 2004), cited in Patricia Ewick, "The Return of Restraint: Limits to the Punishing State," *Quinnipiac Law Review* 31 (2013): 577–98, 584.

12. Some rationales for limiting the death penalty may ultimately entrench the practice ideologically. The Supreme Court's narrowing the class of offenders

subject to a death sentence may have entrenched justices' commitment to the notion that the death penalty is constitutional for those who fall within the newly redrawn boundaries of death eligibility. David Garland, *Peculiar Institution: America's Death Penalty in an Age of Abolition* (Cambridge, MA: Harvard University Press, 2010). An investment in avoiding the execution of the innocent creates an analogous effect: so long as there is no doubt as to innocence, the guilty may be executed. These challenges to the death penalty create a bright line between sympathetic subjects (the mentally disabled, juveniles, the innocent) and unsympathetic subjects (neurotypical adults who are guilty or who do not have smoking gun evidence of their innocence) that may harden our attitudes toward the unsympathetic, silencing the "wider question of what constitutes justice for the guilty." Marie Gottschalk, "The Long Shadow of the Death Penalty: Mass Incarceration, Capital Punishment, and Penal Policy in the United States," in *Is the Death Penalty Dying? European and American Perspectives*, ed. Austin Sarat and Jürgen Martschukat (Cambridge: Cambridge University Press, 2011), 317. The effect is jurisprudential as well. The Court's emphasis on habeas review as an opportunity to exonerate factually innocent defendants has come at the cost of its tolerance for challenges, in such reviews, of due process violations. Carol S. Steiker and Jordan M. Steiker, "The Seduction of Innocence: The Attraction and Limitations of the Focus on Innocence in Capital Punishment Law and Advocacy," *Journal of Criminal Law and Criminology* 95 (2005): 587–624. Last, it is unclear that exonerations are as damning to capital punishment as some have suggested. Studying the effect that concerns about the execution of innocents might have on support for the death penalty, researchers found that 68.6 percent of those who thought an innocent person had been executed in the past five years still supported the death penalty (by contrast, a whopping 86.9 percent of those who saw the penalty as fail-safe supported it), suggesting Americans may have an unexpected tolerance for lethal error. James D. Unnever and Francis T. Cullen, "Executing the Innocent and Support for Capital Punishment: Implications for Public Policy," *Criminology and Public Policy* 4 (2005): 3–37. At a legislative hearing on the death penalty in New Hampshire in 2000, a high school student testified that the execution of innocents was an acceptable price for its deterrent effect, adding that "if she were wrongly executed, she would accept her fate as necessary for saving others' lives." New Hampshire General Court, House Committee on Criminal Justice and Public Safety executive session on HB 1548 FN, February 26, 2000, paraphrased in Koch, Wark, and Galliher, *Death of the American Death Penalty*, 90.

13. By advocating life without parole as an alternative to the death penalty, abolitionists have endorsed a sanction that other Western nations—including, before the punitive turn, the United States—have seen as extraordinarily harsh and accordingly used sparingly. Gottschalk, "Long Shadow of the Death Penalty."

14. Peter Ross Range, "'Will He Be the First?' This Month, Capital Punishment May Become Legal Again," *New York Times*, March 11, 1979.

15. Robert Sherrill, "Death Row on Trial," *New York Times*, November 13, 1983.

16. Austin Sarat, *Gruesome Spectacles: Botched Executions and America's Death Penalty* (Palo Alto, CA: Stanford University Press, 2014).

17. The death penalty is so overwhelmingly used on minorities and the poor that it likely is easy for many middle-class white Americans to support a public policy whose collateral damage is the occasional execution of someone who, while innocent, does not resemble them.

18. Tracy L. Snell, *Capital Punishment, 2013—Statistical Tables*, Bureau of Justice Statistics, US Department of Justice (Washington, DC: Bureau of Justice Statistics, 2014). Available online at http://www.bjs.gov/content/pub/pdf/cp13st .pdf (accessed April 23, 2016).

19. James S. Liebman, Jeffrey Fagan, Valerie West, and Jonathan Lloyd, "Capital Attrition: Error Rates in Capital Cases, 1973–1995," *Texas Law Review* 78 (2000): 1839–65.

20. *Innocence and the Death Penalty: Hearing before the Committee on the Judiciary, United States Senate*, April 1, 1993, 103rd Cong. 70 (1994) (Statement of Miriam Shehane).

21. Peter Catapano, "They Messed with Texas," *New York Times Opinionator Blog*, September 9, 2011, http://opinionator.blogs.nytimes.com/2011/09/09/ they-messed-with-texas.

22. Snell, *Capital Punishment, 2011*.

23. Marilyn Peterson Armour and Mark S. Umbreit, "Assessing the Impact of the Ultimate Penal Sanction on Homicide Survivors: A Two State Comparison," *Marquette Law Review* 96 (2012): 1–131, 98.

24. On the rise of actuarial penology, see Malcolm M. Feeley and Jonathan Simon, "The New Penology: Notes on the Emerging Strategy of Corrections and Its Implications," *Criminology* 30 (1992): 449–74.

25. Ewick, "Return of Restraint," 591.

26. Ibid., 597. Mona Lynch and others have made similar arguments. See Mona Lynch, "The Disposal of Inmate #85271: Notes on a Routine Execution," *Studies in Law, Politics, and Society* 20 (2000): 3–34, and Daniel LaChance, "Last Words, Last Meals, and Last Stands: Agency and Individuality in the Modern Execution Process," *Law and Social Inquiry* 32, no. 3 (2007): 701–24.

27. Mike Ward, "Prisons End Special Last Meals," *Austin American-Statesman*, September 23, 2011. Two details were absent from much of the coverage generated by the department's decision to discontinue customized meals: the state's policy had long been to release the request to the media in its original form, but to pare down gluttonous requests and to replace, when necessary, items not normally stocked by the prison commissary with simpler equivalents.

Those requesting lobster received pollock. In quantity and content, Brewer had been served a much more modest meal than the one he requested and the state had publicized. The meals had long been, as I argued earlier, more about individualizing the condemned than feeding them what they wanted. Timothy Williams, "Ex-Inmate Shares Stories of Stint as a Death Row Chef," *New York Times*, October 18, 2011.

28. Leland de la Durantaye, *Giorgio Agamben: A Critical Introduction* (Stanford, CA: Stanford University Press, 2009), 352–53, quoted in Ewick, "Return of Restraint," 594.

29. Harcourt suggests that it will take more experienced politicians like George Ryan, governor of Illinois, who come out against the penalty in a climate that is mildly in favor of it. Bernard E. Harcourt, "Abolition in the United States by 2050: On Political Capital and Ordinary Acts of Resistance," in *The Road to Abolition? The Future of Capital Punishment in the United States*, ed. Charles J. Ogletree Jr. and Austin Sarat (New York: New York University Press, 2009).

30. Public opinion is relevant not simply to the prospect for legislative abolition, which is unlikely in states like Texas, but for the much more likely prospect of judicial abolition.

31. Michelle Brown, *The Culture of Punishment: Prison, Society, and Spectacle* (New York: New York University Press, 2009), 8, 5.

32. "Timeless time" is a phrase from an untitled poem by former Texas death row inmate Donnie Crawford, quoted in Bruce Jackson and Diane Christian, *In This Timeless Time: Living and Dying on Death Row in America* (Chapel Hill: University of North Carolina Press, 2012), viii.

33. Ewick, "Return of Restraint," 590–91.

34. Lars von Trier, *Dancer in the Dark*, directed by Lars von Trier (2000, Hollywood: New Line Home Video, 2005), DVD.

35. Ibid.

36. A. O. Scott, "Universe without Happy Endings, *New York Times*, September 22, 2000.

# Index

*Page numbers in italics refer to figures.*

abolitionism: DNA tests and, 248n10; economic costs and, 184, 247n7, 248n11; in Europe, 114; Goldberg and, 8; humanizing and, 190; judiciary and, 251n30; LDF and, 28; life sentencing and, 249n13; Scalia and, 23, state legislation, 183–84, 248n11, 251n30; task of, 189
abuse, prisons and, 11, 86, 89, 165, 198n23, 204n8
Adams, Samuel, 4
Addison, Herman, 87, 88
AFI. *See* American Film Institute
African Americans, 108, 238n72; films and, 107–13, *111*, 229n28; *Gregg* decision and, 17, 105, 113; LDF and, 28; liberalism and, 118 (*see also* liberalism); libertarians and, 153 (*see also* libertarianism); Macy and, 152; media and, 229n29, racism and, 105–7, 153, 239n76 (*see also* racism); South and, 17, 22, 34, 105. *See also specific persons*
*Aikens v. California*, 205n21
Alexander, Michelle, 106
*All in the Family* (TV show), 240n4
American Civil Liberties Union, 61
American Film Institute (AFI), 241n19
American Society of Criminology, 33
Amsterdam, Anthony, 69
*Anderson* decision, 67
Andrews, Lowell Lee, 38
Andrews, William, 139
*Angels with Dirty Faces* (film), 24

Antiterrorism and Effective Death Penalty Act, 138, 191
appeals, 16, 18, 131; dropping of, 217n7; *Gregg* and, 186; habeas appeals, 137; LDF and, 28; liberalism and, 137; process of, 167, 175, 186, 187, 191; victims and, 161, 187. *See also specific persons, topics*
Arendt, Hannah, 207n37
Armour, Marilyn Peterson, 187
Aronson, Jay, 247n10
Asch, Solomon, 38, 56
Asian Americans, 17
*Asylums* (Goffman), 56
Atworth, Robert, 95

Baldus, David, 106
Ball, Terence, 198n20
Barker, Vanessa, 202n55
Barnes, Odell, Jr., 97
Bass, Charles, 95
Beathard, James, 95
Beaumont, Gustave de, 4
Bedau, Hugo Adam, 231n58
Bederman, Gail, 151
behaviorism, 51, 53, 61, 63, 67, 214n51
Behringer, Earl, 79
Bennett, William, 240n7
*Berger* decision, 240n3
Berlin, Isaiah, 5
Berns, Walter, 44, 45, 46, 50, 52, 68
*Better Off Dead* (film), 107, 108

*Beyond Freedom and Dignity* (Skinner), 51
Bill of Rights, 5
*Birdman of Alcatraz* (film), 57, 58
Björk, 191
Black, Hugo, 8
Blackmun, Harry, 72
Black Panthers, 59
Blue, George E., 63
Blumer, Robyn, 124
Brennan, William J., Jr., 70, 104, 216n72
Brewer, Lawrence Russell, 188
Bright, Stephen, 101
Brooks, Richard, 34, 43
*Brute Force* (film), 57
Buchanan, Patrick, 159
Bundy, Theodore, 1, 158, 162
bureaucracy, 3, 5, 16, 48, 58, 64, 92, 133–35, 153, 167, 185, 207n37
Burger, Warren, 103
Burgess, Anthony, 60
Bush, George H. W., 50, 135, 240n7
Bush, George W., 124

*Callins v. Collins*, 225n87
Cantu, Ruben, 98
capitalism, 37, 197n17, 228n21
capital punishment. *See* death penalty
Capote, Truman, 27, 35
Carlson, Norman, 214n42
Carrington, Frank, 159
Castillo, David Allen, 98
*Catcher in the Rye* (film), 9
*Catcher in the Rye* (Salinger), 57, 211n18
Cathey, Eric, 90
*Cell 2455, Death Row* (Chessman), 30
*Chamber, The* (film), 19, 107, 114, 115, 120, 122
Charter of Fundamental Rights (EU), 114
chemical injection, 31, 61, 62
Chessman, Caryl, 30, 109, 120
Christianity, 23, 123, 156–58, 232n61
civil libertarianism, 15, 52–60, 63, 75, 153, 200n47. *See also* libertarianism
Civil Rights movement, 10
Claiborne, William, 63
Clark, Jason, 218n13
Clarke, Peter, 152
Clinton, Bill, 137
Clinton, Hillary, 164

*Clockwork Orange, A* (Burgess), 60, 61, 63, 213n31
Clutchette, John, 212n23, 212n25
Cold War, 7, 29, 157, 206n29, 216n75
Cole, Simon A., 247n10
Commission on Criminal Justice Standards and Goals, 71
communism, 197n17, 240n5
conservatism: Christianity and, 23, 156, 158; death penalty and, 44, 68, 134; family values and (*see* family values); films and, 48, 49, 119, 211n19, 226n5 (*see also* films); government and, 44, 185; legalism and, 48, 186; liberalism and, 211n10, 230n42 (*see also* liberalism); libertarianism and, 10, 54, 154, 163–68 (*see also* libertarianism); race and, 35 (*see also* racism); right-wing, 54; social conservatives (*see* social conservatives)
Constitution, US, 5, 28; Eighth Amendment, 8, 28, 62, 64, 69, 74, 214n45, 225n87; ERA, 158; First Amendment, 5; Fourteenth Amendment, 8, 13, 69; Supreme Court and (*see* Supreme Court). *See also specific topics, decisions, persons*
*Cool Hand Luke* (film), 57
Cover, Robert, 235n31
Crawford, Donnie, 251n32
criminology, 32
culture. *See* popular culture; *and specific topics, groups, persons*
Curtis, Gregory, 232n64

*Dancer in the Dark* (film), 191
Darabont, Frank, 109
Davis, Angela, 63, 212n23
Davis, H. G., 81
*Dead Man Walking* (film), 19, 24, 114–19, *118*, 122, 183
death penalty: abolition of (*see* abolitionism); Christians and, 23, 123, 156, 159, 232n61; culture and (*see* popular culture); death row (*see* death row); executions (*see* execution); family values (*see* family values); films and (*see* films); freedom and, 6–9, 125; libertarians and (*see* libertarianism); nihilism and, 27–56; popular culture and, 20–21, 228n21

(*see also* popular culture); psychology and, 66–75, 88–89 (*see also* psychology); rationale for, 88–89, 101, 103; retribution and (*see* retribution); support for, 1–6, 2, 8, 12–13, 16–18, 20, 23–24, 29, 34, 44, 75, 106, 152, 189; Supreme Court and (*see specific persons, decisions*); Texas and (*see* Texas). *See also specific persons, topics*

death row: African Americans on, 229n28 (*see also* African Americans); appeals (*see* appeals); executions (*see* execution); experience of, 96, 137; films and (*see* films); humanizing inmates, 190; population, 220n36; time on, 137, 184, 187, 189; websites, 82–83, 185, 224n83. *See also specific persons, topics*

*Death Wish* (film), 48, 74

DeLombard, Jeannine Marie, 22

*Dexter* (television series), 168–82, *174*, 243n40

*Dirty Harry* (film), 48, 49, 53, 74, 168

DNA evidence, 244n48, 247n10, 248n10

Dobson, James, 158

*Doing Justice* (von Hirsch), 198n21

Dole, Bob, 164

Douglas, William O., 34, 69, 205n21

Drumgo, Fleeta, 212n23, 212n25

Dukakis, Michael, 49, 135, 136

Duncan, Michael Clarke, 109

Dunn, Kerry, 20

Durkheim, Émile, 37, 85, 210n77

Duwe, Grant, 206n30

Eastwood, Clint, 48, 50

Eichmann trial, 207n37

Eighth Amendment, 8, 28, 64, 69, 74, 214n45, 225n87

electrocution, 1, 80–81, 92, 158, 247n9

Eshelman, Byron K., 27

eugenics, 73

European Union, 114

Ewick, Patrick, 187, 200n47

execution, 2, 6, 31, 81, 83, 91–99, 217n7, 218n10. *See also* death penalty; last meals; last words; methods of execution; *and specific persons, topics*

*Executioner's Song, The* (Mailer), 79

*Execution of Raymond Graham, The* (film), 107

Falwell, Jerry, 158

family values: conservatism and, 158–59, 163, 164, 174; defined, 156; *Dexter* and, 168, 174, 175, 243n40; evangelical Christians and, 156, 158; libertarianism and, 156, 157–58, 163–68, 243n40; punishment and, 156, 158–63. *See also* conservatism; libertarianism

Farmer, Mildred, 183

Feeley, Malcolm, 237n61

Ferguson, James, 200n44

films, 16, 23, 24, 211n19. *See also specific films, persons*

financial crisis, 184

firing squad, 80

Ford, John, 47–48

Foucault, Michael, 85, 219n20, 220n43

Fourteenth Amendment, 8, 13, 69

Foxx, Jamie, 123

France, abolition and, 114

Frankel, Marvin, 214n48

Frankfurter, Felix, 237n61

freedom, concepts of, 5–10, 19–20, 200n47. *See also* individualism; negative freedom; punishment; *and specific groups, topics*

frontier myth, 129–54

Fugate, Caril Ann, 36

*Furman v. Georgia*, 9, 103, 125, 198n27, 216n72; arbitrariness and, 12, 69, 106, 216n72; clemency and, 231n58; LDF and, 69–70; legalism and, 74; punishment and, 104, 205n21; racial bias and, 72, 106; states and, 12, 71–74, 184; Texas and, 82, 85, 202n55

Gaines, Ernest J., 112

Garland, David, 72, 204n8

gas, lethal, 31, 39, 50, 92, 121, 247n9

George, Ronald, 205n21

Gilmore, Gary, 51, 75, 79–80

Ginsberg, Raphael, 159

Girard, René, 225n87

Gissendaner, Kelly Renee, 21

Goffman, Erving, 9, 56, 57

Goldberg, Arthur, 8

"Good Man is Hard to Find, A" (O'Connor), 39

government, trust in, 2, 3, 44, 184, 211n13. *See also* libertarianism

Graham, Barbara, 30, 34, 205n21
Graham, Bob, 184
Great Society, 14
Green, Jonathan, 83, 85
Green Mile, The (film), 109, *111*, 112, 185,
    228n22
Gregg vs. Georgia, 73, 79–102, 208n57,
    216n72; abolition and, 248n11; appeals
    and, 186; Christianity and, 23; execu-
    tions and, 92, 99, 138, 162, 231n58; films
    and, 113, 125, 191; guidelines in, 72, 81;
    legalism and, 74; libertarianism and,
    169, 175; methods of execution and, 92,
    99; racism and, 17, 105, 113
Grisham, John, 120, 228n27, 244n48

Hall, Michael C., 169
hanging, 27, 28, 80, 92, 103, 191. See also
    lynching
Hanks, Tom, 110
Harcourt, Bernard E., 189, 251n29
Harris, Danny, 97
Hatch, Orrin, 138
Heritage Foundation, 160
Hickock, Dick, 27, 35, 38
Hispanics, 17, 238n72
Hollywood. See films
Holmes, Johnny, 129–54, 237n69, 238n72
Hoodlum Priest, The (film), 30, 32
Horan, Caley, 203n7
Horton, Willie, 136

ideology, defined, 200n47. See also spe-
    cific topics
In Cold Blood (Capote), 27, 34, 35, 36, 42,
    43, 80
In Cold Blood (film), 32, 34
individualism, 9–10, 17, 58, 65, 104,
    123, 129, 139, 165, 214n53. See also
    libertarianism
injection, lethal, 81, 92, 93, 131, 218n9,
    218n10, 247n9. See also specific persons
Innocent Man, The (Grisham), 229n27,
    244n48
insurance, 203n7
I Want to Live! (film), 30, *31*, 32, 33

Jackson, Derrick Leon, 89
Jackson, George, 59, 212n23, 212n25
Ježková, Selma, 191

Johnson, David T., 216n75
Johnson, Lyndon B., 10, 14
Johnson, Robert, 79, 92
juveniles, 60–61, 62, 90, 124, 135, 249n12

Kafka, Frank, 183
Kant, Immanuel, 22, 67, 211n11
Kaplan, Paul, 20, 220n41
Kaufman-Osborn, Timothy V., 91
Kennedy, Edward M., 214n48, 215n66
Kershner, Irvin, 30
Kesey, Ken, 53
Keynesianism, 14, 197n17
killing state: defined, 20; Dexter and, 169,
    170, 171, 173; films and, 107–9, 113, 120,
    185, 192; ideology of, 156, 185; libertar-
    ianism and, 156; punishment and, 131,
    156; race and, 107–9, 113 (see also rac-
    ism; and specific groups); rehabilita-
    tion and, 120
Kind and Unusual Punishment (Mitford),
    59
King, Rodney, 239n76
Kohm, Steven, 137
Korean War, 56
Kouba, J. Anthony, 66
Krocker, Jan, 140
Kunkle, Troy, 99

Larivee, John J., 136
Last Dance (film), 108, 114
Last Light (film), 114
last meals, 97–99, 101, 188, 218n13, 222n58,
    222n63, 224n87, 225n87, 250n27
Last Mile, The (film), 57
Last Mile, The (Wexley), 204n11
last words, 94–97, 222n63, 223n68, 224n87
law, rule of, 7, 133, 139, 140, 144, 145, 187,
    198n21. See also trials; and specific
    topics
Lawton, Stacey, 97
Legal Defense Fund (LDF), 8, 28, 34, 69
Lesser, Wendy, 224n87
Lesson Before Dying, A (film), 24, 112,
    228n22
liberalism, 7, 11, 29, 32, 137, 199n36,
    200n43, 206n29
libertarianism, 11, 13, 16, 156, 163, 164, 175,
    241n11, 243n40, 244n40. See also civil
    libertarianism; freedom, concepts of

Liebman, James S., 152
life sentence, 85, 86, 135, 136, 146, 212n25, 220n36, 249n13
Linder, Ray Dean, 147
Linder, Robert, 61
Lipton, Douglas, 46
Lithgow, John, 176
Locke, John, 239n3
Luper, Clara, 238n72
Lynch, Mona, 74
lynching, 18, 34, 72, 105, 110, 151, 201n49, 241n18

MacNamara, Donald E. J., 33
Macy, Bob, 233n9, 236n58, 237n69, 238n72, 239n76
Madden, Robert, 97–98
Mailer, Norman, 79
Mann, Abby, 43
Manson, Charles, 44
Man Who Shot Liberty Valance, The (film), 47
Marion program, 61
Marshall, Thurgood, 73, 104, 125
Martinson, Robert, 46
Marx, Karl, 37
masculinity, 10, 80, 129, 230n35, 239n77
mass murder, 29, 37, 44, 206n30. See also specific persons
Masur, Louis, P., 226n5
May, Elaine Tyler, 203n7
Maynihan, Daniel, 118
McCann, Michael, 216n75
McCarthy, Colman, 50
McCarthy, Joseph, 57
McCleskey v. Kemp, 106, 216n72
McCoskey, James, 96
McFarland, Frank, 97
McVeigh, Timothy, 146
media, mass, 83–84, 119. See also popular culture; and specific types, topics
Memory Hole website, 222n63
Menninger Clinic, 32, 33, 36, 43, 61, 205n17
mental illness. See psychology
methods of execution: electrocution, 1, 80–81, 92, 158, 247n9; firing squad, 80; gas, 31, 39, 50, 92, 121, 247n9; hanging, 27, 28, 80, 92, 103, 191; injection, 81, 92, 93, 218n9, 218n10, 247n9; See also executions; and specific persons

Milgram, Stanley, 9, 38, 56, 207n37
Miller, Arthur, 57, 103
Miller, Gary, 95
mimetic theory, 225n87
Mitchell, Alfred Brian, 134, 161
Mitchell, Gerald, 97
Mitford, Jessica, 59, 213n31
Monster's Ball (film), 228n22
Morris, Herbert, 67, 68
Morris, Norval, 213n42
Muggeridge, Malcolm, 43
Murakawa, Naomi, 13

National Association for the Advancement of Colored People (NAACP), 8, 28. See also Legal Defense Fund
National Commission on the Causes and Prevention of Violence, 208n64
National Organization for Victim Assistance, 160
nationalism, 152, 239n74
Native Americans, 17, 130
Native Son (Wright), 24
Nazis, 207n37, 216n75
negative freedom: abolition and, 193 (see also abolitionism); civil libertarianism and, 52, 55, 56, 59, 154, 200n47; decline of, 6–10; defendants and, 13; First Amendment and, 5; Milgram experiments and, 39; negations of, 19–20; neoliberalism and, 15, 19, 200n44, 200n47; nihilism and, 44; positive freedom and, 5; racism and, 17; social conservatives and, 15, 52; state killing and, 19–20 (see also killing state). See also freedom, concepts of
"Negro Family, The" (report), 118
neoliberalism, 14–16; Great Society and, 14; liberalism and, 200n43 (see also liberalism); libertarianism and (see libertarianism); negative freedom and, 15, 19, 200n44, 200n47; parole and, 53–54; punishment and, 15, 16, 115; supply-side economics and, 14; use of term, 200n44
New Deal, 6, 7, 14, 29
newspapers, 242n20. See also specific topics, persons
New York Institute of Criminology, 33
Nichols, Terry, 146, 148
Nigh, George, 233n9

nihilism, 27–28, 37, 40, 43, 44
*1984* (Orwell), 56
Nixon, Richard, 47, 71
Nobles, Jonathan, 97

Oates, Joyce Carol, 41, 43
O'Connor, Flannery, 39, 43
O'Connor, Sandra Day, 166
Ogletree, Charles J., 183
Oklahoma City bombing, 138, 146
O'Mara, Richard, 46
*One Flew over the Cuckoo's Nest* (film), 53
O'Neill, Kevin Francis, 94
Opton, Edward M., 63
Orwell, George, 56, 211n13

Parents of Murdered Children, 160
parochialism, 152–53
parole systems, 11; curtailment of, 12, 134,
    196n8; life without parole, 135, 184,
    187, 249n13; neoliberals and, 53–54, 58;
    racism and, 12, 59; rehabilitation and,
    59, 60, 205n17; sentencing and, 59, 64–
    65, 86
Patuxent Institution for Juvenile Delin-
    quents, 61, 62
*Payne v. Tennessee*, 166, 243n40
penalty phase, 73
*Penry v. Lynaugh*, 86, 89, 90, 220n36
Perry, Rick, 186
Pippin, Robert B., 130
Poe, Ted, 22
Poncelet, Matthew, 190
popular culture: antiauthoritarianism in,
    57; capital punishment and, 20–21,
    228n21 (*see also* death penalty); de-
    fined, 20; family values (*see* family val-
    ues); films (*see* films); individualism
    and, 9–10 (*see also* individualism); lib-
    ertarianism and (*see* libertarianism);
    mass media, 83–84, 119 (*see also types,
    topics*); neoliberalism and, 200n44; in
    1960s, 47; rebel image in, 57; rehabili-
    tation and, 60; sources in, 20, 243n40;
    technocracy and (*see* technocracy);
    television (*see* television). *See also spe-
    cific topics, persons*
populism, 3, 18, 47, 72
poverty, 11, 19, 33, 35, 89, 116, 153, 240n7

Prejean, Helen, 116–21
prisons, 2, 4, 53, 59, 61, 66, 81, 83, 204n8,
    208n64, 213n31, 214n42, 214n43,
    221n55, 250n24. *See also* death row;
    *and specific institutions, topics*
probation, 135, 143
Progressive Era, 5, 7
Proquest database, 241n14
psychology, 30, 53, 60, 66–68, 91, 205n17,
    206n26, 208n57, 208n64, 248n11. *See
    also specific types, topics*
public opinion polls, 1, 2, 146, 183
punishment, 4–8, 13, 15, 16, 22, 27–49, 54,
    63, 68, 187, 190, 204n8, 210n77, 211n10,
    211n11, 219n20, 230n40, 243n40, 247n6.
    *See also* retribution; sentencing

racism, 3, 12, 17, 18, 20, 59, 63, 105–10,
    121, 151, 152, 228n21, 229n29, 231n54,
    238n72. *See also* African Americans
Rafter, Nicole, 211n19
*Rambo* (film), 152
Raspberry, William, 179
Reagan, Ronald, 160, 164, 165, 200n43
Reed, Ralph, 158
rehabilitation, 27–49, 57, 60, 63, 68, 103–26,
    135, 208n64, 230n40, 244n53
retribution, 7, 8, 10, 12, 16; death penalty
    and, 184, 185, 189, 190 (*see also* death
    penalty); *Gregg* decision and, 73, 85,
    125; Kant and, 211n11; neoliberalism
    and, 115; polarization and, 51–75; pop-
    ular culture and, 82, 94, 101 (*see also*
    films; *and specific topics*); punishment
    and, 93–95, 104, 118, 198n21, 204n8 (*see
    also* punishment); redemption and, 125;
    rehabilitation and, 25–75; rise of, 51–75;
    trials and (*see* trials); victims and, 163
risk management model, 221n55
Robbins, Tim, 16, 116, 119
Roberson, Brian, 95
Robertson, Pat, 123, 158
Rogers, Patrick, 97
Roosevelt, Franklin, 6, 7
Rountree, Meredith Martin, 217n7
Ruhe-Much, Nancy, 123
Rush, Benjamin, 226n5
Russell, James, 97
Ryan, George, 251n29

Salinger, J. D., 9, 57
Sanderson, Ricky, 98
San Miguel, Jessy, 97
Santana, Carlos, 97, 99
Santorum, Rick, 165
Sarat, Austin, xii, 20, 183, 218n9, 222n59
Sartre, Jean-Paul, 24
Savelsberg, Joachim, 202n55
Scalia, Antonin, 23, 225n87
Schmid, Charles, 36, 38, 39, 41, 43, 50,
    206n29
Schwarzenegger, Arnold, 123
Scott, Ann, 134
Self, Robert O., 164
sentencing, 12, 13, 14, 22, 59, 64, 72, 73,
    86, 101, 105, 214n48, 217n75, 220n41,
    235n31. See also death penalty; life sen-
    tence; punishment; trials; and specific
    persons, topics
sexism, 105–7, 124, 152
sexual assault, 17, 34, 87, 88, 108, 110, 116,
    159, 201n50, 241n18
Shapiro, Michael H., 67
Shay's Rebellion, 4
Shchane, Miriam, 161, 186
Siegel, Don, 48
Silbey, Susan S., 200n47
Silent Majority, 10 13
Siskel, Gene, 49
Skinner, B. F., 51–52, 63
Slotkin, Richard, 130
Smith, Fern, 239n76
Smith, Jim, 185
Smith, Perry, 27, 33, 35, 43, 79
social conservatives, 54, 74, 151, 158,
    230n42, 240n5, family values and, 157
    68, 175, 200n47, 244n40; legalism and,
    74; libertarianism and, 163–68; nega-
    tive freedom and, 14–15; neoliberalism
    and, 14; punishment and, 10, 54; sen-
    tencing and, 12; Silent Majority and,
    10–11. See also conservatism
social contract theory, 167, 239n3
Soledad State Prison, 212n23, 212n25
solitary confinement, 66, 213n29, 214n51
Somin, Jonathan, 11
Sonnier, Patrick, 183
Souter, David, 167
South, US, 17, 206n25

Spece, Roy, Jr., 66
Special Treatment and Rehabilitation
    Training (START) program, 61, 66
Speck, Richard, 36, 206n29
Spenkelink, John, 81, 184
Spillane, Mickey, 209n68
Stand Your Ground statute, 181
Starkweather, Charles, 38, 39, 162, 206n29
Steinem, Gloria, 16
Stewart, Potter, 70
Stone, Benjamin, 97
Stouffer, B. J., II, 141, 142
suburbanization, 11, 199n34
Sudden Impact (film), 49
supply-side economics, 14–16
Supreme Court, 8, 11, 28, 34, 47, 55, 70, 71.
    See also specific persons, decisions
Sutherland, George, 240n3
Szasz, Thomas S., 59, 75

technocracy, 7, 9, 10, 18, 53, 61, 91, 93,
    203n7
television, 21, 43, 46; killing state and, 169,
    175; late 1960s, 157; neoliberalism and,
    200n44; racism and, 107–8, 125. See
    also specific programs, topics
television shows, 240n4, 243n40. See also
    films; and specific topics
terrorism, 138, 146, 147, 183, 191, 247n6,
    248n11
Texas, 82–100, 123, 124, 145, 202n55,
    219n23, 232n60
Thatcher, Margaret, 200n43
Thomas, Danny Dean, 89
"three strikes" laws, 65
Tocqueville, Alexis de, 4
Top Gun (film), 152
totalitarianism, 207n37, 216n75
Trial by Ordeal (Chessman), 30
trials: appeals and (see appeals); capi-
    tal defendants, 86, 90; error rates, 186;
    Macy and, 145; racism and, 238n72 (see
    also racism); rhetoric in, 145; sentenc-
    ing (see sentencing); Supreme Court
    (see Supreme Court); testimony in, 160,
    166, 202n57. See also specific persons,
    topics
True Crime (film), 228n22
Tucker, Karla Faye, 123

Turner, Frederick Jackson, 129, 151
Tuttle, Charles, 97

Umbreit, Mark S., 187
US Congressional Database, 241n14

Victim and Witness Protection Act (1982), 160
victims' rights, 159, 160, 163, 166, 175, 191
Vietnam War, 157, 233n6
vigilantism, 18, 21, 48, 81, 130, 147–50, 168–71, 177–81, 217n75
violence, 235n31
von Hirsch, Andrew, 198n21
von Hoffman, Nick, 213n31
von Trier, Lars, 191
voyeurism, 31, 224n87

Walking Tall (film), 49
Wallace, Mike, 46
Wanger, Walter, 30
Warren, Earl, 11, 47
Weber, Max, 37
welfare state, 115, 135, 153, 211n10, 216n75
Wells, Robert, 212n25
West, Old, 129–54, 216n75
West, Rebecca, 43
Wexley, John, 204n11
white Americans: crime rates and, 11; death penalty and, 250n17; freedom and, 3, 6; masculinity and, 10, 80, 129, 230n35, 239n77; neoliberalism and,

230n42, 231n50; prison films, 231n49; racism and, 110, 153 (see also racism); rightward drift, 105; social conservatism and (see social conservatives); as victims, 230n35; welfare and, 11, 115. See also specific persons, topics
Whitman, Charles, 37
Whitman, James Q., 22
Wicker, Charles, 97
Wilks, Judith, 46
Will, George, 207n37
Williams, Jeffrey, 89
Williams, Stanley, 123, 222n60
Wills, Garry, 47
Winner, Michael, 48
Wise, Robert, 31
women: death row and, 30–31, 82, 105, 124, 204n12, 226n12, 232n64; feminist protest, 157; Gregg decision and, 113–14; oppression and, 230n35; punishment and, 65, 105; racism and, 151; responsibility of, 124; sexism (see sexism); sexual assault (see sexual assault)
Wood, Ann Louise, 241n18
Woodson et al. v. North Carolina (1976), 71, 217n75
World War I, 241n19
World War II, 6, 7, 28, 29, 72, 162, 241n19

Zalman, Marvin, 211n10
Zimmerman, George, 181, 181
Zimring, Franklin E., 241n11